Rabindranath Tagore was born in Calcutta in 1861. In his household almost everyone wrote, painted, composed music, or staged plays. His first short story appeared in 1876, when he was barely sixteen, and he continued to write prolifically until a few months before his death in 1941, at the age of eighty. He founded the famous Santiniketan, an international school, now a University, in West Bengal. He was awarded the Nobel Prize in literature in 1913, and was knighted in 1915. In addition to his stories, novels, plays, and poems, he also contributed to Indian philosophical and political thought, and was one of the architects of the new Indian nation.

Rabindranath Tagore

THE HOUSEWARMING
AND OTHER
SELECTED WRITINGS

Edited and with an Introduction by
AMIYA CHAKRAVARTY

Translated by
MARY LAGO, TARUN GUPTA
AND THE EDITOR

A SIGNET CLASSIC

Published by The New American Library, New York and Toronto
The New English Library Limited, London

Copyright © 1965 by Amiya Chakravarty

First Printing, December, 1965

SIGNET CLASSICS are published *in the United States* by
The New American Library, Inc.,
1301 Avenue of the Americas, New York, New York 10019,
in Canada by The New American Library of Canada Limited,
295 King Street East, Toronto 2, Ontario,
in the United Kingdom by The New English Library Limited,
Barnard's Inn, Holborn, London, E.C. 1, England

PRINTED IN THE UNITED STATES OF AMERICA

CONTENTS

PLAYS

FABLES AND PROSE SKETCHES

NARRATIVE POEMS

Introduction

Thirty years ago, Rabindranath Tagore's was a name known to all readers, in several languages. Tagore was the sage of the East, the first Asian to win the Nobel Prize for Literature, the master of the story and novella who accommodated Eastern lore and color to Western literary techniques, the teacher who presented India to the rest of the world. Tagore's fame emanated in part from his towering personality, and after his death in 1941, except for a brief period during his birth centennial, which was internationally observed, his celebrity has faded. The comparatively few stories well known in the West—"Kabuliwallah," "The Hungry Stones," "The Postmaster," and others—continue to be read, but the enormous adulation once given Tagore seems in retrospect to have been inadequately premised. In fact, Tagore's reputation during his lifetime was based on only a partial knowledge of his life and work. Many of his stories were not yet translated; they were unknown even in India, except to the comparatively limited group who read Bengali. In this anthology we have attempted to present a broader sampling of Tagore's work than has appeared before in English; we have included some of the well-known material, but the greater part of the book is newly translated for the Signet Classics edition. We hope that this collection will convey to today's readers a fuller impression of the stature of an artist who, despite the vagaries of literary fashion, remains the greatest writer of modern India and one of the greatest writers in world literature.

The sensitive poet, like the storyteller, knows, besides the drama of the moment, the events behind life's most casual encounter. But poetry, till very recently, was prone to use the content without the context; the circumstances were left behind or melted in visionary light instead of being embroidered into art. The storywriter, on the other hand, was often drawn into sequential narratives where any singleness, in technique or in imagination, seemed to be dangerously "poetical." Tagore broke through this overspecialization even in some of his early writings. Freighting his lyrics with unconventional details, he still sailed without trouble; also, as a short-story writer—his first story appeared in 1878, when he was barely sixteen—he was able to make experiences crystallize, as in a sonnet or a song, on a slant or a colored center, unashamedly primal.

Tagore's versatility and craftsmanship derived from the fact that he "wrote with both hands," that is to say, prose and poetry alternated from his boyhood days, shaped by the same passionate urge to transcribe or transcreate life. In a gifted household where everyone wrote, painted, composed music, or staged dramas young Tagore was exposed to natural correlations; different techniques of artistic representation revealed not only parallels but an integral vision. Deeply spiritual family traditions had much to do with this; the mystery and beauty of the manifold drew him to the breath of existence. The root and the flowering, therefore, cannot be separated in his finest art. Actually, no analysis of Tagore's writings, particularly his short stories, can fail to stress the weddedness of life or the sense of the whole, which is holiness.

Tagore spent his early years on the rivers of Bengal. From his houseboat he saw the fluid, changing scenes of daily life framed by the bend of the river, by the marketplace with a temple or a cluster of trees. Life came to him gemmed and set in single or gathered sights, and always with a horizon. A marriage ceremony, a boat carrying the little bride away, the parting on the shore, the waves, and the distant home where the bridegroom lived would be enough to stir an immemorial sadness, and a specific revolt. Such experiences would flow as easily into a poem as into a short story, mirror the rice-green field or the monsoon sky and form an intricate mold with hidden or explicit history. A rural postmaster; a roving actor trying out his part in open-air Yatra theaters, always nostalgic for roles he had not played or for places he had not visited; a gang of boys with a naughty leader rolling logs on the riverbank—appeared as unmistakably in his poems and stories as they belonged to life. Peasants and fishermen battling against the elements; families caught in a seemingly inexorable feud; a Vaishnavite woman who had renounced the world but lived with an ineffaceable incident, radiant but regretful; middle-class homes; town and countryside; village girls with eager eyes suggested to him stories upon stories. Like Indian melodies these are at once grave and sad, and suddenly happy in a fundamental music. Many of the characters and situations sketched above will be recognized in the stories in this collection. Through them the reader will be involved, as the author was, in the universal concrete of experience. Exciting narration, dexterous plots, and acute observation are the texture of one pervasive document.

Scenes from ancient India, from Rajputana to Arakan, jostle with a contemporary moneylender from Kabul who brought dried fruits and nuts to an alien but neighborly land. The Kabuliwallah, like any father, carried a memento of his child—in this case, a little handprint on a piece of paper—and the story, in and out of prison, transcends the merely tragic by its humanity. Tagore, who once roamed the many halls and balconies of an ancient Mughal manor—his brother was the first Indian member of the Civil Service in the British administration and had this palace in Ahmedabad as his residence—chronicled a legendary atmosphere. Blanched by moonlight, the marble stones and stairs brought back scenes of vanished splendor and poignant events to a perceptive artist; these scenes he later transcribed in one of his best-known stories. Familiar with Indian and world history, stimulated by the modern Western novel and short stories and by the Bengali novels of Bankimchandra, which in turn had been inspired by the West, Tagore's avenues to narrative forms were many. His creative milieu was one where any story could be real and any aspect of reality could become a story.

Tagore wrote no less than ninety-four short stories covering the span from 1877 to 1941. One of his last stories, "Scandal," which is included in this collection, was written a few months before his death. This medium, therefore, belonged to him as consistently and variedly as his poetry. In fact, he complained that he did not quite know which of the Muses he was serving, while wistfully serving all, including music and, toward the end, also the Muse of painting. Stories winged their way to him from everywhere, not only from the rural homes and hearts of Bengal but from the intellectual circles of his family and friends, and increasingly, from sparks lighted up by his struggles with social problems. The vivid modern Indian context belongs to his art. Indeed, so many were the stories that came that his pen was able to serve only a small quantum; the rest he gave away to contemporary writers both young and old. Plots, characters, and situations were used by others who only sometimes acknowledged the source. Often Tagore was obliged to use in conversation the stories that had gathered in his subconscious; he would regale his family members and intimate friends in this way. These improvisations, heightening a leisurely rainy afternoon or an evening, were so effective that his listeners would blame him for withholding many more details. Some of these improvisations started from nowhere, but actually the inner accumulations were there; often he would write down the core of a story or novel before it had vanished altogether.

Tales, fables, and epical narrations containing vignettes of stories are to be found in early Indian literature like the *Panchatantra,* the *Mahabharata,* and in a whole range of medieval legends. The *Mahabharata,* in particular, was the storehouse of stories for Tagore: many of them he relived and re-created in his ballads and short dramas. But the short story, in the modern sense, came to India through Western sources. In Tagore's own storytelling, the single most pervasive influences seem to have been Chekhov and Turgenev —the latter's *Sportsman's Sketches,* for instance, were his favorite. He read Tolstoi and Dostoevski, admired their consummate mastery of the novel; Hawthorne and Poe were also well known to Tagore. But it would be hard to tell whether the precision technique of Maupassant—without its content—had not influenced him even earlier. His brother Jyotirindra was a scholar and translator of French literature; Molière's dramas and French short stories, including Maupassant, reached Bengal in translations that Tagore shared. Evidently Tagore learned from the French the secret of compressing a story within a page or two of brilliant and detailed evocation. Frequently he came back to this short *conte,* though he was more at home in the long story.

The impact of Ibsen can be seen in the later Tagore, when

he made the artist's social conscience the vehicle for a needed rebellion, particularly where women's freedom and rights were involved. Tagore's "A Wife's Letter" is a significant example of such art: we know that he had read Ibsen's "A Doll's House" not too long before and was deeply moved by that dramatic masterpiece. Tagore's insistent opposition to social tyranny, caste, and economic injustice was, of course, the decisive factor in his motivation, but Ibsen and, more distantly, Shaw affected his use of "purposive" art.

Some random samples of Tagore's prose sketches with a full story content, of narrative poems and ballads conveying rapid transcripts of historical events have been included in this volume both for providing contrast and for illustrating Tagore's many-sided genius. Contemporary politics and psychological themes appear in some of the stories not as concessions to modernity but as newly perceived dimensions of the unvarying human story. References to the Western world are there, but strangely enough, not with the full life and context that one would expect from a world-renowned traveler. Intimate identities, however, can be seen in his painted configurations of Western life. While retaining some classical harmonies of the East, Tagore as a painter is frankly a modernist both in technique and in the confrontation of other cultures than his own.

Translations from short stories suffer, though not as much as poems, from a changed language of feeling and structure. This book, however, is a work of unique collaboration between Western and Eastern literary minds. I am referring to the translators, Mrs. Mary M. Lago, an American scholar and litterateur, and Mr. Tarun Gupta, a sensitive Bengali artist. The translating team, to which the editor also belonged, did its best to retain the original fabric, but, of course, deviations were inevitable. Abridgments, deletions of untranslatable phrases, and allusions were meant to bring the original text nearer; also, footnotes were grudgingly added with the hope that the readers might afford to ignore them. The more difficult words and phrases appear in the Glossary. Seemingly endless revisions and modifications followed, only to establish the firm ground already laid by the patient and skillful work done by the two translators; I must refer again to their thoroughness and almost unparalleled excellence in dealing with subtle nuances of Tagore. Also, it is a privilege to record the encouragement and help received, at every stage, from

Thomas J. Davis III and Teresa Egan of The New American Library.

To G. C. Sen, the Director of the Visvabharati Publishing Department, Calcutta, I extend my warm felicitations and acknowledgment. This book of translations would not have been possible without his generous cooperation.

Diacritical marks have not been used in this volume to indicate the exact Bengali pronunciation; the genius of English usage will, it is hoped, meet the needs of the "Common Reader."

An anthology never satisfies: though a few stories were retranslated from the original to restore better luster, and examples of many genres, including two plays, added to depict different stages and styles of Tagore's art, old favorites will be missed and some of the new selections not immediately accepted. But inclusiveness and selectiveness had to be balanced, and recognition given to single great stories as well as to the constellations of stories that define stages of Tagore's genius. Modern readers, in any country, will surely feel the sweep and depth of a powerful mind; the nobility and spiritually sensitive touch of a poet and a storyteller will shine through the obscuring layers of translation. If these versions lead them to the original, or to more attempts at new translations, this volume will have justified itself. But the main emphasis has to be laid on the uniqueness of the universal mind, on the fact that Tagore, a writer, prophet, and creative artist of our own days, continues to reach the excited imagination of distant readers.

AMIYA CHAKRAVARTY

Boston University, 1965

DALIYA

When the defeated King Suja fled from Aurangzeb, he
sought refuge with the King of Arakan. Suja was accompanied by his three beautiful daughters, to whom the King
of Arakan wished to marry his princes. When Suja showed
extreme displeasure at this proposal, the King of Arakan
ordered that he and his daughters be enticed into a boat
and taken onto the river. An attempt was made to capsize
the boat. At that moment of danger, Suja threw Amina,
the youngest girl, into the water. The eldest daughter committed suicide. One of Suja's trusted retainers, Rahamat Ali,
took the second girl, Zulikha, swam away with her, and fled.
Suja died in the fray.

Amina was carried off by the swift-flowing current. By sheer
luck she was soon caught up in the net of a fisherman. He
took her into his home, gave her the Arakanese name of Tinni,
and raised her as a member of his family. In the meantime, the
elderly King of Arakan died, and one of the princes was
crowned king.

1

One morning the old fisherman came to reprimand Amina.
"Tinni," he said, "Tinni, what happened this morning? You
haven't done your work. There's no sizing on my new net,
my boat——"

13

Amina came to the fisherman and said lovingly, "Bura,[1] my sister has come today. That's why I've taken a holiday."

"Who might your sister be, Tinni?"

Zulikha appeared from nowhere and said, "It is I."

The old man was astonished. He came up to Zulikha for a closer look at her face.

Upon a sudden thought he asked, "Can you do any work?"

Amina said, "Bura, I'll do my sister's work. I couldn't let my elder sister work."

After a little consideration the old man said, "But where will you live?"

"With Amina," replied Zulikha.

What a problem, thought the old man. He asked, "What will you eat?"

"There is a way," said Zulikha. With this she scornfully threw a gold coin in front of the fisherman. Amina picked it up, laid it in the fisherman's palm, and whispered, "Bura, don't say anymore. You'd better go to work. It's late."

How the disguised Zulikha had journeyed in many places, how at last she came to know about Amina and arrived at the fisherman's hut—all this would make another story. Her rescuer, Rahamat, under the false name of Shekh, was employed in the court of the King of Arakan.

2

A little river flowed by, and in the cool morning breeze of early summer, flowers fell from the blood-red branches of the *kailu* tree.

Zulikha said to Amina as they sat in the shade of the tree, "God has saved us two sisters from the hand of death for the sole purpose of avenging Father's murder. I can find no other reason."

Amina looked into the far distance beyond the opposite bank of the river, looked toward the most deeply shadowed range of the forest, and spoke slowly, "Sister, please don't talk about all that anymore. In a way, I am enjoying this world. If the men want to die, let them kill each other. I have no complaints here."

"Shame on you, Amina," said Zulikha. "Are you the daughter of a king? Where is the throne of Delhi, and where is the Arakanese fisherman's hut?"

---

[1]*Bura* means old man. The term is used affectionately.

Amina smiled and replied, "Dear sister, the throne of Delhi will not weep a single tear if some girl prefers my Bura's hut and the shade of this *kailu*."

"Well, one can't blame you," Zulikha said, partly to herself and partly to Amina. "You were very young then—but just think of it. Father loved you most. That is why he threw you into the water with his own hands. Don't consider your life here more precious than the death that Father intended for you. Your life will have meaning only after you avenge his death."

Amina remained silent and looked into the distance. But it was quite apparent that in spite of all Zulikha's exhortation she was absorbed by this breeze, this shade, her own budding youth, and some pleasant memories.

After a while she sighed deeply and said, "Sister, please wait a little. I have some housework to be done. Bura will have nothing to eat unless I cook something."

3

Quiet and weighed down by melancholy, Zulikha sat thinking about Amina's situation. Just then there was a thump as of someone's jumping, and Zulikha's eyes were covered from behind.

Startled, Zulikha said, "Who is it?"

At her words a young man uncovered her eyes and came and stood before her. Looking at Zulikha, he said unhesitatingly, "You are not Tinni." He spoke as if Zulikha had tried all along to pass herself off as Tinni, but now all her cunning had been exposed by his extraordinary astuteness.

Zulikha adjusted her dress, stood up haughtily, and her eyes flashed fire. "Who are you?" she demanded.

"You don't know me," the young man answered. "Tinni knows. Where is Tinni?"

Amina came out when she heard the commotion. When she saw Zulikha's rage and the young man's amazement and confusion, Amina burst out laughing. "Sister," she said, "don't take him seriously. Is he a man? He's a wild deer from the forest. I'll discipline him if he has done something improper. Daliya, what have you done?"

The young man promptly replied, "I covered her eyes. I thought it was Tinni. But she is not Tinni."

Amina suddenly burst out with unrestrained fury. "Again!

Big words from a little mouth! When did you cover Tinni's eyes? You don't lack courage."

"No one needs a lot of courage to cover the eyes, especially if one has had previous experience," the young man replied. "But I'm telling you the truth, Tinni, today I was a bit frightened."

Saying this, he furtively pointed toward Zulikha and, with his eyes on Amina's face, began to smile silently.

Amina said, "No, you are such a barbarian, you're not fit to stand before the princess. I must teach you some manners. Look, bow to her like this."

Then Amina bent her slim young body gracefully and bowed to Zulikha. With considerable difficulty the young man performed an extremely inadequate imitation.

"Step back three steps, like this," said Amina. The young man retreated three steps.

"Bow again." Again he bowed. Thus Amina brought the young man, bowing and retreating, to the door of the hut. "Go into the house," she said. He went into the house.

Amina fastened the door from outside and said, "Do a little housework. Keep the fire burning." With this she came and sat beside her sister.

"Sister, please don't be angry," Amina said. "The people here are like this. I'm disgusted with them."

But Amina's face and behavior did not proclaim disgust. Instead, she showed an indefensible partiality toward the people of this country.

Zulikha did her best to appear angry as she said, "Really, Amina, your behavior amazes me. For a strange young man to come and touch you—he is very brash."

Amina agreed with her sister. "Yes, think of it. If the son of a king or a nabob had acted like that, I would have snubbed him and had him thrown out."

Zulikha's suppressed amusement could no longer be restrained. She laughed aloud and said, "Tell me the truth, Amina. You were just saying that you like this life very much. Is it because of that barbarous young man?"

"All right, sister," replied Amina, "I'll tell you the truth. He's really a great help to me. He picks fruit and flowers for me, hunts game for me, and if I call him to do anything, he comes running. Many a time I've thought of disciplining him, but that is useless. If I glare at him and say, 'Daliya, I'm really vexed with you,' he looks at me in the best humor and smiles without a word. I suppose humor here is like that; he is overjoyed with a few slaps. I've experimented with that too. Look there, I've locked him inside; he's perfectly happy. As soon as I open the door I'll see his face and eyes all red, and happy as can be; he'll be blowing up the fire. What can I do with him, sister? I can't keep up with him."

"I could try," Zulikha said.

Amina smiled beseechingly. "I'd fall at your feet, dear sister. Don't scold him anymore."

Amina spoke as if that young man were her favorite tame deer. It was still not far removed from its natural wildness and Amina seemed to fear that a stranger might frighten it away.

Then the fisherman came and asked, "Tinni, didn't Daliya come today?"

"He came."

"Where did he go?"

"He disturbed me so much that I locked him in the house."

Somewhat perturbed, the old man said, "If he irritates you, put up with it. Everyone is unruly when young. Don't discipline him too much. Yesterday Daliya gave me a gold coin for three fish."

"Don't worry, Bura. Today I'll collect two gold coins from him, and you won't have to give him a single fish."

Such cleverness and worldly wisdom in his young adopted daughter delighted the old man; he affectionately stroked her hair and left.

4

Curiously enough, Zulikha gradually came to accept Daliya's comings and goings. After consideration, she perceived that there was nothing surprising about the situation because, as a river has both a current and a shore, so women have both a heart's desire and a fear of gossip. But this remote land of Arakan was beyond the pale of civilization. Where were those who would gossip?

In this country there were only trees that blossomed according to the season. The Neela River swelled during the monsoon, became crystal clear in autumn, and wasted away in summer. There was no criticism in the gushing voices of the birds; and now and then the north wind brought the hum of humanity's daily round, but none of its whisperings, from the other shore.

If one stayed here for a time, the solid man-made foundations of etiquette would gradually crumble unnoticed, just as, under the secret onslaught of nature, the trees grow on the fallen mansion until it becomes one with the surrounding natural world. Nothing pleases a woman more than the union of a compatible couple. Nothing else can become so mysterious, so pleasant, and the subject of such inexhaustible curiosity. Therefore, when Zulikha's pride in her high birth and her concern for her own prestige gradually lost their hold in this primitive hut, in the shadow of this lonely poverty, she took great pleasure in watching the game of love between Amina and Daliya under the blossoming *kailu* tree.

Perhaps an unsatisfied longing in her own young heart made her restless with joy and longing. Eventually, if the young man were sometimes late, both Amina and Zulikha anxiously, eagerly, awaited his coming. When the lovers were together, Zulikha watched them with a loving smile, just as an artist looks from a little distance at his newly completed picture. Sometimes she even pretended to quarrel with them, to reproach them, and by shutting Amina in the house she would thwart the young man's desire to meet his love.

The emperor and the forest have a common characteristic. Both are independent, both are sole sovereigns of their domain. Neither must follow the dictates of another. Both possess a natural, an inborn grandeur and simplicity. Those who are mediocre, those who spend their lives day and night by the letter of man-made laws, tend to become rather isolated. They behave like servants before their elders, like masters before their juniors, and when set at a disadvantage are utterly confounded. The barbarous Daliya was the uninhibited son of the Empress Nature. He felt no diffidence before the princesses, and the princesses were able to recognize him as their peer. Smiling, simple, fond of fun, and fearless in all situations, his easygoing nature showed no sign of repression.

But in the midst of all this play Zulikha's heart sometimes cried out in anguish. She would think, Is this the proper end to the life of a princess?

One morning, as soon as Daliya came, Zulikha grasped his hand and said, "Daliya, can you show me the king of this country?"

"I can. But tell me why."

"I have a dagger that I want to plant in his heart."

At first Daliya was quite astonished. Then, as he looked at Zulikha's hate-distorted face, his whole face broke into a smile, as if he had never heard anything so amusing. This

was humor befitting a princess! If at the very first meeting
there were no conversation, no exchange of news, but a dagger
thrust up to the hilt into a king's living body, how taken aback
that king would be at this unseemly intimacy! As this picture
rose in Daliya's imagination, his customarily silent smile slowly
changed into loud laughter.

—

5

The very next day Rahamat Shekh sent a letter privately
to Zulikha: "The new King of Arakan has learned about the
two sisters in the fisherman's hut. He has secretly seen Amina
and is greatly attracted by her. He has made plans to bring
her to his palace and marry her without delay. There could
never be a more splendid opportunity for revenge."

Then Zulikha sternly grasped Amina's hand and said, "God's
intention is quite clear. Amina, the time has come for you to
carry out your life's mission; no more play now."

Daliya was present. Amina looked toward him; she saw that
he smiled in amusement.

His smile cut Amina to the quick. "Daliya," she said, "do
you understand? I'm going to become the queen."

Daliya said with a smile, "That's not for long."

Hurt and surprised, Amina thought, He is really a wild
deer. It's foolish of me to treat him like a man.

Trying to excite Daliya's concern, Amina said, "I doubt
that I can return after the king has been killed."

Daliya thought that point valid and said, "It would be difficult to return."

Amina's whole soul sank into despair. She turned to Zulikha, sighed, and said, "Sister, I am ready."

And turning to Daliya in feigned mockery, she said with
a sinking heart, "When I am the queen, I'll punish you first
for the offense of conspiracy against the king. Then I'll do
whatever must be done."

Daliya seemed especially amused, as if this proposition, if
carried out, would be an occasion for festivity.

6

The fisherman's hut shook to the point of collapse at the
approach of the king's cavalry and foot soldiers, standard-
bearers, elephants, musicians, and torchbearers. The palace
had sent two golden palanquins.

Amina took the dagger from Zulikha's hand. For a long time she looked at its ivory craftsmanship. Then she lifted her dress and tested its edge once against her own bosom. The dagger touched close to the very flower of her heart. Then she sheathed it and hid it inside her dress.

She longed to see Daliya once more before this journey of death, but he had disappeared the day before. Had Daliya's smile concealed an inner wound?

Before she got into the palanquin, Amina looked once more through the veil of her tears at her childhood shelter, that tree of hers near the hut, that river nearby. She held the fisherman's hand and said in a choked, trembling voice, "Bura, I'm going now. Who will look after your household when Tinni leaves?"

The old man cried like a child.

Amina said, "Bura, if Daliya comes here again, give him this ring. Tell him that Tinni left it for him when she went away."

With this, she quickly climbed into the palanquin. It departed amid great pomp. Amina's hut, her riverbank, the shade of the *kailu* tree darkened, became silent and deserted.

In due time the two palanquins passed through the gates and entered the inner rooms of the palace. The two sisters descended.

Amina neither smiled nor wept. Zulikha was pale. When duty had been remote, she had had all the zeal of enthusiasm. Now she trembled with anxiety as she lovingly embraced Amina. She said to herself, "Have I torn this full-blown flower from its stalk and set it afloat on a stream of blood?"

But there was no more time for thought. As the maids led them past the keen, unblinking eyes of countless lamps, the two sisters walked on as if in a dream. Finally, at the door of the bridal chamber Amina stopped for a moment and said, "Sister."

Zulikha held Amina close and kissed her.

Slowly both girls entered the room.

In the center of the room the king, dressed in his royal robes, sat on a muslin-covered bed. Amina stood hesitating at the door.

Zulikha went closer to the king and saw that he smiled in great amusement.

"Daliya!" Zulikha cried. Amina fell unconscious.

Daliya rose, picked her up like an injured bird, and carried her to the bed. When Amina came to herself, she took the dagger from her bosom and looked at her sister. Her sister looked at Daliya, and Daliya silently smiled and looked at both of them. The dagger also peeped out of the sheath, saw this farce, and smiled a sparkling smile.

1892

AN IMPLAUSIBLE STORY
(Akta Ashare Galpa)

1

Far out in the ocean is an island. The King of Cards, the Queen of Cards, the Ace, and the Jack lived there. Others lived there too, from the Deuce and the Three to the Nine and the Ten, but they had no social position.

The Ace, the King, and the Jack—these three comprised the ruling class; the Nines and the Tens were inferior and unworthy of inclusion in the same category.

But it is a marvelous system. The extent of each person's worth and prestige was predetermined and could not get out of alignment. Everyone worked in a prescribed pattern. Successive generations merely continued the work of their forefathers.

All this was difficult for a foreigner to understand. At first glance it looked like a game. Movements were made only according to rules, comings and goings adhered to regulations, getting up and lying down were done by prescription. An invisible hand guided the cards, and they went.

Their expressions were unchanging, imprinted forever on their faces like that of a meaningless picture. From antiquity to the present, from the tops of their heads to the tips of their toes, they have stayed exactly the same.

No one ever thought, no one wondered about anything; everyone went about silently, lifelessly, with inaudible steps. When they fell, they fell soundlessly and lay flat on their backs, staring steadily and serenely at the sky.

No one had hopes or desires or fears, no one explored a new road; there were no smiles, no tears, no doubts, no questions. Birds beat their wings against such a cage; these picturelike creatures showed no signs of inner life or of restless revolt.

Yet, the living once dwelt in these cages. In those days the cages swung to and fro, there was the sound of wings inside, songs were heard. There were memories of the deep forest and the far-flung sky; now there were only the narrow limits of the cage and its neatly fixed iron bars. Who could say whether the bird had flown, had died, or lay moribund?

The silence and serenity were astounding. Complacency and contentment were complete. In the streets, on the landings, at home, everyone was perfectly disciplined, thoroughly restrained. There was no noise, no conflict, no enthusiasm, no excitement; there was only the trifling work and ordinary leisure of the daily round.

With restless, monotonous rhythm, the sea washed the shores with thousands of soft, shining bubbles and kept the whole island wrapped in profound slumber; like the outspread blue wings of a mother bird, the sky preserved the peace of the world. The shore of a foreign land appeared like a deep blue line, far away. No repercussions of its conflicts could reach this shore.

2

On the other shore, in that foreign land, lived a Prince who was the son of a Rejected Queen. He had spent his childhood with his exiled mother and had lived in isolation on the beaches.

As he sat alone day after day he wove an enormous net of desires. He cast that net across the world, gathered in all the new mysteries of an imagined universe, and drew them to his own doorway. His restless thoughts roamed the ocean's shore to the sky's edge, where the horizon ended in a garland of blue hills. He sought the winged horse, the jewel on the serpent's head, the flowering amaranth, the gold wand, and the silver wand; he knew the place beyond the seven seas and the thirteen rivers where the princess lay dreaming in the impregnable castle of the giant.

The Prince went to school; the merchant's son told him stories of his own and other lands; the general's son told him ghost stories.

The rain fell in torrents; the clouds were thick with darkness. The Prince sat in the doorway with his mother, looked toward the sea, and said, "Mother, tell me a story about a faraway country!" His mother recounted a long-remembered childhood story, a strange tale of a strange land. As he listened to that story, mixed with the patter of the rain, the Prince's heart began to wander.

One day the merchant's son came and said to the Prince, "Friend, I have completed my studies. I am going to travel abroad and have come to say good-bye."

"I shall go with you," said the Prince.

"Will you leave me all alone?" asked the general's son. "I shall go with you."

The Prince went to his sorrowing mother and said, "Mother, I am going abroad. When I find some means of ending your sorrows, I shall return."

The three friends set out.

3

The merchant's twelve ships were launched and the three friends came aboard. The north wind filled the sails; like the yearning heart of the Prince, the ships darted forward.

At the conch island one ship was loaded with conch shells; at the sandalwood island a ship was filled with sandalwood; at the coral island one ship was laden with coral.

During the next four years four ships had been filled with ivory and musk and cloves and nutmeg; then a great storm arose.

All the ships sank with the exception of the one carrying the three friends. It was dashed against an island and broken to pieces.

This was the island where the Ace, the King, the Queen, the Jack of Cards, and their lesser-numbered followers dwelt in conformity.

4

For a long time there had been no disturbance in this Kingdom of Cards. Now for the first time disorder was introduced.

After all this time the first controversy arose: how were these three people who had suddenly appeared one evening on the seashore to be classified?

First, what was their category: Ace, King, Deuce, Ten, or Nine?

Second, what was their lineage: Spades, Hearts, Diamonds, or Clubs?

Unless all this were decided, it would be difficult to know how to treat them. What would they eat? With whom would they live? Until that was settled, who would order them to go northwest or southwest, or keep them facing northeast, or tell them to get up or go to sleep?

This kingdom had never faced a problem so enormous and so unsettling.

But the three hungry friends were not the least concerned about these weighty matters. If they could find a way of getting food, they would be secure. When they saw that people hesitated to feed them and that the Aces had called a mass meeting to search for precedents, the friends began to eat whatever they could find.

The Deuce and the Three were astonished by this behavior. The Three said, "Brother Deuce, these people have no discrimination."

"Brother Three," said the Deuce, "it is obvious that they are inferior to us."

When they had eaten and felt refreshed, the three friends sat quietly and noticed that the people of this place were quite unique. They seemed to have no roots in the earth. These regimented people had somehow been pulled up by the hair and stumbled along out of touch with reality. Whatever one person did was copied by the others. They were like the suspended dolls of a puppet show. Hence the lack of expression on their faces, the absence of desires, the excessive solemnity and precision of gait with which everyone moved. It was all extremely odd.

As the Prince looked around at this living lifelessness and the profound solemnity of manner and movement, he threw back his head and roared with laughter. The noise of this hearty burst of hilarity sounded strange in the streets of the Kingdom of Cards. Everyone here was so very proper, so tidy, so venerable, so solemn, that the laughter itself was shocked by the sound of its undisciplined outburst, faded, and was extinguished. The silence of the people streaming by seemed twice as severe as before.

The merchant's son and the general's son were apprehensive and said to the Prince, "Friend, let us not spend another minute in this joyless land. If we stay here two more days we shall have to pinch ourselves to see whether or not we are alive."

"No, brothers," said the Prince. "I am curious about these people. They look like human beings; I must give them a shake and find out if there is any spark of life in them."

5

Thus some little time passed. But these three young foreigners would not be caught up by any system. Whenever they were expected to stand up, sit down, turn their heads, lie facedown, shake their heads, or turn somersaults, they did none of this but instead looked on in amusement and laughed. They were unaffected by the pattern of serious behavior.

One day the Ace, the King, and the Jack came together to the Prince, the general's son, and the merchant's son, and asked with impassive gravity, "Why don't you move according to the rules?"

"Because that's our wish," replied the three friends.

With one voice the three leaders of the Kingdom of Cards spoke like ghosts, "Wish? Who is Wish?"

They didn't comprehend the meaning of "Wish," but little by little they understood. They began to observe that one did not always have to walk the same way, that another direction was possible; there was this road and there was that road. The three lively young foreigners had demonstrated to them that man has a freedom beyond restrictions. Thus they dimly perceived the might of a ruler named Wish.

As soon as this realization dawned, the Kingdom of Cards began to stir, little by little, from one end to the other, just as the many coils of a great sleeping python stir sluggishly when it awakens.

6

Thus far, the Queens were the same lifeless figures; they paid no attention to anyone. They had gone about their own affairs, silent and serene. Now, one spring afternoon, one of them raised her jet-black eyelashes and looked at the Prince with an enchanting sidelong glance.

"I am lost!" exclaimed the astonished Prince. "I thought they were all images. I see that is not the case. This is a woman!"

The Prince called the general's son and the merchant's son to a secluded spot and said, "Brothers, she's charming! In that first glance from her dark eyes I watched the sunrise over a newly created world. Our patient waiting has been worthwhile."

The two friends were enormously amused and said, laughing, "Is that right, friend?"

The unfortunate Queen of Hearts began to forget the rules daily. She made mistakes at every step. When she was supposed to stand next to the Jack, she suddenly went and stood beside the Prince. Unperturbed, the Jack would say gravely, "Queen, you have made a mistake."

At this, the rosy cheeks of the Queen of Hearts became rosier. Her serene, unblinking eyes looked downward.

"There's no mistake," the Prince replied. "From now on, I am the Jack."

Unexpectedly beautiful was this blossoming of a woman's heart; sweetly restless were her movements. The Queen's inmost self seemed visible in her looks; she was like a newly opened flower.

While correcting the errors of this new offender, everyone now began to make mistakes. The Ace forgot to maintain his habitual dignity, a distinction was no longer made between the King and the Jack, and the lesser numbers did not know how to proceed.

The cuckoo had often sung in the spring on this ancient island, but this time it sang as never before. The ocean had murmured its music but with a monotony that proclaimed an immutable law; now suddenly the restless south wind and the unruly young waves broke into a harmony of life's joy and pain.

7

Is this the same Ace, the King, the Jack? What had happened to those expressions of perfect, placid contentment? Now they looked toward the sky or sat by the sea; some could not sleep at night; still others had lost their appetites.

Their faces were stamped with jealousy, with love, sometimes with anxiety, often with doubts. Some laughed, some wept, others sang. Everyone stared at himself and at the others. They compared themselves with their fellows.

The Ace thought, The King is at least not bad-looking, though he's not handsome, but there is such majesty in my bearing that the whole world can't help watching me.

The King said to himself, "The Ace always goes about red in the face and in a huff. He thinks the Queens are watching and breaking their hearts over him." As he spoke he looked at his face in the mirror and smiled wryly.

All the Queens in the land dressed within an inch of their lives, looked one another over, and said, "Ah, I'm mortified! Whom is that snob trying to impress? Her manners are embarrassing!" As they spoke their gestures doubled in eloquence.

Here and there, friends sat by pairs, chatting confidentially in secluded places. They laughed or cried, were sometimes angry. They argued or pleaded with each other.

The young men sat languidly in the shade of the trees beside the forest path, their backs against the tree trunks, their feet scuffing the dry leaves. The girls, wearing dark-blue saris, concentrated upon walking back and forth along that shady road, faces averted and eyes turning from side to side; they walked as if they saw no one or as if they had not come to see anyone.

So, appearing somewhat demented, a reckless young man plucked up his courage and quickly came forward, but the one of his choice said nothing; he stood abashed, the favorable occasion had gone, and the girl, like the opportune moment, gradually vanished in the distance.

Overhead the birds sang, the sighing breeze tossed scarves and curls, the new leaves on the trees stirred and rustled, and the ceaseless surging of the ocean redoubled the inarticulate longings of the heart as it turned this way and that.

In one spring season the three young foreigners, coming to this arid valley, had brought in the floods of the monsoon.

8

The Prince saw that between the tide's ebb and flow the whole country had come to a standstill. No one spoke, glances only were exchanged; for every step forward there were two steps back; sand castles were built out of the longings of the heart, and the sand castles were demolished. It seemed that everyone sat in his own corner, sacrificing himself at his own fireside and daily becoming thinner and more silent. Only the eyes were alight, and lips trembled with the message of the heart as leaves are shaken by the wind.

The Prince called to everyone, "Bring the flutes, sound the bugles, everyone shout for joy! The Queen of Hearts will choose a husband."

At once the Nines and the Tens began to blow upon the flutes, the Deuces and Threes sounded the bugles. This sudden tumult of rejoicing put an end to the staring and the whispering.

With talk and laughter and mirth the festivities brought the men and women together. What intimate, playful conversation, what evasions and suspicions, what boisterous laughter and trivial beginnings! It was like a wind rising in a dense forest that makes the branches and leaves, the vines and trees whisper and lean toward each other.

In the festive hours the flute played the haunting Sahana *raga* from the morning onward. It brought a note of restlessness in union, serenity in joy, beauty in everything visible. New longings seemed to arise as the music went on. Those who had never loved were now in love; those who loved were absorbed in their own happiness.

Wearing a red dress, the Queen of Hearts sat all day in a shady, secluded grove. She heard the Sahana raga in the distance, and her eyes closed. When she opened them, she trembled and sank down, covering her face with her hands.

All day the Prince paced the seashore alone, turning over and over in his mind that startled look, that shrinking shyness.

9

That night, by the light of hundreds of lamps, amid the fragrance of flower-garlands, the music of flutes, a girl came walking slowly with unsteady steps. She carried a garland in her hand, approached the crowd of richly dressed, handsome, smiling young men, and stood before the Prince in the courtyard. She neither lifted the garland to the neck of the chosen one, nor could she raise her eyes to look into his face. Then the Prince lowered his head and the garland slipped into place upon his shoulders. The silent panorama of the court was stirred by a sudden outburst of joy.

Everyone hailed the bride and groom and set them upon the throne. Everyone joined in the Prince's coronation as ruler of the kingdom.

10

The sorrowing Rejected Queen crossed the ocean in a golden boat and came to her son's new kingdom.

The picture-people had suddenly become human beings. Now there was none of that uninterrupted peace and profound

solemnity of former days. For better or for worse, the motion
of the world had filled the new kingdom of this new king
with its own joy and sorrow. Some people were good, some
were bad, some were happy, still others were sorrowful; everyone was human. No one bowed meekly to the rules and regulations but was good or bad according to his own wish.

1892

THE NOTEBOOK
(Khata)

From the time she learned to write Uma had caused a
terrible commotion. She wrote enormous, imperfect, wobbly
letters in charcoal on the walls of every room of the house.
"The rain falls, the leaves tremble."

The novel *The Secret of Haridas* was under her sister-
in-law's pillow. Uma had discovered it and on page after
page had written: "The water is dark, the flower is red."

On the calendar that the family used every day, most
of the astrological signs had been impartially obliterated by
large letters.

In the notebook containing Father's daily accounts this
was written among the receipts and expenditures: "He who
studies rides in the coach and four." This method of the
cultivation of literature met no obstruction until one day a
more serious accident occurred.

Uma's older brother Govindalal appeared extremely
harmless, but he wrote incessantly for the newspapers. None
of his relatives or neighborhood acquaintances mistook him
for a thinker when they listened to his pronouncements.
And in reality no one could accuse him of thinking about
anything, but he wrote and his opinions were in perfect
harmony with those of the majority of Bengali readers.

European scientists espoused certain gravely erroneous
notions about physiology. With the help of thrilling phrases

and without the slightest assistance from logic, Govindalal had composed a splendid essay of refutation.

One quiet afternoon Uma secretly took her brother's fountain pen and wrote all over that essay in huge letters: "Gopal is a very good boy, he eats whatever he is given."

I doubt that Uma meant the name Gopal[1] to refer to any of Govindalal's regular readers, but there were no bounds to the brother's anger. First he slapped her; then he confiscated her only stub of a pencil, her pen smeared with ink from top to bottom, her whole hoard of nondescript writing materials that she had so painstakingly gathered. The insulted little girl did not understand all the reasons for such severe punishment, and sitting in one corner of the room, she began to cry as if her heart would break.

After the term of punishment ended, Govindalal, feeling somewhat repentant, restored the plundered articles to Uma and, in an effort to assuage her hurt feelings, gave her in addition a fine bound notebook with ruled lines.

Uma was then seven years old. From then on this notebook stayed under her pillow at night and all day long; whenever she was in her room, she would hold it in her lap. When she went to the girls' school in the village, her little pigtail braided, the maid accompanying her, she took the notebook along. Some of the girls regarded it with wonder, with greed, or with envy.

That first year she wrote in the notebook with utmost care: "The birds have begun to sing, the night is coming to an end." She would read aloud and write as she sat in the middle of the bedroom and held the notebook close. A great deal of prose and poetry was compiled in this manner.

In the second year a few original compositions appeared here and there, extremely short but extremely cogent, without preface, without conclusion. A few may be quoted here.

She had copied into the notebook the fable of the tiger and the crane; under it was a line found neither in fables nor in contemporary Bengali literature. That line read as follows: "I love Joshi very much."

Let no one think that I am fabricating a tale of love. Joshi was not an eleven- or twelve-year-old neighborhood boy. An old servant in the house was nicknamed Jashoda.

[1] Gopal also means a cowherd.

This sentence gave no one a precise notion of the girl's attitude toward Joshi. Anyone wishing to write a reliable account of this matter would find the statement plainly contradicted a few pages further on.

There were more than a few such instances. Inconsistencies appeared repeatedly in Uma's compositions. In one place could be seen: "I'll never have anything to do with Hari again." (Hari did not refer to a boy, but to her schoolmate Haridashi.) Not far from this statement were others that easily convinced the reader that Uma had no friend in the world as dear as Hari.

When Uma was nine, the *sanai* was heard one morning at her house. It was her wedding day. The bridegroom's name was Pyarimohan, a writer who was a colleague of Govindalal. Although he was not very old and had some schooling, up-to-date ideas scarcely entered his head. Therefore the people of the neighborhood loudly praised him. Govindalal tried to emulate him but only with partial success.

Uma, wearing a Banaras sari, her little face covered by the veil, was about to go tearfully to her father-in-law's house. Her mother said, "Child, mind what your mother-in-law tells you, do your housework, don't spend all your time reading and writing."

Govindalal told her, "Look here, don't go around marking up the walls there; it's not that sort of a house. And never scratch up any of Pyarimohan's writings."

The little girl's heart sank. She understood that where she was going no one would make allowances for her. She would have to learn by means of many scoldings what they considered a fault, an offense, a defect.

The *sanai* was played all morning. There was probably no one in that crowd who understood what went on in the troubled heart of the little girl who was covered by that veil, that Banaras sari, and those ornaments.

Joshi went with Uma. It was decided that Joshi would stay until Uma was settled at her father-in-law's house and then return. The affectionate Joshi, after much thought, had taken Uma's notebook along. This notebook was one bit of her father's house; it was a cherished memento of the birthplace that had been home all too briefly. It was an abbreviated history of the parts of her life spent with Father and Mother, written in very crooked, immature letters.

It was the precious taste of girlhood freedom in this untimely role of housewife.

For the first few days she wrote nothing. She had no time for it. Presently Joshi went back home. That very afternoon Uma shut the door of her bedroom, got her notebook out of her tin box, and cried and cried as she wrote: "Joshi has gone home and I also want to go to my mother."

In the days that followed she scarcely found time to copy a word from *Charupath* and *Bodhodoi*. Perhaps she did not even want to. As a result there were no more of those long excerpts between her own brief compositions. This was written beneath the previous sentence: "If brother would take me home just once, I wouldn't spoil his writing anymore."

It seems that Uma's father tried to take her home occasionally. But Govindalal and Pyarimohan got together to put a stop to that.

"This is the time for Uma to learn devotion to her husband," said Govindalal. "If she is brought back home like that her father's affection would uselessly distract her." Govindalal had written a magnificent essay on this subject, mixing advice and sarcasm. Readers who concurred with him accepted the complete and irrefutable truth of his logic.

Hearing about this from others, Uma had written in her notebook: "Brother, I beg you, take me back once more to your house; I'll never make you mad again."

One day Uma closed her door and wrote some meaningless trifles in her notebook. Her sister-in-law Tilakmanjari was extremely curious; she wondered why Uma sometimes closed her door and wanted to see what went on. Through a chink she saw Uma writing; the sight amazed her. Saraswati had never made such a clandestine entry to their inner rooms.

Tilakmanjari's younger sister, Kanakmanjari, also came and peeked in.

Kanakmanjari's younger sister, Anangamanjari, came too, stood on tiptoe, with considerable difficulty peeped through the crack, and the mystery behind the closed door was solved.

Uma suddenly became aware of three familiar voices laughing and giggling outside the room while she wrote. She understood what was happening. Quickly she closed the notebook and shut it inside her box. In fear and shame she hid her face on the bed.

Pyarimohan became quite perturbed when he heard the news. Once you allowed such education, novels and plays would come next and getting housework done would be a problem.

Besides, after considerable thought he had hit upon an extremely subtle theory. He held that the sacred conjugal power is born out of the unison of female power and male power, but if the female power is overridden by learning and manifests itself only as male power, the result is a clash between one male strength and another, thus producing a destructive force that negates the effectiveness of the conjugal power. Therefore, the woman becomes a widow! Up to now no one had been able to disprove this theory.

Pyarimohan came home in the evening and scolded Uma and even made fun of her a little. He said, "You'll have to order a turban so that the housewife can go to the office with a pen behind her ear."

Uma didn't get the point. She had never read Pyarimohan's essays, and therefore her literary taste had not been fully developed. But she shrank within herself. She thought that if the world would split in two, she could find a place to hide her shame.

For many days she wrote nothing. But one autumn morning a singing beggar-woman sang Parvati's homecoming song. Uma listened silently, her face resting against the window bars. The autumn itself makes one remember everything about childhood days. Added to that, the homecoming song was more than she could bear.

Uma could not sing, but since she learned to write, she had somehow formed the habit of writing down a song as soon as she heard it. Thus she compensated for her inability to sing. On that day the beggar sang:

> The people say to Uma's mother:[2]
> "There comes your lost star."
> Hearing that, the distraught queen runs saying,
>   "Where is Uma, where?"
> The weeping queen says, "My Uma comes,
> Come, darling, come, my darling,

[2] Uma is another name for Parvati.

Come, let me take you on my lap."
Arms outstretched, holding her mother close,
Weeping, Uma says,
    "You didn't come for me."

The heartsick Uma's eyes brimmed with tears. Furtively calling in the beggar-woman, she closed the door of the room and with inconsistent spelling began to write that song in the notebook.

Tilakmanjari, Kanakmanjari, and Anangamanjari saw everything through the crack and, suddenly clapping their hands, cried out, "Sister-in-law, we see everything you're doing."

Then Uma quickly closed the door, went out, and began to plead, "Please, don't tell anyone, I beg you; I won't do it anymore, I won't write again."

Finally Uma saw that Tilakmanjari was eyeing her notebook. Then Uma ran and clasped the notebook to her chest. The sisters-in-law, joining forces, tried to snatch it away. When they had no success, Anangamanjari went to call Pyarimohan.

Pyarimohan came and sat down solemnly on the bed. "Hand over the notebook!" he thundered. Finding his order disregarded, he moderated his voice a few tones and said, "Give it to me."

Holding the notebook to her heart, the girl looked into her husband's face with an expression of utmost entreaty. When he saw this, Pyarimohan stood up to grab the notebook. She threw it down and, hiding her face with both arms, fell on the floor, utterly stricken.

Pyarimohan took the notebook and began to read the little girl's writings at the top of his voice. As she listened, Uma clasped the earth in an ever tighter embrace. The three girls who listened nearby giggled and shook with laughter.

After that Uma never had that notebook again. Pyarimohan also had a notebook filled with essays on subtle and thorny theories, but there was no one at hand to snatch and destroy that notebook for the good of humanity.

1893

PUNISHMENT
(Shasti)

1

When the brothers Dukhiram Rui and Chhidam Rui went out to work in the morning, sickle in hand, a storm of abuse would begin between their wives. All the people of the neighborhood were used to this quarreling, just as they were used to the various recurring commotions of nature. As soon as the neighbors heard the harsh voices, they said one after another, "There they go again." In other words, it was just what they expected, and there was no deviation from the habitual pattern. No one asks questions when the sun rises in the east at dawn, and no one was curious enough to ascertain the reason for this uproar between the two sisters-in-law in the Ruis' house.

This brawl undoubtedly involved the two husbands more than it did the neighbors, but the Rui brothers did not consider this the least inconvenience. They seemed to travel the long road of household affairs in a springless cart whose two wheels ceaselessly creaked and groaned. They had come to accept this noise as covered by the rules that regulate the journey of life's chariot.

On the other hand, when the house was quite silent, an uncanny sense of foreboding descended like the dread of an approaching unnatural disaster. On such a day no one could predict events with any certainty.

When the evening incident of this story occurred, the brothers had returned from work bone-tired and were dumbfounded at finding the house ominously silent. The weather was very sultry. At two in the afternoon there had been a heavy shower. The clouds were still thick in all directions. There was not a breath of wind. In the rainy season a jungle of weeds grew to a great height all around the house, and these and the waterlogged jute field gave off a heavy odor of drenched plants that stood motionless like a solid wall. The frogs croaked from the swamp behind the cowshed, and the still evening sky was full of the sound of crickets.

Nearby the rain-swollen Padma flowed in a mood of unrelenting fierceness beneath the canopy of rain clouds. Most of the grain plants had been washed out and had floated up close to the houses. Along the edge of this backwash, the roots of several mango and jackfruit trees came to the surface, and the outstretched fingers of their helpless fists seemed to try to catch at some last refuge in the empty air.

Dukhiram and Chhidam had gone to work that day at the zamindar's law court. The paddy was ripe in the river-bottom land opposite. All the poor people of the community were at work either on their own or on someone else's part of this land, harvesting the paddy before the rain washed it out. But the bailiffs had forcibly taken these two brothers to the courthouse. Its roof leaked in places, and they had spent the whole day mending it and making a couple of doormats. They could not come home and had eaten a snack at the courthouse. They were wet through by the rain, they had received no reasonable wages, and they had to listen to harsh language that far exceeded their deserts.

As they came home through the mud and floodwater at evening, the two brothers saw the younger sister-in-law, Chandara, lying silently on the end of her sari spread on the ground. She and this cloudy day had both shed many tears during the afternoon. Toward evening she had stopped crying and was in a sultry mood. The older sister-in-law, Radha, looking glum, was sitting on the veranda. Her one-and-a-half-year-old boy had been crying; when the two brothers came in they saw the naked baby lying flat on his back asleep at one side of the courtyard.

Without further ado the hungry Dukhiram said, "Serve the food!" It was like a spark on a sack of gunpowder. The older sister-in-law instantly shouted harshly at the top of her voice, "Where do I get rice to give you? Did you get me any rice? Do I have to go out and earn it myself?"

After the weariness and humiliation of the whole day, the absence of anything to eat in the dark, depressing house, the gnawing of hunger, the harsh words of the wife, and particularly the ugly hidden irony of her last retort, all at once became unbearable to Dukhiram. Like an enraged tiger he roared in a thunderous voice, "What did you say?" With this, he took the sickle and mindlessly struck it against her head. Radha fell into the lap of the younger sister-in-law and died instantly.

Chandara, her clothes bloodstained, cried out, "Oh! What has happened?" Chhidam clapped his hand over her mouth. Dukhiram dropped the sickle, covered his face with his hands, and sat down on the ground as if bewildered. The child awoke and began to scream and cry in terror.

All out-of-doors was then quite peaceful. The shepherd boy was returning to the village with his herd. Five or six of those who had harvested the freshly ripened paddy had crossed from the opposite bottom land singly in small boats; each person carried on his head, as the reward for hard work, a couple of bundles of paddy. Almost all of them had reached their respective homes.

The Chakravartys' Uncle Ramlochan had gone to the village post office to mail a letter and now quietly and peacefully smoked a pipe at home. Suddenly he remembered that the rent of his sublease tenant, Dukhi, was long overdue; he had promised to pay part of it today. Deciding that the Ruis would be home by now, he threw his chador over his shoulder, took his umbrella, and set out.

He had a feeling of foreboding as he entered the Ruis' house. He saw that no lamp had been lit inside. Several dark shadows were faintly visible on the gloomy veranda. A muffled crying burst out at intervals from one corner of the veranda, and as the child kept trying to sit up and cry, "Mother! Mother!" Chhidam held his hand over the baby's mouth.

Ramlochan was somewhat frightened and inquired, "Dukhi, are you here or not?"

All this time Dukhi had sat motionless on the ground, like a statue, but as soon as he heard his name called, he began to weep unrestrainedly like a distraught child.

Chhidam quickly came down from the veranda into the courtyard and approached Chakravarty, who asked, "Are the women taking it easy after fighting? I've heard them screeching all day today."

Chhidam had not yet been able to decide what to do. Many implausible alibis had come into his head. He had decided that for the time being he would move the dead body somewhere when the night was a little darker. He did not dream that in the meantime Chakravarty would show up. Chhidam had no ready answer. On the spur of the moment he said, "Yes, there was quite a squabble to-day."

As Chakravarty walked toward the veranda, he started to say, "But why is Dukhi crying?"

Chhidam saw no other way out. On a sudden impulse he said, "In the quarrel, Chandara hit Radha hard on the head with a sickle."

We do not easily comprehend troubles other than the immediate one. Chhidam was wondering how they could free themselves from the hold of the terrible truth. Furthermore, it did not occur to him that a lie can be more dangerous than the truth. A hurried answer to Ramlochan's question had popped into his head and he had blurted it out.

Startled, Ramlochan said, "Hah! What are you saying? She isn't dead!"

"She's dead," said Chhidam. He threw himself at Chakravarty's feet.

Chakravarty could not get away. He thought, Lord, Lord, what trouble I ran into this evening! I'll have to spend the rest of my life giving evidence in court!

Chhidam wouldn't release his feet; he said, "Respected sir, what can I do now to save my wife?"

Ramlochan was the adviser to the whole village in matters pertaining to litigation and lawsuits. He thought a little and said, "Look here, there's one way out of this. Run right now to the police station. Tell them that your elder brother, Dukhi, came home in the evening and asked for food, and he hit his wife on the head with the sickle because the food wasn't ready. I'm certain that if you say this, the girl will be saved."

Chhidam's throat began to feel dry, and he stood up saying, "Sir, if one wife goes I can get another. But if my brother is hanged, I certainly can't get another." But he hadn't considered all of this when he put the blame on his own wife. He had done the deed in a hurry; now his mind was unconsciously collecting consolation and arguments to support his own action.

Chakravarty felt that Chhidam's statement was logical and replied, "In that case, tell them just what happened. It is impossible to save everyone." After saying this,

Ramlochan left without further delay; in no time it was all over the village that Chandara had flown into a rage and had killed her older sister-in-law by hitting her on the head with a sickle.

The police poured into the village as water flows in when the dam is broken; the guilty and the innocent shared a profound uneasiness.

2

Chhidam thought that he had better hew to the line he himself had drawn. He had told Chakravarty one story, and that had been spread all over the village. If something else came out now, he could not even imagine what might become of what. He thought that in one way or another he had better hold on to that story, and there was no way to save his wife but by adding a few more stories to it.

Chhidam asked his wife, Chandara, to shoulder the blame. She was absolutely thunderstruck. Chhidam reassured her by saying, "Do as I tell you. There's nothing to be afraid of. We'll save you." Indeed, he offered her reassurance, but his throat was dry, his face ashen.

Chandara was no more than seventeen or eighteen. Her high spirits showed in her round face. She was short of stature, compactly built, and in sound health. She was so graceful that whether she came or went, sat or stood, there was nothing awkward about her. She was like a newly built boat, quite small and well proportioned; she moved with great ease, all shipshape. To her everything in the world was an object of interest and curiosity. She loved going about and gossiping with the villagers, and as she went to and from the river, water jar on her hip, with two fingers she would make a tiny opening in her veil and with her bright, restless dark eyes would see everything worth seeing along the way.

Radha had been just the opposite: extremely disorganized, slack, and untidy. She couldn't manage anything: her veil, the care of her child, her housework. She had little work to do, but she never seemed able to get any free time. The younger sister-in-law didn't say a great deal to her; she could make a few sharp, stinging remarks in a low voice and Radha would fly into a rage, scold, shout, and disturb the whole neighborhood.

These two couples shared a remarkable resemblance.

Dukhiram was a hulking man, big-boned and snub-nosed; his eyes seemed not to fully comprehend this visible world yet never questioned anything. He was so harmless, yet so frightening, so strong a man, yet so weak and helpless.

And it seemed as if someone had painstakingly fashioned Chhidam from a shining black stone. Nothing about him was superfluous, and he was without a flaw. Every limb combined strength and dexterity to achieve a high degree of perfection. Let him jump into the river from the high bank, push the boat with the boat hook, climb the bamboo tree and cut out the select branches—a measured orderliness marked every detail of his work with a spontaneous beauty. His deep black hair, oiled and carefully brushed back from his forehead, came to his shoulders; he was unusually fastidious about his clothing and his style of dress.

Although he was not altogether indifferent to the charms of other village women and had considerable interest in making himself as attractive as possible to them, nevertheless he had a special love for his young wife. They would quarrel and they would make up, for neither could defeat the other. There was another reason for the strength of the bond between them. Chhidam thought that he could not entirely trust so restless and charming a wife, and Chandara would think, My husband's eyes are always roving; unless I tie him tightly there will be nothing to keep him from slipping out of my hands some day.

Not long before Radha's death there had been a serious clash between Chhidam and Chandara. She had noticed that her husband occasionally took a trip on the pretext of having employment. He would come back after a day or two, yet he brought back no earnings. Not liking the look of things, she too began to commit a few excesses. She began to go to the river at odd hours, and after making the rounds of the village she would strike up an extended conversation with Kashi Majumdar's second son.

Chhidam felt as if someone had stirred poison into his days and nights. He had not a moment's peace, at work or anywhere else. One day he reprimanded his sister-in-law severely for not restricting Chandara. Radha shook her finger at him so that her bangles jingled. Addressing Chandara's dead father, she had said, "That girl runs faster than the storm. You expect me to manage her? I know some day she'll come to a bad end."

Chandara had come from the next room and slowly said,

"Why, my dear sister, what are you afraid of?" Thereupon the two sisters-in-law broke into a violent quarrel.

Chhidam rolled his eyes and said, "If I hear again that you've gone alone to the river, I'll powder your bones."

"In that case," replied Chandara, "my bones will be sure to get some rest." She immediately prepared to go out.

In one jump Chhidam caught her by the hair, pulled her back inside the house, and then fastened the door from the outside.

When he returned from work in the evening he found the door ajar and no one in the house. Chandara had gone three villages away and had presented herself at the home of her uncle.

Chhidam had brought her home after considerable trouble and entreaty, but this time he accepted defeat. He saw that it was as difficult to hold onto this wisp of a wife as to hold mercury fast in one's folded hands. She seemed to slip through the fingers.

He ceased to coerce her, but he began to live in utter misery. His ever-apprehensive yet passionate love for this restless young wife of his was like a severe throbbing pain. Sometimes he even thought that if she were dead he would be relieved of his anxiety and get a little peace of mind. Human beings are more jealous of each other than of the god of death.

This was the state of things at their house when the tragedy took place.

When Chhidam asked Chandra to take the blame for the murder, she stared at him, astounded; her black eyes seemed to scorch her husband silently like dark balls of fire. Her whole body and mind cringed more and more, and she longed to escape the clutches of this demon of a husband. Her whole inner self turned violently against him.

Chhidam reassured her, "Don't be a bit afraid." He coached her repeatedly in what to say to the police and to the magistrate. Chandara paid no attention whatever to all those lengthy instructions; she sat like a wooden image.

Dukhiram was completely dependent on Chhidam, and when Chhidam told him to put the blame on Chandara, Dukhiram said, "Then what becomes of dear Chandara?" Chhidam said, "I'll get her off." The burly Dukhiram was reassured.

3

Chhidam coached his wife to say that her older sister-in-law came at her with a fish knife and that in warding her off with the sickle, suddenly, somehow, Radha was hit. Ramlochan had fabricated all of this. He gave Chhidam detailed advice as to the supporting rhetoric and evidence.

The police came and began their investigation. Everyone in the village was unshakably convinced that Chandara had murdered her older sister-in-law. All evidence pointed in that direction. When the police questioned Chandara, she said, "Yes, I killed her."

"Why did you kill her?"

"I couldn't stand the sight of her."

"Did you have any arguments?"

"No."

"Did she attack you first?"

"No."

"Did she threaten you?"

"No."

Everyone was astonished by her answers.

Chhidam was terribly upset. He said, "She isn't telling the truth. Radha started to——"

The police inspector stopped him with a sharp reproof. After interrogating her according to regulations, the inspector merely got the same answer over and over: she didn't admit that Radha had attacked her in any way.

Had any girl ever been so obstinate? She was heading for the gallows with all her might and no one could do anything to keep her from it. What a terrible pride this was! In her mind Chandara was saying to her husband, "I'm leaving you and in this prime of my youth I'm going to marry the gallows; the last ties of my life are with it."

Now a prisoner, Chandara, a harmless, restless, playful little village housewife, went along the familiar village road, along the highway, through the market, along the riverbank, past Majumdar's house, the post office, and the schoolhouse, directly in front of all the familiar faces; branded by scandal, she left her home forever. A mob of little boys tagged after her, and the girls of the village, her friends, peeped through their veils or from doorways or stood behind trees and shivered with shame and fear and disgust as they watched Chandara being led away by the police.

Chandara asserted her guilt before the deputy magistrate as well. Nor did she declare that Radha had threatened her in any way at the time of the murder.

But Chhidam came to the court that day to testify, broke into tears, and said with folded hands, "Please, Your Honor, my wife is not guilty." The magistrate immediately stopped his outburst with a reprimand and began to question him, and bit by bit Chhidam told him the truth.

The magistrate didn't believe him, because Ramlochan Chakravarty, the trustworthy gentleman who was the key witness, had said, "Not long after the murder I happened to be at the scene. The witness Chhidam admitted everything to me and fell at my feet and said, 'Please give me some advice on how to save my wife.' I didn't say anything one way or the other. The witness said to me, 'Would my wife be saved if I tell them that my elder brother didn't get food when he wanted it and hit his wife on the head in anger?' I said, 'Be careful, you wretch, don't tell a single lie in court, there is no greater crime.'" And so it went.

At the outset Ramlochan had concocted many stories designed to save Chandara, but when he saw that Chandara had set her face against salvation, he thought, Oh Lord, I'll end up charged with perjury! It's better to say just what little I know. Reasoning thus, Ramlochan said what he knew. Furthermore, he availed himself of the opportunity to say a little more than he knew.

The deputy magistrate sent Chandara off to sessions court.

In the meantime, all the farmwork and marketing, the joy and sorrow of the world went on. And just as in other years, the ceaseless rains of Sravan fell on the freshening paddy fields.

The police, the accused, and the witnesses arrived at the court. Many people sat in front of the courthouse, waiting for their respective cases to come up. A lawyer had come from Calcutta on a case dealing with the division of property, a marshy plot behind a kitchen, and thirty-nine witnesses for the plaintiff were on hand for the occasion. Hundreds of people had come, eager to settle every penny of their accounts with hairsplitting accuracy. They could conceive of nothing else in this world more important at the moment. Chhidam stared absently through the window at this extremely busy everyday world, all of which seemed to him like a dream. A cuckoo called from the banyan tree in the big compound; it had no law, no courthouse of any sort.

Chandara said to the judge, "Oh, sahib, how many times will I have to say the same thing over and over?"

The judge explained, to be sure that she understood, "Do you know the punishment for the offense you are admitting?"

"No," answered Chandara.

The judge said, "The punishment is hanging."

"Oh, sahib, I beg you," answered Chandara, "please give me that punishment. Do whatever you like. I can't bear any more."

When Chhidam was brought to the court, Chandara turned her face away. The judge said, "Look at the witness and tell me who he is."

Chandara covered her face with her hands and said, "Oh, he is my husband."

The question: "Doesn't he love you?"

"Oh, he loves me a lot."

"Don't you love him?"

"I love him very much."

When Chhidam was questioned, he said, "I committed the murder."

"Why?"

"I asked for food and Radha didn't give me any."

When Dukhiram came to testify, he fainted. After he came to, he answered, "Sahib, I committed the murder."

"Why?"

"I asked for food and didn't get it."

After extensive cross-examination and after listening to other witnesses, the judge could see that the two brothers were assuming the guilt in order to save the housewife the disgrace of hanging. But Chandara had been saying the same thing all along, from the police station to the sessions court, without the slightest deviation. Two lawyers, on their own initiative, did their best to save her from execution, but they finally acknowledged defeat.

The day this very young, very short, dark, round-faced girl left her dolls at her father's house and came to her father-in-law's home, at the auspicious moment of that night, who could have imagined such a thing? Her father, who then lay on his deathbed, had said in relief, "At least I have left my daughter in good hands."

In the jail for condemned prisoners, the kind civil surgeon asked Chandara, "Is there anyone you'd like to see?"

Chandara said, "I'd like to see my mother once."

The doctor replied, "Your husband wants to see you. Shall I call him in?"

"I'd rather be dead," said Chandara.

1893

THE GIRL BETWEEN

(Madhyabartini)

Prologue

Nivaran's household was very ordinary, without much cultural refinement. It had never occurred to him that there could be any need in life for art or aesthetic sensitivities. Just as one's feet slide comfortably into familiar old slippers, Nivaran had taken his accustomed place in this old world. Not even inadvertently did he ever think, debate, or wonder about the meaning or design of living.

Nivaran would get up early in the morning and sit in front of his house, which fronted the lane. Shirtless, at peace with the world, he smoked tobacco from a hookah. People came and went along the road, cars and horses passed, a Vaishnava beggar sang, and the man who collected old bottles passed by, calling his trade. All this activity kept Nivaran's mind trivially occupied, and on the days when the vendor came with green mangoes and fish, he purchased some after much dickering and gave special directions for their preparation. Next on his schedule was the oiling of his body and a bath. After eating, he fetched his *chapkan* from its rope hanger, put it on, took one last puff on the hookah, chewed a betel nut, stuffed one more into his mouth, and set out for the office. After his return home, he spent the evening quietly and peacefully at the house of his neighbor, Ramlochan Ghosh. At night he went home to dinner and afterward retired with his wife, Harasundari, into their inner room.

Nivaran felt no regret that poets had missed celebrating his magnanimous gift of specially cooked delicacies sent to the marriage of Mitra's son, that the insubordination of the newly hired maid went unsung in vivid verse, that nobody seemed to notice his important comments on spices and his culinary art; he was satisfied with life and his own self-contained part in it.

One April Harasundari became critically ill. Her fever persisted. The more the doctor gave quinine, the more her temperature rose like a dammed-up stream. Thus her sickness continued for twenty days, for twenty-two days, for forty days.

Nivaran could not go to his office. For a long time he had not gone to the evening sessions at Ramlochan's house; he did not know what to do. Now he went to the bedroom to inquire about the patient, now he went outside and sat on the veranda, smoking and looking worried. He changed physicians twice daily.

In spite of such lovingly disorganized nursing Harasundari recovered. But she had also become so thin and weak that her body seemed merely to be saying faintly, as if from a great distance, "I am alive."

Then, in the spring, the south wind began to blow. On warm moonlit nights, treading silently, it entered the open bedrooms of housewives.

The neighbors' backyard gardens lay beneath Harasundari's window. This was not a particularly beautiful or pleasant place. Out of sheer whim someone had once planted a few croton bushes and had paid no attention to them thereafter. The pumpkin vines had grown up over a scaffolding of dry branches; there was a veritable jungle under the ancient jujube tree. Beside the kitchen some bricks from a broken wall had fallen in a heap and cinders and ashes piled up alongside day by day.

Harasundari, however, lay by the window, looked at this garden, and drank in its beauty, a thing she had never done before in her insignificant life. In summertime, when the current of the village river dwindles and thins out upon the sandbed, the water becomes crystal clear. Under the rays of the morning sun it trembles to its very depths, its body is thrilled by the touch of the breeze, and its limpid water reflects the stars of the sky as distinctly as a pleasant memory. Every one of Mother Nature's fingers seemed to touch the weak fibers of Harasundari's life, and in her heart there arose a music whose nature she did not fully understand.

Whenever her husband would sit beside her and ask, "How are you?" tears would come to her eyes. In her wasted face those great eyes full of love and gratitude gazed at her husband, her emaciated hands would hold onto his arm, and she would remain thus in silence. The husband's heart also felt a new, unfamiliar glow of joy.

Some time passed in this fashion. One night, when a big moon was emerging from behind the trembling branches of the dwarfed fig tree growing atop the broken wall, a sudden breeze sprang up, softening the sultriness of the evening, and Harasundari said as she ran her fingers through Nivaran's hair, "We won't be able to have any children. You should marry again."

Harasundari had been considering this for some time. When one feels a great joy, a powerful love arises that makes one feel that he can do anything. Then a sudden urge toward self-sacrifice gathers momentum. The outpouring of love and happiness wants to cast itself upon a great sacrifice or a great sorrow, as the surge of the current hurls itself against unyielding riverbanks.

In this ecstatic state of mind Harasundari decided one day that she would do something really great for her husband. But alas, who can make ability commensurate with desire? What could she give? She had no wealth, no intelligence, no talent—only a life, and even if that could somehow be given, what was it worth?

"If only I could give my husband a child as fair as cream, as soft as butter, as handsome as Cupid! But even if I tried with all my might, I couldn't do it." Then it occurred to her that her husband should marry again. She wondered why wives got so upset at this idea; it would not be at all difficult. Why was it impossible for one who loved her husband to also love a co-wife? Her bosom swelled at the thought.

When Nivaran first heard this suggestion, he laughed it off. The second and third times he ignored it. The more she noted his adamancy and lack of enthusiasm, the happier she became, the more firm in her resolve.

On the other hand, the more Nivaran heard the request, the less unfeasible it became, and while he sat on his veranda and smoked, the happy picture of a home filled with children began to take shape in his mind.

One day he himself brought up the subject and said, "I can't marry a slip of a girl and bring her up at this late date."

"Don't give that a thought," said Harasundari. "I'll be responsible for bringing her up." As she spoke, there appeared to this childless woman the vision of a shy, delicate, adolescent girl, a bride barely separated from her mother. Harasundari's heart melted with affection.

"I have the office," Nivaran replied. "I have my work. You are here. I'll have no time for the whims of a little girl."

Harasundari said repeatedly, "You won't have to waste any time on her account." And at last she remarked jokingly, "All right, I'll just see what happens to you and me and your work."

Nivaran saw no need to reply; he tapped her cheek with his forefinger in reprimand. Thus ends the prologue.

1

Nivaran was married to a tearful young girl whose name was Shailabala. She was short of stature and wore a nose jewel.

Nivaran thought that the name was very sweet and the face quite bright. He felt an urge to observe closely her expression, her countenance, her movements, but he could not bring himself to do it. He had to pretend instead that this slip of a girl put him in a great predicament and that he would be relieved if he could bypass her and turn his attention to duties befitting his age.

Harasundari was inwardly very amused at Nivaran's predicament. Occasionally she would grasp his hand and say, "Aha, where are you off to? That little girl isn't going to eat you up!"

Nivaran would become doubly flustered and would say, "Wait, wait, I have some special work to do." He sounded as if he felt trapped. Harasundari would close the door and say with a laugh, "You can't get out of it anymore." At last Nivaran, feeling quite helpless, would sit down pensively.

Harasundari would whisper in his ear, "You shouldn't ignore someone else's daughter whom you have brought into the house." With this she would bring Shailabala and make her sit at Nivaran's left, insist on lifting her veil, raise her chin, and tell Nivaran, "Look what a moonlike face she has."

Sometimes she would get the two of them to sit in the same room; then she would get up and leave, saying that she had work to do. As she went out she would close the door with a bang. Nivaran would feel sure that two curious eyes were glued to some chink or other; with vast indifference he would turn aside and prepare to fall asleep. Shailabala, pulling down her veil, cringing, and turning her face away, would disappear into a corner.

Finally Harasundari, getting nowhere, relinquished the helm and felt no particular regrets.

When Harasundari let go, Nivaran took charge. Here at hand was a great curiosity, an enormous mystery. One wants to examine a diamond under many conditions, from many angles, turning it this way and that, and here was a beautiful little human being, a great wonder. This must be touched and caressed, viewed from a distance, from close at hand, sidewise. Sometimes the earrings were tweaked, sometimes the veil was lifted a little. The extent of the new beauties must be ascertained, sometimes with a quick perception like a flash of lightning, sometimes with a long look as steadfast as the stars.

Mr. Nivaranchandra, head clerk of MacMoran Company's office, had never before experienced anything quite like this. He had been just a boy when he married. By the time he became a young man, his wife was altogether familiar to him; married life had become a routine. He certainly loved Harasundari, but love had never grown consciously, step by step, from within.

At first Nivaran gave Shailabala secret gifts such as a china doll dressed in a gown, or a bottle of perfume, or he would buy sweets for her. This began their intimacy. Finally, while Harasundari rested from housework one day, she peeped through the crack in the door and saw Nivaran and Shailabala playing jacks with cowrie shells.

This was a strange old-age pastime. After breakfast Nivaran had acted as if he were going to the office, but had gone instead to Shailabala's room. Why this deception? Suddenly someone seemed to open Harasundari's eyes with a hot poker; in that searing heat her tears evaporated.

Harasundari said to herself, "I am the one who brought

her into the house, I am the one who brought them together. Then why does he treat me like this, as if I get
in the way of their happiness?"

Harasundari had been instructing Shailabala about housework. One day Nivaran finally spoke out. "She's just a child.
You're making her work too hard. Her health isn't that
good."

Harasundari was about to make a harsh retort, but she
held her tongue and said nothing.

From then on Shailabala was given no more chores.
Harasundari herself supervised all the work. It got so that
Shailabala could neither move about nor sit down but that
Harasundari waited upon her like a slave, and the husband
entertained her like a court jester. The fact that doing
housework or caring for others is an important duty was a
lesson Shailabala did not learn.

Harasundari worked uncomplainingly, like a slave, a role
in which she took great pride. She felt neither deprived nor
underprivileged. She would say, "You two children go and
play. I'm taking care of all the chores."

2

Alas, what happened to that strength that had once enabled Harasundari to give up tranquilly and without stint,
for a lifetime and for her husband's sake, half of her claim
to his love? On a full-moon night, when the tide floods
into our lives and inundates both shores, man impulsively
thinks that he can accomplish everything. Solemn promises
are made then, but in the long-drawn ebbing hours of life,
he finds that the lifelong honoring of the promise is too
demanding. It dawns upon him that the pledge for a gift,
made out with one stroke of the pen on the day of prosperity, must be made good bit by bit in the tedious days
of adversity. Then it is obvious that man is very poor, his
heart very weak, his resources extremely limited.

After her long convalescence Harasundari had been
feeble, anemic, pale; she had been like the thin line of the
new moon. She seemed to hover lightly over this world
and felt that she needed nothing. As she gradually became
stronger and her blood gained vigor, from out of nowhere
a host of cosharers besieged Harasundari's thoughts. Loudly they proclaimed, "Well, you have already signed the
pledge for a gift, but we'll not give up our claims."

When Harasundari finally saw her situation clearly, she gave her own bedroom to Nivaran and Shailabala. She went to sleep alone in another room.

After twenty-seven years of marriage Harasundari gave up the room that was hers from her wedding night. When this married woman blew out the earthen lamp and went with a heavy heart to her newly made widow's bed, a fashionable young man was singing the Behag across the lane, another fellow accompanied him on the drums, and his friends shouted admiringly at the end of every refrain.

That song did not sound unpleasantly in the silent, moonlit night to the occupants of the room next to Harasundari's. Little Shailabala's eyes were heavy with sleep, and Nivaran, his mouth close to her ear, was calling her name softly.

By now Nivaran had read Bankimchandra's *Chandrashekhar* to Shailabala, as well as the work of several modern poets. A fountain of youth that had always lain buried deep within Nivaran had been released. At this extremely unlikely time of his life it gushed forth and overflowed. No one was quite prepared for this; therefore, all his senses and sensibilities and all the routine of his household turned topsy-turvy. The poor fellow had never known that such troublesome elements lie hidden inside ordinary people—elements so unruly, so unmanageable, that they can create sudden chaos in a well-ordered life.

It was not only Nivaran. Harasundari encountered a new kind of pain. Why this yearning? What caused such unbearable pain? What the heart now desired, it had never before desired, never received. When Nivaran had gone to the office regularly like a gentleman and when lying in bed before falling asleep they had discussed the milkman's bills, the rising cost of living, and social obligations, there had been no sign of inner conflict. They certainly loved each other, but there had been no warmth or glow. It was a love unkindled and unlit.

It now seemed to Harasundari that someone had kept her from knowing the true meaning of existence. Her heart felt as if it had always been starved. Her life as a woman had been spent in sheer poverty. She had wasted those precious twenty-seven years in slavery, going to the grocery, worrying about fruits and vegetables, the after-dinner betel nuts and spices. Today, at the midpoint of life, she saw that in the very next room a little girl had unlocked the store containing the most cherished treasure and by a sudden coup had become the empress. Women are indeed meant to serve, but they are also meant to be queens. In the process of sharing, one woman had become the servant and the other the queen. But the servant had lost her pride and the queen was not happy.

Shailabala's feminine existence also lacked the flavor of true happiness. She got such unremitting attention that not a moment was left for her to love anyone. The river may be fulfilled by flowing toward the sea and sacrificing its individuality there, but if the sea, drawn by the tide, continually moves toward the river, the river only becomes uncomfortably full within its banks. The world, with all its admiration and affection, moved day and night toward Shailabala; as a result, her self-esteem rose higher and higher. She had no opportunity to reciprocate the world's love for her. All she knew was that everything came her way and she owed nothing to anyone. There is considerable pride but little contentment in such a situation.

3

One day the clouds heaped high and it was so dark that indoor work was impossible. Outdoors the rain fell in torrents. The jungle of weeds and vines beneath the plum tree nearly drowned, and beside the wall the muddy water flowed gurgling through the gutter. Harasundari sat silent in the solitary darkness of her new bedroom.

Just then Nivaran came to her door quietly, like a thief, unable to decide whether to go in or go away. Harasundari saw everything but said nothing.

Then, like a discharged arrow, Nivaran came up to his wife in a rush and said in one breath, "I need a few of your jewelry pieces. You know I have lots of creditors, and they are embarrassing me. I'll have to pawn something. I can get it back very soon."

Harasundari did not answer. Nivaran stood there like a criminal. Finally he added, "Then you won't give them to me today?"

Harasundari said, "No."

It was as difficult for him to leave her room as it had been to enter. Nivaran looked this way and that, stammered, "Well, then, I'll try elsewhere," and departed.

Harasundari understood all about the cause of the debt

and Nivaran's need to pawn the jewelry. She guessed that the night before, the new bride must have scolded her tame and witless husband and said, "My sister Harasundari has a safe full of jewelry. Can't I have even one piece of it?"

After Nivaran left, Harasundari got up slowly, opened her iron safe, and took out all her jewelry pieces one by one. She called Shailabala to her room and made her put on the very Banaras sari that she herself had worn on her wedding night. Then Harasundari proceeded to cover Shailabala from head to toe with all the jewelry. Lovingly she combed Shailabala's hair. She lit the earthen lamp, and that light showed her that the little girl's face was very sweet, like a freshly ripened fruit, fragrant and luscious. When Shailabala walked away jingling, that sound beat for a long time in Harasundari's veins. She said to herself, "What comparison is there today between you and me? But there was a time when I was like you, and I too was filled to the brim with youth. Why didn't anyone tell me about it then? That day came and went, and I never even knew it. But look how Shailabala moves with so much pride and dignity."

When Harasundari had known nothing but housework, this jewelry had been worth a great deal to her. Could she have given it up then at a moment's notice? Now that she had an intimation of something greater than housework, the value of the jewelry and provisions for the future became quite unimportant.

And Shailabala went to her room showing off the gold and jewels; not for a minute did she consider how much Harasundari had given her. She only knew that the normal course of all attention, all wealth, and all good fortune would eventually lead to her because she was Shailabala, she was the darling.

4

In dreams some people walk fearlessly along the most perilous road without a moment's concern. Many men get themselves into a similarly dreamlike state while wide awake, lose their discretion, and keep on along the narrow path of danger to be finally aroused when in the midst of disaster.

The MacMoran Company's head clerk was in such a state. Shailabala became like a powerful whirlpool at the center of his life. Various valuable items from many sources were drawn into it and disappeared. Nivaran's sense of humanity and his monthly salary, as well as Harasundari's good fortune and her clothes and ornaments, felt the pull. At the same time it secretly sucked in small sums from the cash funds of the MacMoran Company. Bundles of currency began to disappear one or two at a time. Nivaran would resolve to replace it in installments from next month's salary. But as soon as that money was at hand, it was drawn toward the vortex; even the last penny, starting with alarm, trembled and disappeared with the speed of lightning.

At last, one day he was caught. His was a hereditary job. His British supervisor, who liked him very much, gave him exactly two days' time in which to return the cash fund.

Nivaran himself could not understand how he had managed to gradually remove two and a half thousand rupees. He went to Harasundari like a madman and said, "I am done for!"

Harasundari listened to his story and turned pale.

Nivaran said, "Quick, get out the jewelry!"

"I have already given all of it to Shailabala," answered Harasundari.

Nivaran became as frantic as a balked child and kept repeating, "Why did you give it to her? Why? Who told you to give it?"

Harasundari evaded the real answer but said, "What harm did it do? It isn't lost."

The frightened Nivaran said demurely, "Oh, if you could get it back from her on some pretense or other! But for my life's sake, don't tell her that I asked for it or why I need it."

At that Harasundari seethed with anger and said in disgust, "Is this the time for pretending or showing off your affection? Let's go." And she took her husband into Shailabala's room.

Shailabala would not understand a thing. To whatever Nivaran said she replied, "What do I know about it?"

Had it ever occurred to her that she might actually have to think about such household problems? Everyone else would look after his own problems and cooperate in thinking up ways of making Shailabala happier. All at once this principle was revised. What a heinous crime!

Then Nivaran fell weeping at Shailabala's feet. She kept repeating, "I don't know anything about it. Why should I give up what's mine?"

It dawned upon Nivaran that the fragile little girl was more stern than the iron safe. Harasundari was full of disgust at her husband's weakness in such a crisis. She tried to seize Shailabala's key from her by force. Shailabala promptly threw the keyring out the window, over the wall, and into the pond.

Harasundari said to her bewildered husband, "Why don't you break the lock?"

Shailabala calmly declared, "Then I'll put a rope around my neck and commit suicide."

"I'll try another source," said Nivaran and, all disheveled, left the house.

Within two hours Nivaran had sold his ancestral home for two and a half thousand rupees.

Thus he narrowly avoided the handcuffs, but he lost his job. Of his movable and immovable belongings, only his two wives remained. Of these, the distraught younger wife became all the more immovable by becoming pregnant. This family took shelter in a damp little house in the lane.

5

There was no end to the misery of the younger wife. She simply would not comprehend that her husband had no income. Why did he marry her if he couldn't support her?

There were only two rooms on the second floor. One was the bedroom of Nivaran and Shailabala. The other was Harasundari's. Shailabala would whine, "I can't spend day and night in the bedroom."

Nivaran would give her false hope. "I'm looking for a little house. Soon we'll move."

Shailabala would say, "Why, there's another room next to this one."

Shailabala ignored her former neighbors. Some heard of Nivaran's difficulties and came to see him. Shailabala bolted the door and refused to open it. After they left, she flew into a rage, wept, wouldn't eat, and let the whole neighborhood know that she was having hysterics. Such tantrums became a regular occurrence.

At last Shailabala contracted a serious illness. It was even possible that she might lose the baby.

Nivaran grasped both of Harasundari's hands. "You must save Shaila."

Harasundari began to nurse Shailabala night and day. Shailabala swore at her for every little oversight, but Harasundari said nothing.

Shailabala would not drink her barley water and threw it about, cup and all. She insisted on having green mangoes when she ran a fever. If she didn't get them, she had a tantrum. Harasundari would call her "My dear" and "My sister," and tried to divert her as if she were a child.

But Shailabala did not live. After gathering a world of adoration and affection, this little girl's unfinished life was pointlessly wasted in utter misery and discontent.

6

At first Nivaran was terribly shaken, but almost at once he knew that a strong shackle had been broken. Suddenly he felt the joy of liberation mixed with his grief. Suddenly it seemed that something like a bad dream had been pressing upon his chest. When he awoke, he found his life instantly and remarkably lightened. This gentle bond that could be torn like a *madhavi* creeper—was this his beloved Shailabala? Not so. He drew a deep breath and suddenly realized that she had been his hangman's noose.

And what of Harasundari, his lifelong companion? He realized that she alone had occupied his world, had sat at the altar in the temple of his joyful and sad memories, but still there was a gulf between them. It was as if a bright and beautiful but cruel little knife had cut his heart into two and had left a grievous line of demarcation.

Once in the dead of night when the whole city was asleep, Nivaran slowly entered Harasundari's lonely bedroom. In silence, in the same old way, he took the right-hand side of the same old bed. But this time he came like a thief into what had once been his province.

Neither Harasundari nor Nivaran said a word. They lay side by side as they had lain before, but precisely in the middle slept a dead girl, and neither of them could pass over her.

1893

THE ATONEMENT

(Prayaschitta)

1

Between heaven and earth there is an indeterminate, lawless realm where King Trishanku circulates, where innumerable castles are built in the air. The name of that becastled continent is It-Might-Have-Been. Those who have achieved immortality by doing great things are greatly blessed; those who have been born with limited abilities, live among ordinary people, and assist with the daily duties of this world in their own simple way are also blessed. But those who by a slip of fate are suddenly caught between these two states of being have no alternative. They could have amounted to something if they would, but that is precisely why they are the ones for whom amounting to anything is most impossible.

Our Anathbandhu was one of those young men fated to dwell in this no-man's-land of procrastination. Everyone believed that he could have succeeded at anything, had he so wished. But he never wished it and was never successful at anything. The general confidence in him remained unshaken. Everyone said, "He'll be first in the examinations"; he didn't take any more examinations. Everyone believed that once he accepted a job, he could easily rise to the highest rank in some department; he didn't take a job at all. He had a great scorn for ordinary people, because they were so insignificant; he had not a shred of respect for those who were outstanding, because he could have been more outstanding than any of them if he had put his mind to it.

All of Anathbandhu's good reputation, his welfare, and good fortune were deposited in a fund of impossibility that was beyond time and place. In the here and now Providence

57

had endowed him only with a rich father-in-law and an amiable wife. Her name was Bindhyabashini.

Anathbandhu did not care for his wife's name, nor did he consider her qualities equal to his, but Bindhyabashini was extremely proud of her good fortune in getting such a husband. Neither she nor he doubted that, of all the husbands of all other wives, hers was the best in all respects, and ordinary people concurred with this belief.

Bindhyabashini guarded against diminution of this pride in her husband. If she could have elevated him to the highest peak of the unshakable, skyscraping mountain of her devotion and spared him all the slurs cast by foolish mortals, she would have dedicated her life, in peace and contentment, to worshiping her husband. But in the material world one object of reverence cannot be held aloft by devotion alone, and many persons in this world did not accept Anathbandhu as the ideal man. This caused Bindhyabashini much distress.

While Anathbandhu was in college he lived in his father-in-law's home. Examination time came, Anathbandhu skipped the examinations, and the next year he left college.

This greatly humiliated Bindhyabashini in the eyes of the general public. At night she spoke softly to Anathbandhu. "It would have been wise to take the examinations."

Anathbandhu laughed scornfully. "Does a person sprout four arms like Shiva by taking an examination? Even Cousin Kedar got through!"

Bindhyabashini was comforted. How would Anathbandhu's glory be enhanced by taking an examination that had been passed by all the common herd?

Kamala came from next door to give her childhood friend, Bindi, the happy news that her brother, Ramesh, had passed the same examination and won a scholarship. When she heard this, Bindhyabashini decided unreasonably that Kamala's joy was not unalloyed, that it hid a thinly veiled dig at Anathbandhu. So, without showing pleasure in her friend's happiness, she went instead to the other extreme, assumed a somewhat quarrelsome tone, and said, "The intermediate examination is no examination at all. Even in English colleges there is no examination below the B.A. level." Needless to say, Bindhyabashini had garnered all this information and logic from her husband.

Kamala had rushed in to share good news with her best friend, and she was somewhat taken aback at being hurt this way. But she too was a female. Therefore she instantly understood Bindhyabashini's motive, and at this insult to her brother a drop of venom flowed to the tip of her tongue. She said, "Dear, you and I haven't been to England or married an Englishman; how could we know all that? I'm a stupid girl. All I understand is that young men in Bengal must take the intermediate examination in college. My dear, not everyone can take it." Kamala said all this in the sweet, innocent voice of a friend and left. The disgruntled Bindhyabashini took it without a word, went to her room, and began to cry softly.

A little later there was another incident. A distant but rich relative came to Calcutta for a short visit and put up at the home of Bindhyabashini's father, Rajkumar, where he was received with unusual pomp. As a mark of special esteem for the newly arrived guest, the son-in-law was asked to relinquish the large drawing room that he had occupied and spend a few days in the room that had belonged to an uncle.

This was an affront to Anathbandhu's self-esteem. First, he went to his wife and took revenge on his father-in-law by criticizing him and making her cry. Then he displayed his sensitiveness by not eating and by other drastic measures. Bindhyabashini was terribly embarrassed. Her inborn sense of self-respect told her that in such a situation nothing is more embarrassing and degrading than a public show of hurt feelings. She got her husband to desist by clutching at his hands and feet, weeping and wailing.

Bindhyabashini was not unreasonable, and therefore she did not blame her parents. She understood that such incidents are trifling and normal, but she also thought of the respect due a relative by marriage.

From that day on, she began to say to her husband daily, "Take me to your home. I don't want to live here anymore."

Anathbandhu had plenty of vanity but no self-respect. He had not the least desire to return to the poverty of his own home. Then his wife became a bit stubborn and said, "If you don't go, I'll go myself."

Inwardly annoyed, Anathbandhu began preparing to take his wife from Calcutta to the tiny village where his family lived in a mud-brick house. At departure time Rajkumar and his wife urged their daughter to stay a little longer in the paternal homestead. Head bowed and face somber, the daughter sat quietly, and her silence told them that that was out of the question.

Finding Bindhyabashini suddenly adamant, her parents suspected that somehow they had unintentionally offended her. Rajkumar asked with a heavy heart, "Daughter, did we hurt you without meaning to?"

Bindhyabashini glanced sadly and tenderly at her father and replied, "Not at all. I have been very happy here with all your care." And she began to weep. But her determination remained unshaken.

Her father and mother sighed and thought, No matter how much love and care you give your daughter, she becomes estranged as soon as she is married.

Finally, in tears, Bindhyabashini said good-bye to everyone and left her father's home, which had surrounded her with love since the day of her birth. She turned her back upon her friends and relatives and got into the palanquin.

2

There is a considerable difference between a rich Calcutta home and the home of a villager. But not once did Bindhyabashini's attitude or behavior show discontent. She cheerfully helped her mother-in-law with the housework. Knowing their modest circumstances, her father had sent a maid with his daughter at his own expense. When Bindhyabashini reached her husband's home, she promptly sent her back. Bindhyabashini could not bear the fear that a maid from a wealthy home would continually turn up her nose at the poorness of her husband's home.

The mother-in-law was fond of Bindhyabashini and tried to dissuade her from doing hard work, but with tireless diligence and pleasant disposition Bindhyabashini helped with every household task and won the mother-in-law's heart. The village girls were also charmed by her virtues.

But this did not produce an entirely satisfactory result because the rules of this universe are not like the simple rules of conduct set forth in literary language in the first primer. A cruel imp who loves mockery pops up, shuffles all the rules of behavior, and jumbles them thoroughly. Thus, apparently good work does not necessarily produce unqualified good, and there is a sudden upset.

Anathbandhu had two younger and one older brother. The latter had a job away from home and his fifty-rupee salary maintained their family and paid for the education of the two younger brothers.

In those days it was absolutely impossible to make household improvements on fifty rupees a month, but the sum was sufficient to swell the pride of the oldest brother's wife, Shyamashankari. Her husband had year-round work, and therefore she assumed the privilege of taking it easy all year around. Proceeding upon the assumption that she had conferred a great favor upon the whole family by becoming the wife of the wage-earning husband, she did no housework.

When Bindhyabashini came to her father-in-law's home and like a true housewife was consistently willing to do the housekeeping, Shyamashankari's narrow mind felt as if it had been clutched and squeezed. Her motivation was obscure; perhaps she thought that ever since Anathbandhu's wife had come to the house, she wanted people to see her doing menial kitchen work only in order to embarrass Shyamashankari. For some reason the fifty-rupee-a-month wife could not stand this daughter of a rich family. She saw signs of intolerable pride in Bindhyabashini's humility.

For his part Anathbandhu established a library in the village. He gathered ten or twenty schoolboys, became their chairman, and began to telegraph dispatches to the newspapers. He even astonished some of the villagers by becoming a special correspondent for several English-language dailies; instead of contributing a penny to his poor family he incurred considerable expense.

Bindhyabashini continually urged him to take some sort of job. He turned a deaf ear. He told his wife that there were jobs worthy of him, but the biased British government employed only very prominent Englishmen in those posts; a Bengali applicant could be a thousand times more capable, but he didn't stand a chance.

Shyamashankari began to make consistently venomous remarks, direct and oblique, about her brother-in-law and Bindhyabashini. She arrogantly boasted of their moderate means and would say, "We are poor people, how can we support a rich man's daughter and son-in-law? Everything was fine there, no problem at her house. Can they stand our hardships and live on rice and lentils?"

The mother-in-law was afraid of Shyamashankari; she did not have the courage to speak up in support of the victims. Bindhyabashini, too, continued quietly swallowing both the food provided by the fifty rupees a month and her sister-in-law's sharp words.

In the meantime the eldest brother came home for a short vacation and was treated to a lot of lively and excited lectures by his wife. At last, when his sleep began to be interrupted every night and every night the interruptions lengthened, he sent for Anathbandhu one day and said calmly and affectionately, "You ought to look for a job. How can I run the family all by myself?"

Anathbandhu hissed like a trampled snake and snapped, "I can't stand being pressured like this, just for two handfuls of coarse, inedible rice twice a day." He immediately resolved to take his wife and go to his father-in-law.

But the wife would have none of it. According to her the younger brother is entitled to the older brother's support and the younger sister-in-law puts up with the abuses of the older one, but it was too humiliating for her husband to live under his father-in-law's roof. Bindhyabashini could bear being at her father-in-law's with her head bowed like a pauper, but in her father's home she wanted to maintain her dignity and hold her head high.

At this point a position for a third-grade teacher became vacant in the village elementary school. Anathbandhu's older brother and Bindhyabashini both urged him to take this job. Even this took a contrary turn. Anathbandhu was highly insulted that his own brother and his legally wedded wife could think him fit for such a contemptible job, and he thereupon became four times as indifferent to the family and all its activities.

Then his older brother had to take him aside again and beg him to calm down. Everyone felt that it was useless to say anything more to him. The family would be best out of it by finding some means of keeping him at home.

His older brother went back to work after the vacation. Shyamashankari glowered and set her jaw so that she looked like a menacing wheel of fate. Anathbandhu came to Bindhyabashini and said, "It is impossible to get a decent job these days without training in England. I've decided to go to England; you go to your father's and make some excuse for collecting money."

Bindhyabashini was thunderstruck by this idea of going to England. Nor could she think how to go to her father and beg for money; she was shamed by the very thought of it. Anathbandhu's pride prevented his asking in person for money from his father-in-law; still, he could not understand why the daughter would not go and extract money from her father by pretext or pressure. Anath supported his argument with temper tantrums, and the hurt Bindhyabashini shed copious tears.

Things went on this way while household routine suffered and the air filled with unhappiness. At last the autumn Puja holidays were imminent. Rajkumarbabu dispatched a palanquin in great style with a cordial invitation for the daughter and son-in-law to pay a visit. After a whole year she and her husband returned to her father's house. This time the son-in-law received a welcome even better than that which he had found so intolerable when extended to the rich relative. Bindhyabashini, after all this time, took off her veil, reveled in the unceasing affection of her relatives, and joyfully rode the waves of festivity.

It was the sixth day of the Puja. Tomorrow the seventh day's worship would begin. The din and bustle were endless. Every room of the big house was filled with near and distant relatives.

That night Bindhyabashini went to bed very tired. She was not in their former bedroom. With a special indulgence, her mother had given up her own room to her son-in-law. Bindhyabashini did not know when Anathbandhu had come to bed. She was then sound asleep.

Early in the morning the *sanai* began to play, but the exhausted Bindhyabashini did not wake up. Her two friends, Kamala and Bhuban, tried unsuccessfully to peep through the bedroom door and, still outside, finally broke into loud laughter. Then Bindhyabashini quickly awoke and found that her husband was already up. Feeling ashamed of herself, she got out of bed and saw that her mother's iron safe was open and her father's cash box was gone from its place inside.

Then she recalled that there had been a great commotion in the house the previous evening over the disappearance of her mother's keyring. Obviously, the thief who stole that keyring had done this. Then she had a sudden fear that the thief had somehow hurt her husband. Her heart shook and pounded. Looking under the bed, she found a letter weighted down by her mother's keyring near one leg of the bed.

It was her husband's handwriting. She opened the letter and read that a friend had helped him to get the fare to London. Now, since he was unable to find other means of defraying his expenses there, he had stolen his father-in-law's money and had gone down the wooden stairs from the adjacent veranda into the garden, had jumped the wall, and fled. The ship had left early that morning.

When Bindhyabashini read the letter her blood froze. She sat there holding on to the leg of the bed. Inside her body, against her eardrums, throbbed a sound like the call of crickets in the still night of death. Added to that were many *sanais* playing on many pitches in the courtyard, in the neighbors' houses, and in distant homes. All Bengal was in a frenzy of festivity.

The autumn sun, blazing with festival colors, jovially entered the bedroom. Bhuban and Kamala, finding the door still closed so late on a festival day, began to pound on it with their fists, laughing loudly and joking. When that got no response, they were a little frightened and began to shout at the tops of their voices, "Bindu, Bindu!"

Bindhyabashini spoke in a choked, broken voice. "I'm coming. You all go away now."

Afraid that their friend was ill, they brought her mother, who came and said, "Bindu, darling, what is the matter? Why is the door still closed?"

Bindu checked the flow of her tears and said, "Bring Father here."

Deeply disturbed, her mother immediately brought Rajkumarbabu and stood outside the room. Bindu opened it, drew them inside, and quickly closed the door.

Then Bindu fell on the floor at her father's feet and burst into tears that seemed to tear her heart to pieces. "Father, forgive me! I have stolen money from your safe."

The astonished parents sat on the bed. Bindu said that she had done it in order to send her husband to England.

"Why didn't you tell us you wanted it?" her father asked.

"You would keep him from going to England."

Rajkumarbabu was very angry. Mother and daughter cried, and from every part of Calcutta the cheerful music of the Puja sounded in a variety of tunes.

That Bindu who had never been able to ask her father for money, that wife who would try with all her might to conceal from her relatives the slightest dishonorable act of her husband, was now crushed; amid this festive crowd her wifely pride, her dignity as a daughter, her self-respect, were like dust beneath the feet of all those she loved and those she disliked, people known and unknown. The news spread like wildfire through the house filled with relatives: that the deed was premeditated, that the keys were stolen by conspiracy, that Anathbandhu had stolen the money with the help of his wife and fled to England. Bhuban, Kamala, and many others—neighbors, servants, and housemaids—had stood near the door and had heard every word. Everyone had come, inquisitive and eager with anticipation, when the head of the house and his wife had anxiously entered the closed room of the son-in-law.

Bindhyabashini would not see anyone. She lay in bed behind closed doors without anything to eat. No one pitied her in her sorrow. Everyone was amazed at the conspirators' evil-mindedness and decided that Bindhyabashini's true character had been hidden all this time. The Puja festival passed somehow in this joyless household.

3

Bowed with humiliation and fatigue, Bindhyabashini came back to her mother-in-law's house. There a bond was established between the widowed mother-in-law, who was overwhelmed by the defection of her son, and the daughter-in-law, who was separated from her husband. The two women drew closer to each other under the silent shadow of their sorrow and with profound patience continued to perform every detail of household work with their own hands. Bindhyabashini's own parents became more remote as the mother-in-law became closer. Bindhyabashini said to herself, "My mother-in-law is poor, I too am poor. We are tied by the same bond of sorrow. My parents are wealthy; they are worlds away from us." Bindhyabashini was remote from them, first of all, because she was poor; now she had fallen even lower by confessing herself a thief. Can the bonds of affection withstand such great strains?

At first Anathbandhu wrote regularly to his wife from England. But gradually his letters became less frequent and a note of unconcern crept in. Many English girls who were superior in knowledge, education, appearance, and everything else to his uneducated, hard-working wife regarded Anathbandhu as eligible, intelligent, and handsome. Under such circumstances it was not at all remarkable that Anathbandhu would consider his unsophisticated, old-fashioned, dark-complexioned wife unworthy to share his lofty status.

But when he needed money he didn't hesitate to send

a cable to this helpless Bengali girl. And she, who wore only two pairs of glass bangles on her arms, sold all her jewelry in order to keep sending the money. Because there was no place in the village where they could be kept safely, all her most valuable ornaments were at her father's house. On the pretext that she had invitations to visit her husband's relatives, Bindhyabashini brought all the jewelry to the village a piece at a time. At last, after selling the last of her bracelets, her silver bangles, and even her Banaras sari and shawl, after making many humble pleas and promises, after blotting every line of her letter with tears, Bindhyabashini begged her husband to come home.

The husband, now a barrister, returned with his hair cut short, his beard shaven, wearing coat and trousers, and moved into a hotel. It was impossible to live in his father's house. In the first place, there was no suitable room; in the second place, the villagers were backward, and once a householder had forfeited his caste by going abroad he was helpless. His father-in-law's family were very orthodox Hindus. They too would be unable to shelter an outcaste.

Very soon he was so low in funds that he had to leave the hotel for a rented room. He had no intention of bringing his wife to that house. After returning from England he had paid his wife and his mother only a few daytime visits and had not seen them again.

The two sorrowful women had only one consolation: Anathbandhu was living near his own relatives. At the same time, they took unbounded pride in Anathbandhu's extraordinary achievement in becoming a barrister. Bindhyabashini began to reproach herself for being unworthy of her renowned husband. Her pride in him was increased all the more by her own feeling of unworthiness. She was ill with unhappiness and exalted by her pride. She hated non-Hindu customs; still, when she thought of her husband, she said to herself, "So many people become sahibs these days, but no one else looks as proper as he does! He is like a real Englishman! There's nothing to show that he's a Bengali."

When Anathbandhu could not meet his expenses; when he sorrowfully decided that there was no respect for talent in this accursed India and his malicious colleagues were secretly obstructing his promotion; when there were more vegetables than meat in his meals, and fried shrimp gradually took over the honored place of roast chicken; when the nattiness of his clothes and the resplendence of his well-shaven face became dulled; when the uppermost note in the chord of life slowly descended from the high seventh to a melancholy low note—then a serious mishap in Rajkumar's family changed the course of Anathbandhu's miserable, muddled life. While returning by boat from his uncle's home on the Ganges, Rajkumarbabu's only son, Harakumar, his wife, and his little boy were killed when their boat collided with a steamer. This left no one in Rajkumar's line of descent except his daughter, Bindhyabashini.

After this terrible sorrow had faded a little, Rajkumar went to Anathbandhu and made a request: "Son, you'll have to undergo the cleansing ceremony and be restored to your caste. I have no one but you."

Anathbandhu agreed enthusiastically to that proposal. He thought this was the way to get even with all those office- and library-bound Indian barristers who envied him and showed insufficient respect for his uncommon talents.

Rajkumar consulted the pundits. They said, "If Anathbandhu has not eaten beef, there is a way to restore him to his caste."

Anathbandhu unashamedly refused to admit that the proscribed four-legged animal had been among his favorite foods in the foreign country. To his close friends he said, "When society voluntarily listens to lies, I see no crime in telling it what it wants to hear. The tongue that has eaten beef must be purified with cow dung and lies; our modern society orders purification by means of nastiness and equivocation. I don't want to fly in the face of that order."

An auspicious day was set for his atonement and restoration to society. In the meantime Anathbandhu not only donned dhoti and chador, but he began to use arguments and advice to blacken the English and to whitewash Indian society. He delighted everyone who heard him.

The proud, happy Bindhyabashini's tender heart filled to overflowing with love and adoration. She told herself, "Whoever returns from England returns as a full-fledged English sahib, and it's hard to recognize him as a Bengali. But my husband has returned absolutely unspoiled. In fact, his devotion to Hinduism is much greater than before."

On the designated day, Rajkumarbabu's home was full of Brahman pundits. No expense was spared. Food and transportation were provided. In the inner part of the house magnificence was unlimited. The courtyard and all the rooms swarmed with invited friends, relatives, and neighbors. The smiling Bindhyabashini floated happily through that great uproar and bustle like a feathery cloud blown by the morning breeze and touched by the autumn sun. Her husband was the hero of an occasion of universal significance. All Bengal seemed like a theater that day, and as soon as the curtain rose, Anathbandhu would be displayed alone before a world oblivious of all else. Atonement was not an admission of guilt; it was an expression of favor. Anathbandhu, by returning from England and reentering Hindu society, had ennobled it; this new glow was diffused throughout the land in thousands of beams, fell on Bindhyabashini's face, alight with love, and reflected in extraordinary splendor. Now, after all the misery of her unimportant life and her trifling humiliations, she rose to the peak of glory in her father's house before all her friends and relatives. Today her husband's greatness commanded the respect of the world for the unworthy wife.

The ceremony ended. Anathbandhu was reinstated. The guests, relatives, and Brahmans had sat in the same room with him and had finished their meal with relish.

The relatives called the son-in-law to the inner rooms. Calmly, chewing betel nut, smiling, he strolled lazily toward the inner rooms while the corner of his chador swept the floor.

While payment of the Brahmans' fee was being arranged after the meal, they sat together and made a tumultuous display of scriptural knowledge. The head of the house, Rajkumarbabu, was resting briefly, listening to this learned uproar and mulling over the arguments when the doorman gave him a card and said, "An English lady has come."

Rajkumar was astonished. The very next instant, as he looked at the card, he saw written in English: "Mrs. Anathbandhu Sarkar." In other words, this was Anathbandhu's wife.

For quite some time Rajkumarbabu stared at this simple card without being able to make head or tail of it. In the meantime the lady herself, newly arrived from England, rosy-cheeked, auburn-haired, blue-eyed, fair as milk, light-footed as a doe, walked into the room and for a long interval stood looking from person to person. She did not find the one familiar, loving face. All the scriptural arguments had stopped the moment the lady arrived, and the room became as silent as a cemetery.

Just then, with his chador trailing, Anathbandhu languidly reentered the scene. At once the English lady ran and embraced him, and a kiss from her red lips left the imprint of a conjugal meeting.

The scriptural debate was not resumed that day.

1894

APPEASEMENT
(Manbhanjan)

Gopinath Sil's wife, Giribala, lived on the top floor of Ramnath Sil's big three-story house. A few jasmine plants and a rosebush grew in a planter at the north door of the bedroom. The rooftop terrace was surrounded by a high wall; a few bricks had been removed here and there to provide a view. In the bedroom hung many framed engravings of European actresses in different stages and styles of dress, but they were no lovelier than the reflection of the sixteen-year-old lady of the house that appeared in the big mirror by the door.

Giribala's beauty was like an unexpected burst of light, a sudden surprise, an awakening. It made an instant impression and was quite overwhelming. The beholder would think, I wasn't prepared for this. She's so different.

Giribala was conscious of her own loveliness. Her youth and beauty overflowed her body as wine foams and overflows the glass. She was inordinately concerned with her clothes and carriage, her gestures, the angle of her neck, the quick rhythm of her step. It was all her own: the music of her ankle bells, the jingling of her bracelets, her rippling laughter, her vivacious manner of speaking, the flash of her eyes.

Giribala was intoxicated by her own beauty. Dressed in a pastel sari, she walked on the roof terrace; her body felt an urge to dance to the rhythms of an indistinct, unknown song. She seemed to take pleasure in every movement as she stretched, whirled, and turned. As she stirred up the waves of her own beauty, she felt an ebb and flow of extraordinary excitement in her blood. She would suddenly tear off some rose petals and with her right arm toss them skyward to be carried off by the wind. Her bracelets jingled, the end of her sari fluttered loose, the movement of her lovely arm was like that of a caged bird set free and flying away into the boundless cloud kingdom of the sky. All at once she would pick up a lump of soil from the planter and throw it away for no apparent reason. Standing on tiptoe, she could peep through the wall for a quick glimpse of the great outside world. The end of her sari would twirl as she moved and the bunch of keys tied to it would clink and jingle. Perhaps she would stand in front of the mirror and let down her hair at midday. Raising her arms and holding a hair ribbon between her teeth, she would coil her hair firmly into a braid at the back of her head. When it was braided she had nothing more to do. She would lazily stretch on the soft bed like a shaft of moonlight that had slipped through the leaves of the trees.

She had no children and no housework in this wealthy home; she spent her days alone till she could stand it no longer. She had a husband but he was beyond her control. He did not notice that Giribala had left childhood behind and blossomed into the full beauty of youth.

He had paid more attention to her as a little girl. In those days he would give his dozing teacher the slip and run away from school for an afternoon alone with his girl-wife. He wrote her letters on fancy stationery, even though they lived in the same house. He proudly showed those letters to his friends at school. No friction arose between him and Giribala over trifles and imaginary issues.

About this time Gopinath's father died, and Gopinath became the head of the house. The worm quickly penetrates the unseasoned plank; young Gopinath soon found himself the prey of all sorts of odd creatures. His outside distractions began to increase, and his visits to the inner rooms became less frequent.

There is excitement in leadership. Men are stimulated by the company of other men. Like Napoleon, who felt compelled to extend his power over countless men and the panorama of history, this minor head of a minor salon had a compulsion to create a miniature empire out of his own little circle. It was exciting to collect a crowd of down-and-outers as his regular cronies, wield influence over them, and cheer them on. He was prepared to shoulder all the failures, debts, and scandals in his mighty task.

Gopinath found the leadership of a clique increasingly stimulating. He grew more jovial every day, more proud of himself. His cronies began to say, "Gopinath is more fun than anyone!" That pride and excitement blinded him to all other considerations of pain, pleasure, or duty; the misguided fellow was spun around and steadily swallowed up as by a whirlpool.

Giribala, for her part, was enthroned in her empty bedroom. Her conquering beauty ruled the untenanted kingdom. She was well aware that the gods had awarded her the scepter, she knew that one glance from her would subjugate the wild world that she saw through the chink in the wall, but so far she had not been able to capture a soul in that world.

Giribala had a droll maidservant named Sudho. She sang, danced, recited jingles, praised the beauty of her mistress, and fretted over a heedless husband's neglect of such beauty. Giribala couldn't have managed without Sudho; she would listen to the lengthy eulogies of her own beautiful face, the shape of her figure, and the fairness of her complexion. Now and then she protested and would scold Sudho with a great show of horror, calling her liar and flatterer. Sudho would protest on her honor that no one was more innocent than she, and Giribala was very easily convinced.

Sudho would sing for Giribala: "I have enslaved myself at your feet." Giribala heard eulogies of her own beautiful lac-tinted feet and conjured up in imagination the picture of a slave prostrate before her feet, but, alas, although two exquisite feet could make the whole empty rooftop resound triumphantly with the music of their anklets, no one came of his own free will to write her a bond of indenture.

Gopinath had signed himself over to a girl named Labanya. She was an actress with a marvelous aptitude for fainting on the stage; when she panted and whimpered in her nasal stagy voice and lisped "Lord of my heart!" or cried "My dearest one!" the audience, wearing flimsy vests over their dhotis and long socks, stood up and shouted in English, "Excellent! Excellent!"

Giribala's husband himself had already given Giribala

many glowing descriptions of the wonderful actress Labanya. But even though Giribala was unaware of her husband's infatuation, she had been jealous. She couldn't bear
knowing that some other woman could make herself so
attractive. Giribala had often expressed a desire, which
arose from envious curiosity, to be taken to the theater,
but she could never get her husband to humor her.

Finally one day she gave Sudho the price of a ticket
and sent her to see the play. Sudho came back frowning,
fervently invoking the name of Ram, and declaring that
actresses should be disposed of with the broom and that
the same treatment should be meted out to all those men
who drooled over their disgusting figures and artificial pos-
turing. Giribala was greatly reassured.

But when her husband became footloose, her doubts re-
vived. If she appeared skeptical about Sudho's words, Sudho
would touch Giri and say that her figure was ungainly and
as dried out as a dressed-up piece of firewood. Giri could
not divine a reason for this criticism, and the telling blow
struck at her pride.

At last she took Sudho with her one evening and sneaked
out to the theater. The special excitement in forbidden
things fluttered her heart. The lighted, crowded place, the
sound of the musical instruments, the brightly colored sce-
nery, all doubled in splendor before her eyes. She was transported from those walled-in, joyless rooms of hers to the
fringe of this happy, well-dressed festive crowd. The whole
thing was like a dream.

The play that evening was *Appeasement*. When the bell
rang, the music stopped, the restless audience immediately
quieted down. The footlights brightened, the curtain rose,
and a corps of dancers beautifully dressed as women of
Vraja began to sway in time to the accompanying song.
The theater shook with the noise of prolonged applause
and shouts. The blood began to race and surge through
Giribala's young body. The rhythm of the song, the lights
and the dazzling setting, and the chorus of praise made
her for the moment oblivious of society, the world, and
everything else. She felt that she had come to a place
that promised glorious deliverance from restrictions.

Now and then Sudho came and whispered in her ear
in a frightened voice, "Ma'am, let's go back home now. If
my master hears about this, nothing will save us." Giribala
paid no attention. She was not a bit afraid now.

The play was very long. Radha was in a towering fit of pique, and Krishna could make no headway in this sea of resentment. How he pleaded and implored and wept! It availed him nothing.

Then Giribala felt a bursting inner pride. At the sight of Krishna's humiliation she imagined herself as Radha. She began to perceive the unlimited scope of her own power. No one had ever so humored her; she was an ignored, despised, deserted wife; still, in that one extraordinary moment of delusion, she too had the power to be cruel and to make someone weep. She had heard that beauty had power and might, but she had only speculated about it. Now she saw it all very clearly in the light of the lamps, in the tunes of the songs, on the lovely stage. Her whole being was intoxicated.

At last the curtain fell, the gaslights were turned down, and the audience gradually thinned. Giribala sat there as if enchanted. She forgot that she would have to get up and go home. She had thought the play would never end, that the curtain would rise again. Nothing existed except Krishna's downfall at the hands of Radha. "Ma'am," said Sudho, "what are you doing? Get up, all the lights will soon be turned off."

It was very late when Giribala returned to her bedroom. A lamp flickered in one corner, no one stirred, there was not a sound; at one side of the room over her unused bed, an old mosquito net moved a little in the breeze. Her everyday world seemed terribly ugly, joyless, and cluttered with trivialities. Where was that world full of beauty and lights and music where her own beauty could be diffused and fill the center of the universe, where she would not be just an unknown, neglected, insignificant, ordinary young woman?

Now she began to go to the theater every week. As time passed, her first enchantment diminished. Now she saw the actresses' makeup, their lack of beauty, all the artificiality of the theater. But she was still fascinated by it. When the curtain rose, her heart pounded with joy as a soldier's heart leaps at the sound of martial music. Where could a world-conquering beauty queen find a better imaginary throne than this self-contained world of the lovely, lofty stage, bordered with gold lettering, arranged like a painting, filled with the illusory magic of poetry and music, the focus of innumerable enchanted spectators, mysterious with the secrecies of the greenroom, strung with garlands of lights and displayed before everyone?

The first time she saw her husband in the theater and Gopinath began to rave about the performance of an actress, Giribala felt a powerful resentment toward him. She thought bitterly that if the day ever came when her husband fell at her feet like a singed moth drawn by her beauty and she could walk out on him showing resentment from head to toe, her wasted youth and beauty could be put to some good use.

But that happy day did not come. It became difficult to catch even a glimpse of Gopinath. He was whirled away like a dust eddy in the storm of his own infatuation, and no one knew his whereabouts.

One night in mid-April Giribala, dressed in a yellow sari whose bordered end floated on the south wind, sat on the roof terrace. Although her husband did not come home, she nevertheless decked herself out daily with her newest jewelry. Her fingers and toes, ornamented with diamonds and pearls, dazzled as she moved; a surge of glitter and jingling enveloped her. Today she wore bracelets, a necklace of rubies and pearls, and a sapphire ring on the little finger of her right hand.

Sudho sat on the floor, and now and then stroked Giri's soft, rounded feet, stained with red ocher along the soles, sighed deeply, and said, "Oh, ma'am, if I were a man, I'd let myself be trampled to death by these feet."

Giribala laughed haughtily. "It seems no one's going to let himself be trampled, so what else can be done with feet? Don't sit there. Sing that song."

On the lonely rooftop flooded with moonlight, Sudho began to sing:

> I am enslaved by your beautiful feet,
> The dwellers at Vrindavan are my witnesses.

It was ten o'clock. Everyone else in the house had eaten dinner and gone to bed. At that hour Gopinath suddenly appeared, with his scarf flying, reeking of perfume. Sudho hurriedly pulled up her veil and fled breathlessly.

Giribala thought that her day had come. She did not look up. She remained sitting, like Radha, profoundly aloof. But the scene did not open. The tail of the peacock did not collapse at her feet. No one began the song. "Why does the full moon hide its face?"

In a dull, dry voice Gopinath said, "Give me your keys."

In the moonlight, in the spring, after such a long separation, what kind of opening line was this! Did those who wrote poetry, plays, and novels produce nothing but lies from start to finish? A stage lover fell singing at one's feet, but to capture the heart of the beholder, this fellow had come to the roof terrace in the middle of a spring night and said to his own incomparable wife, "My dear, give me your keys!" There was no background music, no love scene; there was no illusion, no grace to it; it was a terrible letdown.

The wind began to blow from the south like a long, deep sigh for all the wasted romance of the situation; the fragrance from the tub of blooming jasmine swept across the roof. Giribala's humiliation showed in her wide-open eyes and in her expression, and the scented scarf of her yellow sari fluttered frantically.

Giribala abandoned all her pride. She took her husband's hand and said, "I'll give you the keys. You go inside." She firmly intended that he would now weep and wail, all her lovely daydreams would come true, all her infallible weapons would be brought forth to triumph.

"I can't stay long," said Gopinath. "Give me the keys."

"I'll give them to you and I'll give you all that goes with them, but you can't go anywhere tonight."

"That's impossible. I have urgent business."

"Then I won't give them to you," said Giribala.

"Of course you won't. I can see that." He had seen that there were no keys tied to the end of Giribala's sari. He went into the room and opened the drawer of her mirror stand; it held no keys. He smashed open her cosmetic box; it contained a mascara jar, a box of vermilion, hair ribbons, and an assortment of similar items—but no keys. Then he tore up the bedding and lifted the mattress, forced open the wardrobe and ransacked it.

Giribala was as stiff as a stone image. She stood holding the door and looked out at the rooftop.

The frustrated Gopinath, growling angrily, went up to her and said, "I told you to give me the keys, and you'll be sorry if you don't."

Giribala did not say a word. Then Gopinath pushed her

down, pulled off the bracelets, the necklace, and the ring, gave her a kick, and made his exit.

No one in the house awoke. No one in the vicinity knew anything about it. The moonlit night was as silent as ever. Peace was undisturbed. But if the heart had cried aloud, the sound of its anguish would have torn to shreds the moonlit serenity of the April night. Thus the tearing of a heart occurred in complete silence.

Still, she got through the rest of the night. Giribala could not report such a defeat, such humiliation, to Sudho. She thought of suicide, of destroying this matchless beauty with her own hands, of avenging her rejection herself. But at once she remembered that no one else would benefit by such an act; not a soul in the world would feel the least distress. There was neither pleasure in life nor consolation in death.

"I'll go to my father's," said Giribala. Her father lived a long way from Calcutta, but she neither listened to the objections of her mother-in-law nor took anyone along. Gopinath was away on a boat trip with his friends and no one knew where he had gone.

Gopinath's love of the drama took him to the theater almost every day. Labanya was appearing as Manorama in the play of that name, and Gopinath and his friends, sitting in the best orchestra seats, shouted "Bravo!" at the top of their voices and tossed bouquets onto the stage. Now and then the audience became intensely annoyed by the daily hubbub. Nevertheless, the theater managers never got up the courage to put a stop to it.

Finally one day Gopinath, who was a little drunk, went into the greenroom and caused a big commotion. Considering himself insulted by some trifling imaginary slight, he gave an actress a vicious slap. Her shrieks and Gopinath's storm of abuse electrified the room.

That day the managers could stand it no longer and got the police to throw Gopinath out.

Gopinath vowed revenge for this insult. For a month before the Puja holiday, the theater management had been announcing with considerable fanfare the opening of the new play, *Manorama*. They covered the city with posters and newspaper notices; it seemed they had inscribed that illustrious playwright's name upon the metropolitan roll of honor.

At this point Gopinath boarded a boat with their leading

lady, Labanya. She disappeared no one knew where, and their search produced no results.

The play producers were suddenly cast adrift. For a few days they waited for Labanya. Finally, they began to train a new actress for the role of Manorama; this caused a lag in their production schedule.

But little damage had been done. The regular theater-goers were not deterred. They came back by the hundreds, and there was no end of the eulogies in the papers.

Gopinath heard that chorus of praise in the far reaches of the country. He could stay away no longer. Full of spite and curiosity, he came to have a look at the play.

The curtain rose. Manorama appeared in the first act as a destitute drudge in the home of her father-in-law; humble and gently reticent, she went about her household chores. She didn't speak one line, and her face could not be plainly seen.

In the last act, Manorama was sent back to her father's house by the greedy husband who was about to marry the only daughter of a millionaire. After the wedding, when the husband looked beneath his wife's veil in the bridal chamber, he found that the bride was Manorama, no longer a drudge. Now she was dressed like a princess; her peerless beauty, heightened by the splendor of her clothes and jewels, shone radiantly. Manorama had been kidnapped from her wealthy home as a child and carried off to a poor household. Much later, her father had found her, had her brought home and remarried with the pomp of her new circumstances to the same husband.

Thereupon a process of appeasement commenced in the bridal chamber. But in the meantime a towering commotion broke out in the audience. As long as Manorama had worn the dirty veil of the drudge, Gopinath had watched quietly. But when she stood in the bridal chamber, glittering with jewels and dressed in the red wedding sari, the veil fallen from her head and her beauty revealed; when she turned with an indescribable pride and dignity to face the audience and Gopinath, and withered him with a look like a lightning bolt; when the whole audience joined in prolonged applause that shook the theater—then Gopinath suddenly leaped to his feet shouting, "Giribala! Giribala!" He tried to run and jump onto the stage, but the musicians held him back.

The members of the audience were enraged by this abrupt

interruption of their enjoyment and began to shout in English and in Bengali, "Get him away from there! Throw him out!"

Like a madman, Gopinath kept shouting hoarsely, "I'll murder her, I'll murder her!"

The police came, arrested Gopinath, and took him out. The whole city of Calcutta went to feast its eyes on Giribala's play; Gopinath was the only one who could not get admission.

1895

THE TROUBLEMAKER

(Apada)

As evening approached, the storm became progressively more violent. The lashing rain, the roaring thunder, the glittering lightning made the sky seem like a battlefield of demons. The black clouds flew on every side like victory flags at the millennium; the rebellious waves tossed from one shore of the Ganges to the other in a tumultuous dance; and the great trees in the garden flapped all their branches and sprawled to left and right in terror.

In this setting a man and his wife in a garden house in Chandernagore sat opposite each other on a cot and a low bed, and talked behind closed doors.

Sarat was saying, "If you stay a few days longer you'll be fully recovered; then we can go back home."

"I am completely recovered," Kiranmayee replied. "It won't hurt me to go back to the country now."

Married readers will know that there was more to the conversation than is reported here. The problem was not particularly complex; nevertheless, the debate did not seem to proceed toward a decision; it went in circles like a rudderless boat and got nowhere. The probable outcome appeared to be a sinking beneath waves of tears.

"The doctor said that it would be wise to stay a few more days," said Sarat.

"Your doctor knows everything!" Kiran retorted.

"You know how many epidemics break out at this time of the year in the country. It would be wise to spend a few more months here."

"So no one ever gets sick here!"

Kiran was popular with everyone—at home, in the neighborhood, even at her mother-in-law's. When she became seriously ill everyone was upset, and when the doctor suggested a change of climate, neither her husband nor her mother-in-law objected to her going away from home and housework. However, the village elders questioned the whole thing, declaring that to expect a change of climate to effect a recovery and to make such a to-do over a wife was a shameless demonstration of the newfangled extremes of wife pampering. Had no one's wife ever been seriously ill before? Were the people immortal in the place to which Sarat proposed taking his wife? And in what region is one's fate inoperative?

Nevertheless, Sarat and his mother ignored all such arguments. The life of their beloved Kiran seemed more important to them than all the wisdom of the village. Human beings often labor under this delusion when their dear ones are threatened.

Sarat, his wife, and his mother took up residence in the garden house at Chandernagore and Kiran recovered, but she still had not fully regained her strength. Her face was pathetically thin, so that those who saw her shuddered and said, "Ah, she has had a narrow escape!"

But Kiran's was a friendly and fun-loving nature. She didn't want to be there alone anymore; she had no housework, no neighborhood friends. It wasn't interesting to be concerned all day with only one's own sick self. Take the medicine as directed every hour on the hour, keep warm, stick to the prescribed diet—she was sick of all this. This was what husband and wife argued about behind closed doors on the stormy evening.

As long as Kiran argued back, the battle seemed an even match, but when she finally fell silent and protested by turning her head away in indifference, the poor, helpless man was disarmed. He was about to accept defeat when the bearer loudly shouted something outside the door.

Sarat got up and opened the door. He was told that a Brahman boy whose boat had capsized had made his way into their garden.

This news disposed of Kiran's pique. Immediately she took dry clothes from the rope hanger, warmed some milk, and had the Brahman boy called to her room.

He had long hair, large eyes, and no beard as yet. Kiran served him herself and inquired about his family.

She learned that his name was Nilkanta and that he was an apprentice in a touring theatrical troupe. They had been called to give a performance at the Sinhas' house; on the way the boat had capsized, and the fate of the others in the troupe was unknown. Nilkanta was a good swimmer and had managed to save himself.

The boy stayed on. Kiran's sympathy was aroused by the fact that he had almost lost his life.

Sarat thought it a good thing that Kiran had a new interest to occupy her; it would help pass the time. The mother-in-law too was cheered by the prospect of accumulating merit by serving a Brahman. And Nilkanta was especially relieved that he had passed from the hands of Yama and the troupe manager into the hands of this well-to-do family.

But it was not long before Sarat and his mother began to think otherwise. They decided that the boy was no longer needed and that they could avert trouble by getting rid of him.

Nilkanta began to smoke Sarat's hookah on the sly. On rainy days he took to roaming the village in search of new friends, never hesitating to use Sarat's favorite silk umbrella. He pampered a dirty, mangy, stray dog until it had the audacity to go uninvited into Sarat's nicely furnished room and leave indelible evidence of its call in four dirty paw-prints on the spotless embroidered bedspread. A large following of adoring boys gradually attached itself to Nilkanta, and that year the green fruit was never allowed to ripen in the mango grove.

Kiran indulged this boy too much, there was no doubt of it. Sarat and his mother would order her to stop it, but she ignored them. She dressed Nilkanta like a gentleman in Sarat's old shirt and socks, his new dhoti, chador, and slippers. Calling Nilkanta to her now and then would satisfy both her need to give affection and her curiosity. Laughing and smiling, Kiran would sit on the bed, a box of betel nuts beside her, while the maid brushed her wet hair dry, and

Nilkanta would stand before her, acting out with appropriate gestures the drama of Nala and Damayanti. The long afternoons passed very rapidly this way. Kiran would try to get Sarat to join her as a member of the audience, but Sarat would become very fidgety, and before him Nilkanta's talents never showed off to the best advantage. The mother-in-law joined in once or twice, drawn by the hope of hearing stories about the gods, but soon her long-standing habit of a mid-afternoon nap overcame her and she took herself off to bed.

Sarat gave Nilkanta repeated slaps, scoldings, and ear-twistings, but he felt neither insulted nor injured, since he had been accustomed to harsher treatment all his life. It was Nilkanta's settled conviction that the earth consists of equal parts of water and dry land, and man's life consists of food and punishment, with punishment predominating.

It was difficult to ascertain Nilkanta's exact age. If he was fourteen or fifteen, his face had certainly matured beyond his years; if he was seventeen or eighteen, his face seemed too young for his age. He was either precocious or immature.

As a matter of fact, he had belonged to the theatrical troupe since childhood and had been assigned the roles of Radhika, Damayanti, Sita, and the companion of Vidya.[1] The gods favored the manager's necessity by arresting Nilkanta's growth at a certain point. Everyone regarded him as a little boy, he thought of himself as a little boy, and he did not get treatment commensurate with his years. On all these accounts, natural and unnatural, at the advanced age of seventeen he looked more like a precocious fourteen. This impression was further reinforced by his beardless state. Whether because of the use of tobacco or of language unfitted to his age, the area around his lips seemed rather more mature, but there were simplicity and youthfulness in his dark eyes. One would trust that he possessed some inner tenderness, but it was evident that the theatrical troupe had left exterior marks of sophistication.

While Nilkanta stayed at Sarat's Chandernagore garden house, the laws of nature became operative again. After all this time his long unnatural adolescence ended, and all at once it became apparent that he had silently crossed a barrier. He looked all his seventeen years.

There was no external change, but when Kiran treated him like a little boy, he was hurt and humiliated. One day

---

[1] Famous heroines in Indian literature.

the jolly Kiran asked him to wear girl's clothes and act a girl's dramatic role; the suggestion distressed him, but he could find no precise explanation for his reaction. He would disappear if asked to mimic the actors. He could not get used to the idea that he was anything more than an unlucky boy from the theatrical troupe.

He decided to learn a little reading and writing from the estate superintendent. But the superintendent could not stand the sight of Nilkanta because he was Kiran's favorite, and since Nilkanta was not accustomed to concentrated study, the letters drifted away before his very eyes. He sat for hours on the bank of the Ganges, leaning against a champac tree with an open book in his lap. The water rippled; the boats floated past; on the branches of the tree a restless, preoccupied bird chirped to itself; and what Nilkanta thought about was known only to himself—perhaps it was unknown even to him. He could not progress from one word to the next, but he was very proud of the fact that he was reading a book. Whenever a boat passed near him, he would raise the book with great éclat and, mumbling to himself, would pretend to read. But he could not maintain his enthusiasm for reading after the spectators had gone.

Formerly he had sung his repertoire of songs as a theatrical routine; now the tunes of those songs stirred up a new restlessness in him. The words were very ordinary, full of meaningless alliteration, and their allusion was not fully intelligible to Nilkanta, but when he sang,

> O swan, of twice-born lineage,[2]
> Why have you become so cruel?
> Tell me why, in this forest,
> You threaten the life of the princess, . . .

he was reborn in another world. Then the song transformed him and his unimportant life. The tale of the swan and the princess projected a marvelous picture upon his imagination; it would be difficult to say whether he had a clear picture of himself, but he would forget that he was an orphan boy from a theatrical troupe.

When he had been a dirty, neglected child in a poverty-stricken home, he had lain in bed listening to the story of the prince, the princess, and the treasures of the seven kings.

---

[2] Twice-born: a spiritual man is thus described in Indian scriptures.

In the gloomy, dimly lighted corner of the shabby room his thoughts escaped from the bonds of poverty and deprivation, and he found a new form, splendid clothes, and unending indulgence in the everlasting fairy-tale kingdom. Now with the tunes of those songs this boy from the theatrical troupe could still create a new form for himself and for his world. By some alchemy of music the sounds of the water, the rustling of the leaves, the call of the birds were transformed into a goddess of good fortune who protected this unfortunate boy with her smiling face, her favor-filled hands, and her rosy feet, incomparably beautiful and flower-soft. When this musical intoxication had passed, Nilkanta the actor would appear with his usual ruffled hair and would be smartly slapped by the superintendent of the mango grove next door, who had heard complaints from the neighbors. The leader of a gang of admiring boys, he would create renewed havoc among the fragile branches.

About this time, Sarat's brother, Satish, came from Calcutta to spend his college vacation at the garden house. Kiran was delighted; she had someone else to look after. Her merriment grew as she saw to the food and clothes of her young brother-in-law, whose age was the same as hers. Sometimes she covered his eyes with hands rubbed in vermilion. Sometimes she wrote "Monkey" on the back of his shirt. Sometimes she slammed the door, locked it from the outside, and ran off laughing gaily. Satish did not give in; he took revenge by stealing her keys, putting red pepper in her betel nuts, and tying the end of her sari to the end of the chair when no one was looking. Thus it went all day long as they argued, chased each other, laughed, and occasionally fought, shed tears, begged forgiveness, and made up all over again.

Who knows what demon seized Nilkanta? He didn't know what to quarrel about or whom to quarrel with, but he was filled with a burning resentment. He made his faithful young followers cry for no good reason. He beat that pet stray dog so that it filled the air with its yelps. As he walked along the road he even whipped the weeds savagely and flattened them out with a cane.

Kiran loved to feed people who enjoyed eating. Nilkanta was a good eater, and never before had requests for him to eat gone unheeded. Kiran had called him regularly, served him herself, and been gratified to see that this Brahman boy was well fed. After the arrival of Satish, Kiran had less free time and was occasionally absent while Nilkanta ate.

Formerly, when he had to eat alone, it had not bothered him at all; he would finish up the milk, take a drink of water, and leave; but now if Kiran herself did not call him to his meal, there was a pain in his chest, his food had no taste, and he would get up without eating. In a tightened voice he would say to the maid, "I'm not hungry." He thought that Kiran would hear of this, penitently send for him, and insist on his eating. When she did, he would continue to decline her invitations and would say, "I'm not hungry."

But no one reported to Kiran, nor did Kiran send for him. The maid ate up the leftover food. Then Nilkanta would go to his room and throw himself down on the bed in the dark; his chest would heave, and he would press his face into the pillow and cry. But what was his complaint? Against whom should he bring charges? Who would come to comfort him? When no one came, sleep, which tenderly nurses the world, came and slowly soothed the injured pride of this unhappy motherless boy.

Nilkanta firmly believed that Satish continually maligned him to Kiran. Whenever for any reason Kiran sat quietly, Nilkanta would think that she was angry with him because of Satish's intrigues.

From then on Nilkanta prayed to the gods with an intensely concentrated purpose: "Let me be Satish in the next life, and let Satish be me." He knew that the solemn curse of a Brahman never goes unheeded; therefore he tried to scorch Satish with his Brahman might as he himself had been scorched, while he listened to the outbursts of laughter and merriment from Satish and his sister-in-law in the next room.

Nilkanta obviously did not have the courage to harm Satish, but he gloried in inconveniencing him whenever he could. When Satish started to dive into the Ganges, Nilkanta would whisk the soap from the river-landing steps and run off. When Satish looked for it, it was gone. One day while he swam, he spied his favorite muslin shirt floating on the surface of the Ganges; he supposed it had been blown by the wind, but who could tell which way the wind blew?

Once Kiran called Nilkanta and told him to entertain Satish with a theatrical song. Nilkanta was silent.

Kiran was surprised. "What has happened to you?" she asked.

Nilkanta did not reply.

Kiran repeated, "Won't you sing that song?"

Nilkanta went out saying, "I've forgotten that one."

At last it was time for Kiran to go home. Everyone began to pack. Satish was to go with them. But no one said a word to Nilkanta. It didn't occur to anyone to tell him whether he was to go or stay.

Kiran proposed that Nilkanta be taken along. At that the mother-in-law, the husband, and the brother-in-law unanimously objected, and Kiran abandoned her idea. At last, two days before their departure, Kiran sent for the Brahman boy and suggested affectionately that he return to his own district. After all the days of indifference he couldn't stand the kind words and burst out crying. Kiran's eyes also filled with tears. She was full of remorse at letting someone think that he would stay on indefinitely, keeping him under the illusion that all was well by being nice to him for a few days.

Satish arrived on the scene. He was annoyed to see such a big boy cry and said, "Oh, what a sissy! No one said a word, but he started to cry!"

Kiran scolded Satish for his harshness.

"Sister-in-law," said Satish, "you don't understand. You trust everyone too much. He rules here like the King of Heaven—who knows whether he's all right or not? He's shedding crocodile tears because he dreads having to be what he was before; he knows perfectly well that a tear or two will make you melt."

Nilkanta hurriedly went away. But though he thought of a knife slashing an image of Satish, a needle piercing it, a fire consuming it, nothing happened to the real Satish except that he carried an inner wound of his own making.

Satish had brought a stylish inkstand from Calcutta. It had two shell-shaped inkwells with a German silver swan between them, its wings spread, its open beak holding the pen. Satish took great care of it. At regular intervals he dusted it meticulously with a silk handkerchief. Kiran continually teased him by tapping the silver swan with her finger and saying, "O swan, if you are twice-born, why are you so inhuman?" And the sister-in-law and brother-in-law would wrangle cheerfully over it.

The morning of the day before the departure, the inkstand was missing. Kiran laughed and said, "Brother-in-law, your swan has flown off in search of your Damayanti."

But Satish flew into a rage. He had not the slightest doubt that Nilkanta had taken it. The servants had told Satish that Nilkanta had been seen prowling near Satish's room the previous evening.

The criminal was brought before Satish. Kiran too was there. Satish spoke out at once: "Bring my inkstand from wherever you put it when you stole it."

Nilkanta had swallowed all sorts of affronts, and except for this one by Satish, he had borne them all cheerfully. But when he was falsely accused in Kiran's presence of having stolen the inkstand, his big eyes flashed fire, his heart pounded in his throat. If Satish had said one more word he would have pounced on him and clawed him like an angry kitten.

Kiran called Nilkanta into the next room and said softly, "Nilu, if you have the inkstand, give it to me quietly. No one will say a word."

Nilkanta's eyes filled and overflowed, and then he covered his face and began to sob.

Kiran came out of the room and said, "Nilkanta has never stolen!"

"Obviously no one but Nilkanta has stolen it," both Sarat and Satish kept saying.

"Never!" Kiran declared emphatically.

Sarat wanted to question Nilkanta. "No," said Kiran, "you cannot ask him a single question about this theft."

"We should search his room and his trunk," said Satish.

"If you do that, " Kiran answered, "I won't have anything to do with you for the rest of my life! You can't suspect the innocent like that."

Teardrops hung on her eyelashes as she spoke. After the appeal from those eyes the investigation was dropped.

Kiran was deeply moved by pity for the innocent boy who had been so outraged while under her protection. She went into Nilkanta's room that evening carrying two pairs of handwoven dhotis and chadors, two shirts, a pair of new shoes, and a ten-rupee note. She wanted to put all those tokens of affection in Nilkanta's trunk, quietly, without telling him. The tin trunk too was her gift.

Silently she opened the trunk with a key from the bunch tied to the end of her sari. But she couldn't put her gifts inside. In the trunk were a spool for kite string, pieces of bamboo, polished shells for cutting green mangoes, the bottoms of broken glasses, and all the various odds and ends that boys collect, piled in a heap.

Kiran decided to rearrange the contents of the trunk in

a more orderly fashion. With that in mind, she began to empty it. Out came first a spool of string, a top, a knife, a cane, and other such items; then came a few soiled clothes and a few clean ones; then from the very bottom there suddenly emerged Satish's cherished swan inkstand.

Astonished and flushed, Kiran held it in her hand and thought for a long time.

She was unaware that Nilkanta had come to the door during the time she sat there. He saw it all and thought, Kiran came in like a thief herself to catch me instead, and she's been caught red-handed. How could he explain that his motive was not that of the common thief, that he had taken it only out of a desire for revenge, that he had intended to throw the thing into the Ganges, but in a moment of weakness had not thrown it but had hidden it in the trunk? He was not a thief, he was not! Then what was he? He had stolen but he was no thief; Kiran had suspected him: this was the crushing injustice that he could not understand and could not bear.

Kiran sighed deeply and replaced that inkstand in the trunk. Like a thief, she covered it over with the soiled clothes, the string, the sticks, the shells, and all the other odds and ends, and on top of the heap she arranged her gifts and the ten-rupee note.

But the next day no one could find the Brahman boy. The villagers said they had not seen him. The police found no trace of him.

"Now," said Sarat, "let's examine Nilkanta's trunk."

"You'll do no such thing," Kiran replied obstinately.

She had the trunk taken to her own room, got out the inkstand, went out when no one was watching, and threw it in the Ganges.

Sarat took his family home. In one day's time the garden was deserted. Only Nilkanta's pet stray dog was left. It refused to eat and howled as it wandered back and forth along the riverbank.

1895

THE RETURN OF KHOKABABU
(Khokababur Pratyabartan)

1

Raicharan was twelve years old when he first came to work at his master's house. He was from Jessore District, a dark, slim boy with long hair and big eyes. He was Kayastha by caste. His employers, too, were Kayastha. His chief duty was to look after his master's one-year-old boy and to assist in his upbringing.

In due time this child, Anukul, left Raicharan's side and went to school, then to college. After college he became a member of the judiciary. Raicharan was still his servant.

Another source of authority had been added. A wife was part of the household; consequently, most of Raicharan's previous authority over Anukul passed into the hands of the new mistress.

But although Raicharan's authority was somewhat curtailed, the mistress compensated by giving him a new responsibility. When Anukul's son and heir was born, Raicharan, by a display of sheer determination and perseverance, assumed complete charge of the boy.

He rocked him so vigorously, held him in his arms and tossed him skyward with such skill, stood waggling his head so boisterously in front of the boy, asked such utterly nonsensical questions without expecting answers, addressing them to him in a singsong voice, that this miniature Anukul was always delighted to see Raicharan.

When the child began to cross the doorsill, crawling very cautiously on all fours, he would burst into laughter and quickly tried to hide in a safe place if anyone pursued him. Raicharan would be amazed at this extraordinary cleverness and capacity for decision. He would go to the boy's mother and say with pride and wonder, "Mother, when your son grows up he will be a judge and make five thousand rupees a month."

It was inconceivable to Raicharan that any other human child of comparable age could muster the dexterity requisite for exploits as impossible as the scaling of a doorsill. But nothing was impossible for a future judge.

At last the boy began to toddle, an astonishing event; and when he addressed his mother as "Mama," his aunt as "Nana," but Raicharan as "Channa," Raicharan began to proclaim this incredible news to whomever he met: "The most amazing thing is that he calls his mother Mama, calls his aunt Nana, but calls me Channa." Really, it was hard to imagine how the boy had acquired such wisdom. If any adult had ever displayed such extraordinary qualities, ordinary people would not have seen in him the makings of a future judge.

Presently Raicharan was obliged to assume the role of a horse with a rope over his head. And he had to become an athlete to wrestle with the child; then if Raicharan didn't fall to the ground and acknowledge defeat, there would be a serious insurrection.

At this time Anukul was transferred to a district on the banks of the river Padma. Anukul ordered a stroller from Calcutta for his son. Raicharan would dress the child in a satin suit, a gold-lace cap, and gold bangles on his wrists and ankles, and he would take the boy out for an airing twice a day.

The rainy season came. The ravenous Padma began to devour villages, gardens, and paddy fields one by one. It submerged the reeds and casuarina groves on the sandbars. The *jhup-jhup* sound of the crumbling banks never stopped, the roar of the water echoed throughout, and the swiftness of the rushing foam testified to the violent state of the river.

The afternoon was overcast, but rain was unlikely. Raicharan's capricious little master refused to stay indoors. He climbed into the stroller. Pushing it slowly, Raicharan came to the paddy fields at the edge of the river. There was not a boat on the river, not a person in the fields. On the uninhabited sandy shore opposite, a break in the clouds showed that sunset was approaching with silent but brilliant pageantry. In that silence the little boy suddenly pointed his finger and said, "Channa, fla—"

A huge kadamba tree stood on the muddy ground not

far away. A few flowers had blossomed on its top branches. They drew the child's greedy eyes. A few days before, Raicharan had made him a car by stringing kadamba flowers on a stick; the boy had had such fun pulling it on a string that Raicharan had not had to wear the bridle that day; he was promoted all at once from horse to groom.

Channa did not care to wade through the mud to pick flowers; he quickly pointed in the opposite direction and said, "Look, look there—look at that bird—it's flying—it's gone! Oh, birdie, come back!" Continuing a constant chatter about this and that, he began to push the stroller at a rapid pace.

But it was useless to employ such inept measures to divert the attention of a boy who was destined to be a judge—particularly since there was nothing nearby to catch his attention. One cannot manage for very long with imaginary birds.

"Then you stay in the stroller," Raicharan said. "I'll go in a wink and bring the flowers. Take care, don't go near the edge of the water." He pulled his dhoti above his knees and proceeded toward the kadamba tree.

The fact that he was forbidden to go near the water's edge immediately turned the child's attention away from the kadamba flowers and straight toward the water. He saw how it sped past, hissing and slapping as if a hundred thousand streams of children, playing pranks and dodging the outstretched hand of some enormous Raicharan, laughed sweetly as they ran headlong toward the forbidden place.

Their bad example made the human child restless. Slowly he got down from the stroller and went to the water's edge. He picked up a long reed and, imagining it as a fishing rod, leaned over to catch a fish. The mischievous mass of water murmured insistently to the child, inviting him into its playroom.

There was a thud, but such sounds are frequent on the banks of the Padma in the rainy season. Raicharan filled the end of his dhoti with kadamba flowers. He descended the tree, came smiling toward the stroller, and found no one there. He looked in all directions, but there was no sign of anyone anywhere.

Raicharan's blood ran cold. The whole universe turned as murky, as colorless, as smoke. His heart in his mouth, he called and shouted with all his might, "Babu, Khokababu, my dear big brother!"

But no one answered. No laughing childish voice teased him in reply. There was only the rushing Padma still hissing and slapping as if it knew nothing and could not pay a moment's attention to all the trivial happenings of the world.

When it grew dark, the anxious mother sent people out in all directions. Lanterns in hand, they came to the river-bank and saw Raicharan running all over the field like a midnight windstorm and shouting in a broken voice, "Babu, my dear Khokababu." Finally Raicharan returned to the house and fell with a headlong crash at the feet of his mistress. The more they questioned, the more he wept and said, "Mother, I don't know."

Everyone knew in his heart that the river Padma was responsible; nevertheless, there was persistent suspicion of a band of Gypsies who had gathered at the edge of the village. And the mistress even suspected that Raicharan himself had kidnapped the child. She went so far as to call him and implore, "Give back my child; I'll give you as much money as you want." At this Raicharan only beat his forehead. The mistress turned him out of the house.

Anukul had tried to disabuse his wife of this unfair suspicion of Raicharan. Why, he asked, would Raicharan do such a monstrous thing? "Why?" his wife replied. "There was gold jewelry on him."

2

Raicharan returned to the country. All this time he had had no child of his own, nor was there much hope of one. But contrary to expectations, his middle-aged wife gave birth to a son and then died.

Raicharan developed an intense dislike for his newborn son. He felt that this boy had come to deceive him and to usurp the place of Khokababu. He felt that it was a great sin to enjoy a son of his own after letting the master's only son drown in the river. If Raicharan had not had a widowed sister, this child would not long have enjoyed life in this world.

Curiously enough, after a while this boy also began to cross the doorsill and displayed humor and intelligence in overriding all restrictions. His voice, as he laughed and cried, even seemed like the voice of that other child. Sometimes, when Raicharan heard his son cry, his heart would suddenly pound; it seemed that his Khokababu was crying somewhere because he had lost Raicharan.

Phalna (the boy was named by Raicharan's sister) in due time addressed his aunt as "Nana." One day, when Raicharan heard that familiar word, it suddenly seemed that Khokababu, unable to escape his attachment to Raicharan, had been born into his family.

A number of irrefutable arguments supported this belief. In the first place, this boy was born soon after the death of the other. In the second place, the fact that his wife had suddenly become pregnant and borne a child after so long a time could not be due to her merits in this life. In the third place, this boy also crawled on all fours, tottered as he walked, and called his aunt Nana. This boy showed all those signs indicative of future judgeship.

Then Raicharan recalled his mistress' appalling suspicion of him; astonished, he said to himself, "Aha, the mother's intuition could tell who had stolen her child." Then he felt deep remorse over his long neglect. Once again he devoted himself to a little boy.

Raicharan now began to raise Phalna like a rich man's son. He bought a satin suit. He brought home a gold-lace cap. He had his dead wife's jewelry melted down to make bangles and anklets. He did not permit Phalna to play with the neighborhood boys; day and night he himself was the boy's only playmate. The other boys seized every opportunity to make fun of him, calling him a nabob's son, and the country people were amazed by Raicharan's irrational behavior.

When Phalna was old enough to go to school, Raicharan sold all his land and took the boy to Calcutta. With considerable difficulty, he found a job there and sent Phalna to school. He himself lived any old way, but he never failed to provide the boy with good food, good clothes, and a good education. He would say to himself, "My dear, you came to my home because you love me. I'll never neglect you, you may be sure of that."

Twelve years passed in this manner. The boy did well in his studies. He was quite handsome and well built, with a light-olive complexion. He was very particular about the style of his hair; his disposition was quite genial and his tastes refined. He was unable to think of his father as a real father because Raicharan loved him like a father but waited upon him like a servant. Raicharan had another handicap: he had told no one that he was Phalna's father. The Bengali students in Phalna's hostel constantly joked about the rustic Raicharan, and Phalna was not innocent of joining in the fun behind his father's back. Yet all the students really loved the innocent and affectionate Raicharan, and Phalna also loved him, but not as a father. Phalna's love contained a little condescension.

Raicharan grew old. His master continually found fault with his work. To tell the truth, he had become feeble; he could not concentrate and was forgetful, but he who pays a full wage does not care to hear the excuses of approaching age. But the cash acquired from selling Raicharan's property was running out. Now Phalna began to complain continually about his shortage of good clothes.

3

One day Raicharan suddenly quit his job, gave Phalna some money, and said, "I must go to the country for a few days." He went to Barashat, where Anukul was a magistrate.

Anukul and his wife had had no second son, and she still brooded over the loss of her son.

One evening, when Anukul rested after returning from court, and his wife, still hoping for a child, was buying an expensive herb and a blessing from a holy man, a voice spoke in the courtyard, "Long live the lady of the house."

Anukul asked, "Who is it?"

Raicharan came and touched Anukul's feet and said, "I am Raicharan."

Anukul's heart softened when he saw the old man. He asked him a thousand questions about his present situation and offered to employ him again. Raicharan smiled sadly. "I'd just like to pay my respects to the mother of the house," he said.

Anukul took him along to the inner rooms. The lady of the house did not receive Raicharan with the same warmth; Raicharan seemed not to notice that. With folded hands he said, "Mistress, Mother, I stole your child. It was not the Padma or anyone else. I did it, I, this vile, ungrateful——"

"What are you saying?" Anukul burst out. "Where is he?"

"Sir, he is with me. I'll bring him the day after tomorrow."

Day after tomorrow was a Sunday, and the court was closed. From early morning husband and wife watched the road in a fever of impatience. At ten o'clock Raicharan appeared with Phalna.

Without question or comment the mother had the boy sit on her lap, touched him, savored his scent, gazed at his face as if she could never get enough of looking at him, cried and laughed incoherently. Really, the boy was handsome. Neither his dress nor his manners bespoke poverty. His air of shy modesty was most becoming. As he watched, Anukul too felt an unexpected surge of affection. Nevertheless, he assumed an undemonstrative expression and asked, "Is there any proof?"

"How could there be proof for such an act?" Raicharan asked. "Only God knows that I stole your son; no one in this world knows about it."

Anukul considered this and decided that in view of the eagerness with which his wife had accepted the boy, it was inadvisable to try to gather evidence now. Whatever had happened, it would be wise to have faith. Apart from that, where would Raicharan get such a boy? And would his old servant deceive him for no good reason?

Anukul talked with the boy and learned that although he had lived with Raicharan since childhood and had known him as his father, Raicharan had behaved more like his servant than his father.

Anukul brushed doubt aside. "But, Raicharan," he said, "I won't allow you even to tread on our shadows."

Hands folded, Raicharan said in a choking voice, "Master, where can I go in my old age?"

"Oh, let him stay," said the mistress. "May God bless my boy. I forgive Raicharan."

"He cannot be pardoned for what he has done," said the upright Anukul.

Raicharan clasped Anukul's feet and said, "I didn't do it, God did it."

Anukul became even more irritated at Raicharan's attempt to shift his guilt onto God. "A person who has behaved so treacherously cannot be trusted again," he said.

Raicharan let go of his master's feet and said, "That was not I, master."

"Then who was it?"

"My fate."

But such an explanation can never satisfy an educated man.

"I have no one else in this world," said Raicharan.

Phalna was inwardly indignant when he discovered that Raicharan had stolen him, a magistrate's son, so long ago and had demeaned him by calling him son. Nevertheless, he spoke magnanimously to Anukul, "Father, forgive him. If you won't let him stay in our house, give him a little monthly pension."

Raicharan said no more. He looked once at his son's face, then bowed low to everyone. He went out to mingle with the uncounted people of this earth. At the end of the month Anukul sent a small pension to Raicharan's country address. The money was returned. No one lived there anymore.

1891

A LAPSE OF JUDGMENT
(Durbuddhi)

I have had to leave my homestead. I won't speak candidly of how this came about; I shall give only a hint.

I am a native village doctor. My house is just across from the police station. I depended no less upon the police inspector than upon the god of death. As a result I was familiar with all the assorted ills that mankind inherits from both man and God. Just as the bracelet and the jewels enhance each other's beauty, my collaboration with the police inspector and his collaboration with me created an increasing sense of financial well-being.

And these intimate conditions set the terms of my rather special friendship with this erudite inspector, Lalit Chakravarty. At one time or another he had asked me to do him the favor of marrying the eligible daughter of a relative, and by so doing he had almost made me eligible too.

But Shashi, my only daughter, was motherless. I could not hand her over to a stepmother. Year after year many days that the current almanac designated as auspicious were wasted. Before my very eyes many worthy and unworthy bridegrooms had ridden in the wedding palanquin. I merely joined the bridegroom's party, was served sweets in the reception room, and returned home with a sigh.

Shashi was twelve and soon would be thirteen. I hoped that if I could lay my hands on some money I could get my daughter married into a family of wealth and distinction. This latter arrangement expedited, I could turn my attention to the arrangement of another auspicious ceremony.

Just as I mulled over the matter of those essential funds, Harinath Majumdar from the Tulsi District came and fell at my feet in tears. This was the gist of it: his widowed daughter had suddenly died in the night, and his enemies had written the inspector an anonymous letter containing the false accusation of an abortion. At that very moment the police were all set to examine the body.

Along with grief at the loss of a daughter, the shock of such an insult was unbearable. I am a doctor as well as a friend of the police inspector. Somehow I must save Majumdar. When Lakshmi wants to come in, she arrives uninvited, sometimes at the front door and sometimes at the back. Shrugging my shoulders, I said, "The matter is very serious." I cited a few fictitious cases, and the shaky old Harinath began to cry like a child.

I need not recount all the details. Harinath went bankrupt providing for his daughter's last rites.

My daughter, Shashi, came and inquired sadly, "Father, why was that old man crying at your feet like that?" I scolded her and said, "Go away, go away, why do you have to know so much about it?"

Now the way was clear to getting my daughter married. The day was set for her wedding. As she was my only daughter, I arranged for a sumptuous feast. Since I was a widower, my sympathetic neighbors came to help me. The bankrupt but grateful Harinath worked night and day.

On the night before the marriage, when the bride is ceremonially marked with yellow ocher, Shashi was suddenly stricken, at about three o'clock in the morning, with cholera. The disease became increasingly critical. After many experiments I threw those useless bottles of medicine on the floor, ran to Harinath, and clasped his feet.

"Forgive me, brother," I said. "Forgive this blasphemous man. This is my only daughter. I have no one else."

Harinath was distraught. "Doctor, sir," he said, "what are you doing? What are you doing? I'm indebted to you for life. Don't touch my feet."

"I ruined you in your innocence," I replied. "My daughter is dying because of that sin."

Then I cried out before the whole crowd, "Listen, everyone, I have ruined this old man and I am being punished for it. God save my Shashi!"

I took the slippers from Harinath's feet and began to beat myself on the head. The old man hastily snatched the slippers from my hand.

At ten o'clock the following morning, Shashi, wearing the ceremonial yellow ocher, left this world for good. The very next day the police inspector said, "Well, why wait any longer? Go ahead and get married now. Don't you want someone to look after you?"

Such cruel disregard for a human being's heartbreak and sorrow doesn't become even the devil. But on various occasions I had displayed such indulgence toward the police inspector that I didn't have the nerve to say a word. That day was the first time the inspector's friendship seemed to humiliate me like a whiplash.

No matter how depressed the heart, the round of work goes on. Food to eat, clothes to wear, wood for the fire, and even laces for the shoes must be assembled and brought home in the routine manner with the usual perseverance.

During leisure hours, when I sit alone in my room, I hear the occasional echo of that question asked in a sorrowful voice, "Father, why was that old man crying at your feet like that?"

I paid for new thatching for poor Harinath's dilapidated house. I made him a present of my milch cow. I redeemed his mortgaged property from the moneylender.

For some time, during lonely evenings made unbearable by this grief and during sleepless nights, I kept thinking that my tenderhearted daughter had relinquished the joys of earth but could get no peace in heaven because of her father's cruel and evil deed. It seemed that in her distress she was continually returning to ask me, "Father, why did you do that?"

For some time I could not bring myself to press my poorer patients to pay for my treatment. If any little girl were sick, I would feel as if my Shashi herself were suffering for all the sick girls of the village.

Then, at the height of the rainy season the village was flooded. Traveling over the paddy fields and around the houses must be done by boat. Morning and night the rain kept on, still without a break. I received summons to appear at the zamindar's law court. His boatman, unwilling to be delayed, turned arrogant and threatened to leave. When I had to go out in such bad weather in the past, there had been someone to open up my old umbrella to check it for leaks, and an anxious voice had warned me repeatedly to protect myself from the strong wind and the driving rain. Today, as I searched for the umbrella myself in the quiet, empty room and recalled that loving face, time went by unnoticed and I was a little late. As I looked at her closed bedroom, I was thinking that God had no obligation to preserve love and affection in the home of the man who feels no concern for the sorrow of others. Pondering this, pausing near the door of that empty room, my heart contracted with despair. I heard the rich man's servants shouting outside. I quickly restrained my grief and went out.

As I climbed into the boat, I saw a skiff tied up at the landing by the police station and a farmer in a loincloth standing drenched in the rain. "What's the matter?" I asked. I was told that his daughter had been bitten by a snake the night before and the poor wretch had carried her from a far-distant village to report the death at the police station. I saw that he had taken off his only garment and had covered the dead body with it. The zamindar's impatient boatman shoved off.

When I came home about one o'clock I saw that man still there, squatting in the rain with his hands clasped about his knees. He had been unable to see the inspector. I sent the man a little food from my own meal. He didn't touch it.

After rushing through my meal, I had to go out again to the case at the courthouse. When I came home in the evening, the farmer still sat there as if dazed. When questioned, he was unable to answer and only stared at my face. To him now this river, this village, this police station, and this wet, muddy, cloud-covered world were like a dream.

After repeated interrogation I learned that one constable had come and asked whether he had anything in his pocket. He had replied that he was really poor, he had nothing. The constable had said, "All right then, keep waiting."

I had often observed such a scene but had never given it a thought. That day I found it unbearable. My Shashi's indistinct voice, choked with grief and compassion, seemed to echo all over that rainy sky. The immeasurable sorrow of that speechless farmer who had lost his daughter seemed to well up beneath my heart.

The inspector was comfortably seated in a cane chair and smoking tobacco from a hookah. His uncle, who had a marriageable daughter, had recently come to the country with his eye on me and sat on a mat gossiping. In an instant, I had stormed into the room. I shouted, "Are you men or fiends?" I threw down in front of them all the money I earned in fees that day and said, "If you want money, take this! When you die, see that this goes along. Now let that farmer go. Let him arrange for his daughter's funeral."

The love that had grown between the inspector and myself as we had wiped the tears of the sorely oppressed was razed to the ground in that storm. In no time I had fallen at the feet of the inspector. I referred with fulsome praise to his magnanimity and reproached myself for my own lapse of judgment. But in the end I had to leave my homestead.

1900

THE TUTOR

(Mastarmashai)

Introduction

It was almost two o'clock in the morning. A large horse-drawn carriage coming from Bhawanipur made a tiny ripple in Calcutta's sea of silence and stopped near the junction of Birjitallau Street. One of its passengers hailed another carriage that was standing there. Seated beside him was a young Bengali wearing Western-style clothes, slightly intoxicated, feet up on the opposite seat, shoulders sagging. This young man was being given a lift partway after a party celebrating his return from England. His friend poked him several times, awoke him, and said, "Mazumdar, there's a carriage for you. Go on home."

Mazumdar awoke with a start and, swearing in English, got into the hired carriage. His friend carefully gave its driver an address and went to his own destination in his own carriage.

The hired carriage went straight ahead for a time, came near Park Street, and then turned toward the Maidan. Mazumdar swore again in English and said to himself, "What's going on? This isn't the way!" Then, sleepy and befuddled, he thought, Maybe this is a shortcut.

As soon as the carriage entered the Maidan, Mazumdar had a presentiment of something amiss. Although no one sat beside him anymore, it suddenly seemed that the vacant seat was filling up; its empty portion seemed to solidify and press against him. Mazumdar thought, What's happening? Why is the carriage doing this to me? "Hey, driver! Driver!"

The driver did not reply. Mazumdar raised the shutter at his back, grasped the groom's arm, and said, "You come and sit inside."

The groom replied fearfully: "No, sahib, I can't get inside!"

At this Mazumdar broke into gooseflesh. He grasped the groom's arm forcibly and said, "Quick, get inside!"

With a mighty pull the groom freed his arm, jumped down, and ran away. Then the frightened Mazumdar turned to see what was beside him. He saw nothing, but still it seemed that some immovable substance was planted there. He managed to get some sound from his voice and said, "Driver, stop the carriage!" The driver seemed to stand up and haul on the reins in an effort to stop the horses, but nothing could stop them. Instead, they took the Red Road and turned south. Terrified, Mazumdar cried, "Driver, where are you going?" There was no reply. Then he glanced sidewise at the empty space and began to perspire all over. He

tried to squeeze himself into the smallest possible area, but
what little he relinquished seemed to fill up again.

Mazumdar began a debate with himself: Some ancient
European scholar said, "Nature abhors a vacuum." That's
obvious. But what is this? Is this Nature? If it will spare
me, I'll jump out right now and let it have the whole space.

He lacked the nerve to jump; some unknown thing might
grab him from behind. He tried to shout "Police," but
such an odd and feeble little sound resulted from his pro-
digious effort that even in his terror, he felt like laughing.
The trees of the Maidan seemed to stand facing each other
in the darkness like a silent parliament of ghosts, and the
flickering gas streetlamps winked as if they knew everything but would not say a word.

Mazumdar thought of making one quick jump to the
driver's seat. Immediately he felt himself the object of a
disembodied stare. There were no eyes, nothing but a stare.
Mazumdar could remember that stare as belonging to someone but could not recall whose it was. He did his best to
shut his eyes tight, but he was too frightened to close them.
He returned that vague stare so steadily that he was unable
even to blink.

Meanwhile, the carriage continued to circle the Maidan
road from south to north and north to south. The horses
became increasingly wild. Their speed kept increasing. The
carriage's shutter began to shake and rattle.

Then the carriage seemed to collide with something and
came to a sudden stop. Startled, Mazumdar saw that it
stood on his own street. The driver was shaking him and
saying, "Sahib, tell me where to go now."

Mazumdar asked angrily, "Why did you make me go
around and around in the Maidan all this time?"

The driver was astonished. "Why, I didn't make you go
around the Maidan."

Mazumdar didn't believe him. "Is this only a dream,
then?"

The driver thought briefly and said apprehensively, "Sahib,
this may not be just a dream. Three years ago something
happened in this carriage of mine."

By now Mazumdar's intoxication and drowsiness were
gone. He ignored the driver's story, paid the fare, and
left the carriage.

But that night he did not sleep well, he kept wondering
whose stare that had been.

1

This young man was Benugopal, the son of Adhar Mazumdar. Adhar Mazumdar's own father had begun as an ordinary shipping clerk and had risen to the post of chief accountant in a large accounting firm. Adhar had put his father's hard-earned cash to work earning interest and so did not have to work himself. His father had gone humbly to the office in a palanquin with a white towel around his head; still, he was both pious and generous. He took pride in the fact that people of all classes sought his help when they were in need.

Adhar, however, had built a huge house and kept a carriage and pair. He had no contacts with people other than calls from the broker who came and smoked a hookah reserved for him, or discussions with clerks from the attorney's office about the terms of the stamped documents. He was so miserly about his personal expenditures that even the most persistent boys in the neighborhood soccer club could not make a dent in his treasury, no matter how hard they tried.

One day a guest arrived in his household. For a long time his wife, Nanibala, had had no child, but finally, after all that time, she had a son. The boy had his mother's features: big eyes, straight nose, a complexion like petals of the tuberose. Whoever saw him said, "Well, that's no boy, that's Kartik." Adhar's devoted servant, Ratikanta, said, "He is just what a rich man's son ought to be."

This was Benugopal. Nanibala had never pitted her opinion against her husband's with respect to household expenditures. They certainly had occasional disputes about a few of her indulgences or arrangements for her entertaining, but the upshot was that while the wife despised her husband's miserliness, she quietly capitulated.

After the advent of Benugopal Adhar could not cope with Nanibala; Benu's demands began to make Adhar's account books beat a steady retreat. Anklets for Benu's feet, bangles for his arms, a chain for his neck, a cap for his head, the indigenous and English clothes of various styles and colors for which Nanibala put in a claim—she achieved each and every one, sometimes by quiet tears, sometimes by loud volleys of harsh words. Whatever Benu needed or did not need had to be provided. Pleas of empty coffers or depleted savings for future projects were not effective even for a day.

2

Benugopal began to grow up. Adhar got into the habit of spending money for Benu. He engaged a high-salaried elderly tutor with many academic degrees. Until this assignment the tutor had always maintained professional dignity through enforcement of strict discipline; now he did his utmost to win Benu with pleasant words and good manners. But his sweet words and benign manner seemed out of tune, and the boy was unconvinced. Nanibala said to Adhar, "What sort of tutor did you get? The boy is upset as soon as he sees him. Discharge him."

The old tutor was dismissed. Nanibala's son set about choosing his own tutor as women in ancient times chose their own husbands. Whoever was unacceptable to him held degrees and certificates in vain.

At this point Haralal appeared in a dirty shawl and torn tennis shoes, looking for a position as tutor. His widowed mother had cooked and husked rice in other people's homes in order to send him to the district school and somehow or other had gotten him through high school. Now Haralal was determined body and soul to go college in Calcutta. He had set out toward this goal. He had gone without food for so long that his face had become thin and shrunken, as thin as India's Cape Comorin except for his wide forehead. It had broadened like the Himalayas and overshadowed his eyes, to which poverty had given an unnatural sparkle, like sunlight on desert sand.

The gateman asked, "What do you want? Whom do you want to see?"

Haralal was intimidated and replied, "I want to see the head of the house."

"You can't see him," said the gateman.

At a loss for words, Haralal was wavering there when the seven-year-old Benugopal, who had been playing in the garden, appeared in the portico. The gateman saw Haralal's hesitation and said again, "Babu, go away."

Benu suddenly became obstinate. "No," he said, "he will not go." With this, he took Haralal by the hand, led him up to the second-floor veranda, and presented him to his father.

That gentleman had just finished his afternoon nap and sat quietly on a cane chair and swung his feet. His old servant

Ratikanta smoked a hookah on a wooden bench nearby. That afternoon, that very hour, thus casually, Haralal was installed as tutor.

"How far have you gone in school?" asked Ratikanta.

Haralal lowered his head a little and said, "I graduated from high school."

Ratikanta raised his eyebrows. "Only a high-school graduate? I would have said you had gone to college. You don't look very young."

Haralal was silent. Ratikanta, whose principal pleasure was harassing those sheltered in the house and those who sought shelter there, caressed Benu and tried to pull him onto his lap, saying, "So many B.A.'s and M.A.'s came and went; none of them were chosen. And will Sonababu finally study under a tutor who is a high-school graduate?"

Benu jerked his hand out of Ratikanta's affectionate grasp and said, "Go away."

Benu could not abide Ratikanta, but Rati considered this antipathy part of his childish charm, tried to humor him, and drove the boy to a fury by calling him Sonababu, Chandbabu, and the like. Haralal's situation as a successful applicant was becoming increasingly difficult. He thought to himself, Now if I can just get off this bench somehow and get outside, I'll be safe.

It suddenly occurred to Adharlal that he could get this young fellow at a very low salary. It was finally decided that Haralal would live in the house, have his meals there, and get five rupees a month. Letting him stay in the house would be a useful display of benevolence, compensated for by getting more work out of him.

3

This time the tutor survived. From the very first Haralal and Benu were as close as two brothers. Haralal had no relatives in Calcutta; this beautiful little boy won his heart completely. Never before had the unfortunate Haralal had the opportunity to love any other human being this way. He had taken great pains to gather books in the hope of improving his situation, and by virtue of nothing more than his own perseverance had done nothing day and night except study. Because his mother had had to work for others, the boy had spent a withdrawn childhood. He had never had the pleasure of playing pranks to defy restrictions or the joy of proving his boyish strength. He belonged to no group; he was all alone among his torn textbooks and broken slates. Who on earth is more deserving yet is more deprived of pity than the boy who is obliged to be quiet and well behaved all his life? He must carefully consider his mother's tribulations and his own situation. His fate never allows him freedom to be completely irresponsible. He can neither chase after pleasure nor weep when disappointed; he must renounce both pleasure and tears because he fears the inconvenience and disapproval of others, and must use all his childish strength to suppress these natural desires.

Haralal, crushed by the weight of the world, had never even dreamed that he possessed so much stored-up affection awaiting its opportunity. As he played with Benu, tutored him, nursed him during sickness, Haralal perceived plainly that human beings have a concern other than improvement of their lot; once that concern takes hold, it knows no bounds.

It was a relief to Benu to get Haralal, for Benu was the only son. He had a baby sister and another three-year-old sister, but Benu did not consider them worthy of his company. There was no shortage of boys his age in the neighborhood, but since Adharlal considered his family very superior and intended to maintain that station, Benu had not been able to mix with boys his own age. Consequently Haralal became his sole companion and had to put up with all the naughtiness that would have been tolerable if portioned out among ten others. Haralal's affection grew stronger under the burden of this daily tyranny. Ratikanta kept saying, "The tutor is ruining our Sonababu." Sometimes it would occur to Adharlal that the relationship between tutor and pupil was not an appropriate one, but who was strong enough to separate Haralal from Benu now?

4

Benu was eleven. Haralal had passed his intermediate examination with a scholarship and was in the third year of his college. He had a few friends at the college, but this eleven-year-old boy was closest. When Haralal returned from classes he would take Benu out to Goldighi, and sometimes they even went to Eden Gardens for a walk. Haralal would tell Benu the hero tales from Greek history; he told him the stories of Scott and Victor Hugo a little at a time in Ben-

gali. He recited English poems, translating and explaining
them. He read and explained Shakespeare's *Julius Caesar*,
and tried to get Benu to memorize Antony's speech. The
small boy seemed to be the golden wand that had brought
Haralal's heart to life. Haralal had never taken such delight
in English literature when he sat alone memorizing his lessons. Now if he found pleasure in whatever he read—history, science, literature—he was eager to share it with Benu.
His own powers of understanding and enjoyment seemed
doubled by the attempt to transfer that pleasure.

When Benu returned from school, he would hurriedly finish
his snack and be impatient to go to Haralal. His mother
could not keep him in the inner rooms by any pretense or
enticement. Nanibala did not like this. She felt that Haralal
was making such an effort to influence her son only in order
to keep his job. One day she sent for Haralal and spoke
from behind the purdah curtain: "You are a tutor, you're
only supposed to teach the boy one hour in the morning
and one hour in the evening. Why do you stick to him day
and night? He ignores his mother and father these days.
How did he get so wrapped up in education? He used to
come running when I called; now he doesn't answer. My
Benu is a boy from a high-class family. Why are you getting so thick with him?"

Ratikanta had told Adhar a tale about several tutors of
rich men's sons who won over the boys in order to become
dictators and rule them after they came of age. This hint
was not wasted on Haralal. He had borne everything in silence, but today Benu's mother's words broke his heart. He
could see what the title of tutor means in a rich man's home.
There was a cow in the cowshed to provide milk for the
boy, and a tutor was hired to provide him with knowledge.
No one, from a house servant to the housewife, can tolerate the audacity of a tutor's establishing an affectionate
relationship with a student. Everyone knows that it is a
ruse to further one's own interests.

Haralal spoke in a trembling voice: "Mother, I will only
tutor Benu. There will be no other relationship between him
and me."

That evening Haralal did not return from the college for
his playtime with Benu. He walked the streets, and only he
knew how he passed that time. When he came at dusk
for the lessons, Benu had a sullen look. Haralal set to work

without explaining his absence; studies did not go well that evening.

Haralal had been accustomed to get up while it was still dark and study in his room. Benu would run to him as soon as he had arisen and washed. One of their morning duties was feeding puffed rice to the fish in the garden pond. There were some stones in one corner of the garden, and Benu had built tiny roads, constructed a little gate and a fence, and laid out a miniature garden fit to be the hermitage of Balakhilya, the happy patron saint of children. Their second morning task was the care of this garden, over which the gardener had no authority. Afterward, as the sun grew stronger, they would return to the house, and Benu would sit down to study with Haralal.

Benu got up as early as possible on this particular day and came running out to hear the rest of the story that remained unfinished last evening. He thought that he had outdone his tutor at early rising. He found no Mastarmashai in Haralal's room. He questioned the gateman and was told that the tutor had gone out.

That day also, Benu, in the anguish of his little heart, looked sullen at lessontime. He didn't even ask why Haralal had gone out in the morning. Haralal didn't look Benu in the face and conducted the lesson with his eyes on the book. When Benu sat down to eat with his mother, she asked, "Tell me what has happened to you since yesterday afternoon. Why do you have such a long face? You haven't eaten well. What's the matter?"

Benu did not reply. After his meal, when his mother pulled him closer and stroked his arm with great affection and kept repeating the question, he couldn't bear it any longer. He whimpered aloud. He said, "Mastarmashai—"

His mother said, "What about Mastarmashai?"

Benu could not tell what the tutor had done. It was hard to put his complaint into words.

Nanibala said, "I believe Mastarmashai complained to you about your mother!"

Benu was unable to follow her meaning and went away without answering.

5

In the meantime some of Adhar's clothes were stolen from the house. The police were informed; they included

Haralal's suitcase in their search. Ratikanta remarked with an air of utmost innocence, "That fellow who stole the stuff— would he keep it in a suitcase?"

The things were not found. Adhar could not tolerate such a loss. He was angry with everyone in the world. "There are so many people in the house," Ratikanta said. "Whom will you accuse, whom do you suspect? Everyone comes and goes as he pleases."

Adharlal sent for the tutor and said, "Look, Haralal, it won't be convenient for me to keep any of you in the house. From now on you live somewhere else and come and tutor Benu at the proper times. This seems to be the best arrangement. I am prepared to increase your salary by two rupees at the most."

Ratikanta kept on puffing at the hookah and said, "This seems quite a sound idea—good for both parties."

Haralal listened with his head down. He could say nothing just then. He returned to his room and wrote a letter to Adhar saying that for many reasons it would not be convenient to tutor Benu; therefore he was ready to leave at once.

When Benu returned from school that afternoon, he found the Mastarmashai's room empty. Even his almost worn-out tin trunk was gone. His chador and towel had hung on a line; the line was there but chador and towel were not. Books and papers had lain strewn carelessly over the table; in their place were goldfish that swam shimmering up and down in a large glass jar. A label fastened to the bottle bore Benu's name in the handwriting of Mastarmashai. And there was also a new English picture-book, well bound; Benu's name was at one edge of its fly leaf and beneath that the date and the year.

Benu ran to his father and asked, "Father, where did Mastarmashai go?"

The father pulled him close and replied, "He quit and went away."

Benu pushed his father's arm aside, went to the next room, lay facedown on the bed, and began to cry. Adhar was worried but couldn't think what to do.

About ten-thirty the next morning, Haralal sat listlessly on a wooden cot in his hostel, wondering whether to go to class. Suddenly he saw Adhar's gateman. Behind him came Benu, who threw his arms around Haralal's neck. Haralal's voice choked. He couldn't say a word for fear that his tears would overflow. Benu said, "Mastarmashai, come to our house."

Benu had begged their old gateman, Chandrabhan, to take him, one way or another, to his Mastarmashai. Chandrabhan inquired of the neighborhood porter who had carried Haralal's luggage, then brought Benu past Haralal's hostel as he went to school in the carriage.

Haralal could not explain why it was absolutely impossible for him to go to Benu's house, for going there was the one thing he could not do. For many days and nights the touch of Benu's arms around his neck and the memory of the words "Come to our house" made Haralal catch his breath, as in a sigh. Then, gradually, another day came when everything was over between them. The pain no longer clung to the inner nerve as the bat clings to the dark.

6

Despite all his efforts Haralal could no longer concentrate on his studies in the old way. He would try to read, then would slam the book shut, go out, and walk rapidly and aimlessly through the streets. Sometimes there were big gaps in his class lecture notes, and the occasional doodles in those notebooks bore no resemblance to any script except Egyptian hieroglyphics.

Haralal realized that things were not going well. Even if he got through the examinations, there was no possibility of his getting a scholarship. Without a scholarship he couldn't manage for a single day in Calcutta. Furthermore, he had to send a few rupees to his mother in the country. After considering the possibilities, he went out in search of a job. Getting a job was difficult, but not getting one would be even worse. He could only hope against hope.

When Haralal applied at a big English business firm, he had the good fortune to come to the notice of the manager. The Englishman believed that he could judge people by their faces. He summoned Haralal, exchanged a few words with him, and told himself that this fellow would do. He asked, "Do you have any experience?"

"No," said Haralal.

"Are you bonded?"

"No" was the answer to that too.

"Can you bring recommendations from some prominent person?"

He knew no prominent person.

The Englishman seemed even more pleased at this and said, "Jolly well. Get started at twenty-five rupees. We'll increase the pay as you improve." Then he looked at Haralal's clothes and said, "I'm going to give you fifteen rupees in advance. Get some proper office clothes made."

The clothes were made. Haralal joined the office staff. The manager began to make him work like some superhuman being; when all the other clerks went home, Haralal was not excused. He had to go to the Englishman's home now and then and report on his work.

Haralal soon learned his job. His fellow clerks did their best to slow his progress and to malign him to his superiors, but none of them could harm this quiet, meek, insignificant Haralal.

When his pay rose to forty rupees, Haralal brought his mother from the village and set up a tiny household in a tiny lane. Now the long days of his mother's misery were over. She said, "Son, now I'll bring a daughter-in-law to this house." Haralal touched his mother's feet in respect and replied, "Mother, you'll have to forgive me on that score."

His mother had another request. She would say, "You always talk about your pupil Benugopal; invite him here for dinner some day. I'd like to meet him."

"Mother, where would I put him in this house?" was Haralal's reply. "Wait a bit, I'll get a bigger house; then I'll invite him."

7

When Haralal's salary increased, he moved from the little lane to a wider street and from the small house to a larger one. Still, for some unformulated reason he was unable to decide about going to Adhar's house or inviting Benu to his own house.

It seemed that he would never overcome his diffidence. Just then, Benu's mother died unexpectedly. When Haralal heard this news he went at once to Adhar's house.

Those two friends of disparate ages met once again. After Benu's mourning period ended, Haralal continued to call at his house. But nothing was the same. Benu was now grown up enough to twirl his new moustache between thumb and forefinger. He lived like a dandy and had plenty of compatible friends. He entertained his cronies by playing cheap film songs on the phonograph. Where were that old broken bench and marked-up table that once stood in the study? The room seemed puffed out with mirrors, pictures, and furniture. Benu now went to college but seemed to have no incentive to get through his second year. His father had decided that passing a few examinations would increase his son's value on the marriage market. But Nanibala knew his value and used to spell it out: "My Benu does not have to prove his superiority by passing examinations like common boys. Hold onto the securities in the iron safe." The son too understood his mother's point very well.

Haralal understood that under these circumstances he was quite unnecessary to Benu, and he kept recalling that morning when Benu had suddenly arrived at his hostel, thrown his arms around his neck, and said, "Mastarmashai, come to our house." That Benu was gone; that house was changed. Now who would ask for Mastarmashai?

Haralal once thought of inviting Benu to his home occasionally, but he did not get up the courage to do it. One day he would think, I'll invite him; then again he would think, What's the use? Perhaps Benu would accept his invitation, but—let it go.

Haralal's mother didn't give up. She insisted that she would cook for Benu herself—ah, the poor motherless boy!

At last Haralal went to issue the invitation and said, "Let me go and get Adharbabu's permission."

"You don't need to ask his permission," said Benu. "Do you think I'm still that same kid?"

Benu came to dinner at Haralal's. Haralal's mother fed this boy who looked like Kartik and blessed him with loving eyes while she served him. She thought only of what Benu's mother must have felt when she passed away, leaving so young a son whose future she would never know.

As soon as Benu had eaten, he said, "Mastarmashai, I'll have to be excused a little early. A couple of my friends are coming to see me." He took out his gold pocket watch and looked at the time. Then he briskly took his leave and got into his carriage. Haralal remained standing at the door of his home. The carriage shook the whole street and instantly disappeared.

"Haralal, invite him now and then," said his mother. "I feel so sorry when I think that at his age he has lost a mother."

Haralal was silent. He saw no reason for consoling this

motherless boy. He sighed and thought, That's it. Never again will I invite him. Once I tutored him for five rupees a month, but I am still the insignificant Haralal.

8

One evening after coming back from the office Haralal found someone sitting in the dark on the first floor of his house. He would have gone upstairs without noticing anyone, but as he came to the door he smelled the air heavy with the scent of cologne. Haralal went into the room and asked, "Who is it, sir?"

Benu stood up and said, "Mastarmashai, it is I."

"What's the matter? When did you come?"

"A long time ago," Benu replied. "I didn't know that you came from the office so late."

Long ago Benu had been invited to dinner again but he had not come. Suddenly this evening, without a word of warning, he sat waiting in this dark room. Haralal felt uneasy.

They went upstairs, turned up the light, and sat down. Haralal inquired, "Is everything all right? Is there some special news?"

Benu said that school was becoming increasingly boring. How could he stay stuck in the second year, year after year? He had to study with boys much younger than himself; he felt terribly embarrassed. But his father did not understand this at all.

"What do you want to do?" Haralal asked.

Benu said that he would like to go to England and become a barrister. One fellow in his class, a worse student than he, had decided to go to England.

"Did you tell your father what you wish to do?"

"I told him. My father says he won't listen to my proposal until I pass my examination. But I'm discouraged, I certainly won't be able to pass if I stay here."

Haralal sat quietly thinking. "Today my father gave me a dressing-down about this," Benu said. "That's why I've left the house. This could never have happened if my mother were alive today." He began to cry in self-pity.

"Let's both go to your father," said Haralal. "We can discuss the matter and decide on the best thing to do."

"No," said Benu, "I don't want to go there."

Haralal did not like the idea of Benu's staying at his house after an argument with his father. At the same time it was very hard to say "You can't stay here." He thought, After a while, when he calms down a bit and I can get his mind on something else, I'll take him home. He asked Benu, "Have you eaten anything?"

"No, I'm not hungry. I'm not going to eat today."

"How can you do that?" Haralal quickly went to his mother and said, "Mother, Benu is here. I'd like something for him to eat."

Very pleased, his mother went to prepare a meal. Haralal changed from his office clothes, washed, and came to Benu. He gave a little cough, hesitated a moment, put an arm over Benu's shoulder, and said, "Benu, I don't think you're doing the right thing. It isn't right for you to quarrel with your father and leave the house."

Benu stood up at once. "If this inconveniences you," he said, "I'll go to my friend Satish." He was on the point of leaving. Haralal held his arm and said, "Wait, don't go without eating."

In the nick of time Haralal's mother brought a plate of the food that had been prepared for Haralal. She came and stood before Benu. "Where are you going, child?" she asked.

"I have work to do. I was leaving," Benu answered.

"How can that be, my child? You can't go without eating something." And she set a place for him on the veranda, prepared to serve him, and had him sit down.

The angry Benu ate nothing and was only toying with the food when a carriage stopped at the door. First came a gate-man and behind him, Adharbabu himself. Shoes squeaking, he marched straight upstairs. Benu's face paled. The mother went to the inner room.

Adhar came up to his son and, while looking toward Haralal, said in a voice that trembled with anger, "So this is it! Ratikanta warned me, but I didn't believe you had so much deceit in you. Did you think you would win Benu over and live off him? But I won't permit that. You'd alienate the boy! I'll report you to the police. I'll not stop until I have you in jail." Next he turned to Benu and said, "Let's go. Get up." Benu followed his father out without a word.

That evening Haralal was the only one who could not eat.

9

Haralal's mercantile house now began to purchase a very large quantity of rice and lentils from the country districts. This project obliged him to travel early every Saturday morning by train, carrying seven or eight thousand rupees to the villages. In order to pay the wholesalers in cash, he would take the money to the company's district office and change it into ten- and five-rupee note and coins. There he would examine the ledger and the receipts, check the voluminous accounts of the preceding week, and leave some funds there for the coming week's transactions. Two company guards went with him; there was some talk in the office about the fact that Haralal was not bonded, but the manager had assumed all the liability and said that bonding was unnecessary.

This work began in November, and there was a possibility that it would last until April. Haralal was particularly busy on this assignment. He often returned from work late at night.

Returning thus one night, he heard that Benu had come and his mother had fed him and fussed over him. As she chatted with him, she became all the fonder of him. This happened on several other occasions. Haralal's mother said, "His thoughts don't stay at home because his mother isn't there. I think of Benu as your younger brother, my own child. He comes here merely to get affection and to call me Mother." As she said this she wiped her tears with the end of her sari.

One evening Benu waited for Haralal. They talked until far into the night. "Father has become so unbearable these days that I can't live in the house anymore," Benu said, "especially since I've heard that he is preparing to remarry. Ratibabu is the go-between; Father consults him all the time. It used to be that if I went somewhere and came home late, my father would get very upset. Now if I don't come home for several days, he feels safe. If I stay home he has to discuss his marriage plans secretly, so if I am not there he heaves a sigh of relief. If this marriage goes through, I won't be able to live in that house. Please tell me a way to get out of this mess. I want to be on my own."

Haralal's heart filled with sorrow and affection. The fact that Benu had come with his troubles to his Mastarmashai, instead of to anyone else, gave him joy. But it also brought sorrow, because there is so little that a Mastarmashai can do.

"Whatever happens," said Benu, "if I can go to England and become a barrister, I'll be out of this mess."

"Would Adharbabu let you go?" Haralal asked.

"He'll be relieved if I go. But he's so fond of money that it won't be easy to get anything out of him for my expenses abroad. There'll have to be some trick."

Haralal smiled at Benu's worldly wisdom. "What trick?"

"I'll borrow money by signing IOU's," Benu said. "When the creditors bring action, my father will have to pay off the debts. With that money I'll run away to England. Once I'm there he can't withhold my allowance."

"Who would lend you money?" Haralal inquired.

"Can't you do it?"

Haralal was astounded. "I!" He couldn't say another word.

"Why, I saw your gateman bring a lot of money to the house in bankrolls."

Haralal smiled and said, "Just as the gateman is mine, so the money is mine." Then he explained the use of this money. "These office funds take shelter for only one night in this poor man's house. In the morning they move out in ten directions."

"Can't your boss give me a loan? I can pay him higher interest."

"If your father puts up some collateral, perhaps my boss would give you a loan at my request."

"If Father would put up collateral," said Benu, "why wouldn't he give me the money?"

Their discussion ended here. Haralal kept thinking, If I had any property, I'd sell it and give him the money. There was only one drawback; he owned neither house nor land.

10

One Friday night a carriage stopped in front of Haralal's home. When Benu got down, Haralal's office orderly made him a deep bow and scurried in to inform his superior. At that time Haralal was sitting on his bedroom floor counting the money. Benu came in. Tonight he was dressed quite differently. Instead of a fine-spun dhoti and chador, a parsi coat and trousers encased his vigorous body, and he wore a cap on his head. Expensive jewels and pearls glistened on the fingers of both hands. Around his neck was a long, thick gold chain leading to the breast pocket which contained his watch. There were diamond cufflinks on his shirt-cuffs.

Surprised, Haralal stopped counting. "What's this about?" he asked. "Why so dressed up so late at night?"

"Day after tomorrow my father will be married," answered Benu. "He has kept it a secret from me, but I've heard about it. I told him I'd like to go to our Barrackpore garden house for a few days. He was very happy and gave me permission. So I'm going to the garden house. I feel like not coming back. If I had the courage I'd drown myself in the Ganges."

Benu began to weep. Someone seemed to pierce Haralal's heart with a knife. Some unknown woman would come to take over Benu's mother's room, her bed, her place. With all his heart Haralal could feel how painful it would be for Benu to live in that house that was wrapped in loving memories. He thought to himself, Even if you are not born poor there is no end to misery and humiliation in this world. At a loss for words of consolation, he took Benu's hand in his.

Immediately a question arose. How could Benu be so dressed up at such a sad time?

Benu noticed Haralal's eyes fixed on the rings and seemed to anticipate the question. He said, "These are my mother's rings."

With a great effort Haralal held back his tears. Presently he said, "Benu, have you had anything to eat?"

"Yes, haven't you eaten?"

"I can't leave the room until I count all the money and put it in the iron chest."

"Why don't you go and eat?" suggested Benu. "I have many things to discuss with you. I'll stay in the room. Your mother is waiting with your food ready."

Haralal hesitated for a moment, then said, "I'll eat and be right back."

Haralal ate quickly and returned to the room with his mother. Benu touched her feet and she patted his chin and kissed him. She had heard the whole story from Haralal and her heart was breaking because even all her affection could not make up for Benu's loss. The three sat with money strewn all around them and began to talk about Benu's childhood

days. So many incidents, so many occasions, were bound up
with Mastarmashai. From time to time their talk turned to
the mother whose affection had been poured out so unrestrainedly.

Thus the night wore away. Suddenly Benu took off his
watch and said, "No more. If I wait any longer I'll miss the
train."

"Son, why don't you stay right here tonight?" asked Haralal's mother. "Tomorrow morning you can leave with Haralal."

"No, Mother, don't ask that," Benu begged. "I must leave
tonight." To Haralal he said, "Mastarmashai, it isn't safe to
take this jewelry and this watch to the garden house. I'll
leave these with you and pick them up when I come back.
Tell your orderly to bring the leather handbag from my carriage. I'll put everything in that bag."

The office orderly brought the bag from the carriage. Benu
took off his chain, watch, rings, cufflinks, and stuffed them
into the bag. The cautious Haralal immediately put that bag
into his safe.

Benu touched Haralal's mother's feet. She blessed him and
said in a choked voice, "May the Mother of the world be
your mother and watch over you."

Then Benu touched Haralal's feet in respect. He had never
done this before to Haralal. Haralal did not say a word.
He put his hand on Benu's back and went downstairs with
him. The lamps on the carriage were lighted, and the two
horses became restless. The carriage disappeared with Benu
into the gaslit Calcutta night.

Haralal went to his room and sat in silence for a long
time. Then he sighed and began to count the stack of coins
and put them into a sack. The notes had been counted earlier
and deposited in the safe.

11

Very late that night Haralal went to bed in that room with
the money, the key to the safe under his pillow. He did not
sleep well. He dreamed that Benu's mother scolded him loudly
from behind the purdah curtain. He couldn't hear the words
clearly, but along with her disembodied voice, the red and
green and white rays from her emeralds, rubies, and diamonds
pierced the dark curtain and swung back and forth. With all
his might Haralal tried to call Benu but could not make a

sound. Then with a tremendous noise the curtain tore and disintegrated. Startled, Haralal awoke and saw a thick-layered darkness. A sudden gust of wind boisterously opened the window and put out the light.

Haralal was drenched with perspiration. He got up quickly and struck a match. His clock showed it was four in the morning and too late for more sleep. He would have to prepare to take the money to the villages. He washed his face, and when his mother heard him, she said from the other room, "Are you up already, son?"

Haralal's first act each morning was to go into his mother's room and receive her blessing. She accepted his respects, blessed him from the fullness of her heart, and said, "Son, I was just dreaming that you were going to get yourself a wife. Can the morning dream be wrong?"

Haralal smiled and went into his room. He took the sacks of bank notes and coins from the safe and was about to put them in the packing box when his heart suddenly began to pound: two or three of the bank-note sacks were empty. He thought he was dreaming. He picked up the sacks and banged them against the safe. This did nothing to disprove their emptiness. Still, hoping against hope, he opened the drawstrings and shook the sacks upside down. Two letters fell out. They were written in Benu's hand. One was addressed to his father, the other to Haralal.

Quickly he got his letter open. His eyes seemed unable to focus. He felt that there was not enough light; he kept turning up the lamp. What he read he did not comprehend; he seemed to have forgotten the Bengali language.

The letter said that Benu had taken 3,000 rupees' worth of ten-rupee notes and had set out for England. His ship was to leave at dawn. Benu had done this while Haralal ate. He had written: "I am also writing to my father. He will pay off this debt. In addition, if you open the bag you'll see my mother's jewelry. I don't know its exact value. Perhaps it will come to more than 3,000 rupees. If my mother were alive today, and my father wouldn't give me money to go to England, she would certainly have used this jewelry to get the money for me. I can't bear to have my father give my mother's jewelry to anyone else. Therefore in doing this I have exercised my rights. If my father delays in repaying you, you can very easily get the money by selling this or putting it up as collateral. These are my mother's things; they are my own property."

There was much more, but it was not important. Haralal locked the door, quickly took a carriage, and raced to the Ganges landings. He didn't even know the name of the ship on which Benu had taken passage, but he went as far as Metiaburuj. He learned that two ships, both bound for England, had left that morning. He had no idea which one Benu was on, nor could he think of any way to catch up with it.

When his carriage turned back from Metiaburuj toward his home, the city of Calcutta had awakened in the morning sun. Haralal saw nothing. His uncomprehending mind seemed to push with all its might against a terrible formless adversary but could not make it move an inch. The carriage stopped in front of that house where his mother lived, where all his weariness and tension after a day's work had always vanished instantly. He paid the driver and entered in a state of immeasurable fear and despair.

His mother stood anxiously on the veranda. "Where did you go?" she asked.

Haralal burst out, "Mother, I went to get you a daughter-in-law." He laughed and laughed with a dry voice and fell unconscious on the spot.

"Oh, heavens, what happened?" she cried as she quickly brought water and sprinkled it on his face.

Haralal presently opened his eyes and sat looking with a vacant stare. "Mother, don't be upset," he said. "Let me stay alone for a little while." He went straight to his room and bolted the door from inside. His mother sat down on the floor outside the door. The April sun fell full on her. She stayed there with her head against the bolted door, calling, "Haralal, dear Haralal."

"Mother, I'll come out very shortly," said Haralal. "You go away now."

She sat there in the sun and began to count her prayer beads. The office orderly came, pounded on the door, and said, "Sir, if we don't go right now, we won't get another train."

"We won't be going by the seven-o'clock train today," Haralal said from inside.

"When will you go, then?" asked the orderly.

"I'll tell you that later."

The orderly nodded his head, threw up his hands, and went downstairs.

Haralal began to think, To whom can I tell this? This is embezzlement. How can I put Benu in jail?

Then he remembered the jewelry. He had forgotten all about it. It seemed that he had found a solution. Opening the bag, he saw not only rings, a watch, cufflinks, a gold chain; there were bracelets, necklaces, hair ornaments, strings of pearls, and many other expensive pieces. The value of all this was much more than 3,000 rupees. But this was also theft. These did not belong to Benu either. As long as this bag remained in his room, he was in danger.

At once Haralal left his room with Adhar's letter and the bag, and went downstairs. "Where are you going, son?" asked his mother.

"To Adharbabu's."

The great burden of undefined fear fell from his mother's heart. She decided that last night's news about Benu's father's marriage had deeply perturbed Haralal. Ah, how he loves Benu! "Won't you go to the village today?" she inquired.

"No." Haralal hastily went out.

He heard from a distance the opening strains of wedding music, but as soon as he entered Adhar's house he saw that the marriage festivity was mixed with unrest. There was a strict guard of gatemen, none of the servants was allowed to leave the house, and there was fear and anxiety on every face. He was told that a lot of expensive jewelry had been stolen from the house during the night. Several servants were prime suspects, and plans were under way for handing them over to the police.

Haralal went to the upstairs veranda. Adhar sat there in a rage, and Ratikanta smoked.

"I have something to tell you in private," said Haralal.

Adhar flew into a passion. "I have no time now to discuss anything privately with you. Whatever you have to say, say right here."

He thought that Haralal had come to him at this time for a favor or a loan.

"If you're ashamed to speak to my master in front of me, I can leave," said Ratikanta.

Annoyed, Adhar snapped, "Hah! Sit still! Why should you go?"

"Last night," said Haralal, "Benu left this bag at my house."

"What's in it?" asked Adhar.

Haralal opened the bag and gave it to Adhar.

"Tutor and pupil have started a fine business," said Adhar. "You knew that you'd be caught if you tried to sell this stolen stuff. That's why you've brought it back. Did you think you'd get a reward for your honesty?"

Then Haralal gave Adhar his letter. As Adhar read it, his rage increased. He said, "I'll report this to the police. My son is still under age; you made him do the stealing and sent him off to England. Perhaps you loaned him 500 rupees and made him write 3,000. I will not repay this debt."

"I have made him no loan," said Haralal.

"Then where did he get the money? Did he break into your trunk and steal it?"

Haralal did not answer that question. Ratikanta pointedly remarked, "Why don't you ask him why 3,000 rupees? Has he ever seen 500 rupees with his own eyes?"

As soon as the mystery of the stolen jewelry was solved, the house was in an uproar over Benu's running away to England. Haralal took all the blame on himself and left the house. When he reached the street, his mind was benumbed. It lacked even the capacity for fear or worry. It refused to dwell upon the consequences of this affair. When he came to his lane he saw a carriage standing directly in front of his house. He was startled by a sudden hope that Benu had come back. It must be Benu! He could not believe that his trouble would be driven to such utterly hopeless extremes.

He hurried up to the carriage and saw an Englishman from the office sitting inside. When the sahib saw Haralal, he stepped down, took him by the hand, and led him to the house. "Why didn't you go to the country this morning?" the Englishman asked.

The office orderly had become suspicious, had gone to the manager; he had sent this man.

"I am missing 3,000 rupees in notes," Haralal said.

"Where did they go?"

Haralal could not even reply, "I don't know." He was silent.

"Show me where you kept the money."

Haralal took him to the room upstairs. The sahib counted all the money and searched every corner of the room. He thoroughly searched every room of the house.

As she watched this, Haralal's mother could bear no more. She stood right in front of the Englishman and asked anxiously in Bengali, "Oh, Haralal, what happened?"

"Mother, the money is stolen."

"How could the money be gone? Haralal, who has done such a dreadful thing?"

"Mother, be still," said Haralal.

The Englishman closed the investigation by asking, "Who was in this house last night?"

"The door was closed and I slept alone. There was no one else," Haralal replied.

The Englishman put the coins in the carriage and said to Haralal, "Well, let's go to the manager."

Seeing that Haralal was leaving with the Englishman, his mother stood in their way and said, "Sahib, where will you take my boy? I've starved myself to raise this boy. My boy would never touch that money."

The sahib did not understand Bengali. He said, "All right, all right."

"Mother, why are you upset?" Haralal asked. "I'll come back as soon as I've seen the manager."

The mother said in distress, "You haven't eaten anything all morning."

Without replying Haralal got into the carriage and went away. The mother fainted and lay there on the floor.

The manager said to Haralal, "Tell me the truth. What's this all about?"

Haralal said, "I didn't take the money."

"I have complete faith in your word. But you must know who took it."

Haralal continued to look down and made no reply.

"Did someone take this money with your knowledge?" the manager asked.

"As long as I am alive no one could ever take this money with my knowledge."

"Look here, Haralal," said the manager. "I trusted you and gave you this responsibility on the job without bonding you. Everyone at the office was opposed to this. Three thousand rupees is not a lot of money. But you'll put me to shame. I give you the whole day today to offer you a chance to get the money together and turn it over. If you can raise the money, I won't discuss it further. You'll work just as you do now."

With this the manager got up and left. It was then eleven o'clock. When Haralal came out with his head hanging, the office staff were extremely pleased and began to discuss his downfall.

Haralal had one day's time. He had one more long day in which to stir up the silt of despair during the increased time allotted to him.

What way, what way, what way out? With this one thought in mind Haralal began to walk the streets under the blazing sun. Finally he stopped thinking but could not stop his aimless wandering. Calcutta, which was a place of refuge for thousands and thousands of persons, had in one moment's time become a monstrous trap for Haralal. There appeared to be no way out. The whole of society stood ranged to hem in this insignificant Haralal. He knew no one, and no one bore him any malice, but every man was his enemy. Yet passersby brushed against him on the street. Office clerks ate snacks from paper bags. No one noticed him. At the edge of the Maidan people at leisure lay under the trees with legs crossed and their heads on their hands. Open carriages full of Hindustani girls went to Kalighat.

A messenger carrying a letter came up to Haralal and said, "Sir, please read this address for me," as if he were no different from other pedestrians. Haralal read the address and explained it.

Office closing time approached. The carriages turned homeward and rushed along the streets that had led to the offices. Clerks crowded the trolleycars and read theater advertisements on their way home. Now Haralal had no office, no closing time, no rush to catch the homeward-bound train. All the din and bustle of the city, all the buildings and homes, the movement of traffic, the comings and goings, sometimes seemed like a creature of truth, fangs exposed, and sometimes like a formless dream hanging over him. He had had no food, no rest, no shelter; he couldn't even tell how he had spent the day.

The gaslights were lit on every street; their thousands of shifty eyes seemed to unite in peering at the alert darkness, which was like a monster silently poised to pounce upon its prey. Haralal didn't even wonder about the time. The nerve in his forehead began to throb, his head felt as if it would split, his whole body burned, his feet could move no longer.

All day long, thoughts of his mother had alternated with pain, fatigue, excitement, and numbness. Out of this great mass of people in Calcutta only this one name came into his dry throat: Mother, Mother, Mother. There was no one else to call.

He thought that when the night would be far-gone and no one was awake to accuse the utterly insignificant Haralal for a crime not of his doing, then he would quietly go to his mother, fall asleep with his head on her lap, and hope never

to waken again! He could not go home now for fear the police or someone else would come to humiliate him in front of
his mother. When it seemed that he could no longer bear his
own weight, he saw a carriage for hire and hailed it. "Where
do you want to go?" asked the driver.

"Nowhere," Haralal answered. "I want to ride around this
Maidan road for a while."

The driver was suspicious and was about to drive on, and
Haralal paid him one rupee in advance. Then the carriage
began to take him around and around the Maidan road.

The weary Haralal put his burning head on the sill of the
open window and closed his eyes. All his misery gradually began to recede. His body became cool. A profound, impenetrable peace filled with joy began to gather in his mind. A great
deliverance embraced him from all sides. It seemed that in
a single moment all that he had thought throughout the day—
that there was no way out, no one to help him, no pardon,
no end to his humiliation, no bounds to his misery—became
untrue. Now only fear remained, but that was not true either.
He refused to accept that which had seized his life and crushed
it in an iron fist. Freedom filled the whole sky and peace was
boundless. In this whole universe there was no power, no
emperor who could imprison this insignificant Haralal inside
his misery, humiliation, injustice. The terror with which
he had bound himself fell away.

Then in the limitless sky around his liberated soul it appeared to Haralal that he saw his poor mother grow in size
and splendor until she encompassed the whole of the darkness.
Nothing could contain her. The streets and the landings of
Calcutta, the buildings and the homes, the shops and bazaars,
one by one merged with her. She filled the breeze, the sky,
and the stars one after another were lost in her. All his pain,
all his anxiety, his entire consciousness gradually emptied
into her. Everything was gone, the warm mist seethed and
burst. Now there was neither light nor darkness, only a profound fulfillment.

The clock in the church tower struck one. The driver
finally became annoyed at going around and around in the
dark Maidan. "Sir," he said, "the horses can't go any longer.
Tell me where to go."

He heard no response. He came down from the driver's
seat, shook Haralal, and repeated his question. There was
no reply. Then the driver was frightened. He looked more

closely and found that the body was stiff and breath had ceased.

The question, "Where do you want to go?" went unanswered.

1907

A WIFE'S LETTER
(Strir Patra)

To One Whom I Respect:[1]

We have been married for fifteen years; until today I have never written a letter to you. You have heard me and I have heard you. There has never been occasion for letter writing.

Today I have come to Srikshetra on a pilgrimage; you are working at your office. Calcutta is to you what the shell is to the snail; it has been fastened tight to your body and your mind. That is why you don't request a leave from the office. My being here is God's intention. He has approved my request for a leave.

I am the second daughter-in-law in your family. Now after fifteen years I have come to realize, as I stand on the seashore of Srikshetra, that I stand in a second relationship, which is that between my world and God. That is why I have dared to write this letter. This is not the letter of your family's second daughter-in-law.

No one except He who wrote the decree of fate that placed me among you would have thought it possible that my brother and I had typhoid fever together when we were children. My brother died, I lived. All the neighborhood girls said, "Mrinal survived because she is a girl. If she were a boy, would her life have been spared?" Yama is a canny thief and covets the things that are really valuable.

---

[1] The salutation in the original, *Sricharankamaleshu*, may be translated literally as: Dedicated to your lotus feet (an ancient form of address).

Dying is not in my fate. I sat down to write this letter in order to make you fully comprehend that fact.

I was twelve years old when your distant uncle brought your friend Nirod to see the bride. We lived in a remote village where the jackals howled in the daytime. A covered carriage came fourteen miles from the station, and the passenger arrived at our village after traveling in a palanquin the three remaining miles of unpaved road. How annoyed you all were that day! On top of that, the food in our house was prepared in the East Bengal style; Uncle still hasn't forgotten that terrible cookery.

Your mother was firmly determined that the second daughter-in-law should make up for the elder sister-in-law's lack of beauty. Otherwise, why would you have taken so much trouble to get to our village? Bengal was full of men with diseased spleens and livers, and yet they could easily pick up a bride. But if they saw a pretty girl they put extra pressure on her; they didn't want to let her escape from being married to even an inferior person.

My father's heart began to pound; my mother began to call upon Durga. Would the village worshipper please the city god? Hope lies in the girl's beauty, but if she boasts none of that beauty, those who have come to look her over will pay whatever they think she is worth. Therefore, girls with a thousand graces and other merits need never get over their shyness.

The whole house, even the entire neighborhood, was permeated by this terror, which pressed against my heart like a stone. All that sky's daylight and all the might of the world seemed to transfix a twelve-year-old village girl so that two people could hold her before them for examination by two pairs of eyes. There was no place for me to hide.

As the wedding flute began to play, I came to your house. My shortcomings were noted in detail, totted up, and acknowledged by the housewives of that joint family, but I was pronounced, on the whole, beautiful. When she heard that, my elder sister-in-law looked somber. But I wonder why I needed beauty? If some old priest had made an image out of Ganges clay, it would have been revered, but when God Himself fashions a form out of joy, it has no value in your pious world.

It didn't take you long to forget my looks, but the fact that I had intelligence rankled in your minds. It is so much a part of me that it has endured even through all this time spent among you as a housewife. My mother was always worried about my intelligence, for it is a calamity for a woman to possess it. If one who must live according to rules tries to use her mind, she is sure to stumble and be cursed. But tell me what I could do. In an unwary moment God had given me more sense than was necessary for a house-wife in your family. Can I return it now to someone else? Morning and evening you all called me "precocious girl." The harsh words were consolation for the weak. I forgive all of that.

I had something else beyond keeping house for you, which none of you knew about. I wrote poetry in secret. This was not important; it never passed the barrier of the inner rooms at your house. But there was my freedom, there was my real self. You neither liked nor recognized whatever in me amounted to more than the second daughter-in-law. That I am a poet is something you haven't discovered in all these fifteen years.

Your cowshed is foremost among my first memories of your house. The shed is just beside the stairway that ascends to the women's apartments, and except for a tiny court-yard in front, the cows have no space in which to move about. In a corner of that courtyard is a wooden tub for their fodder. The bearer has all sorts of morning chores; in the meantime the hungry cows licked and chewed at the handful of fodder around the edges of the tub. My heart wept for them. I am a village girl; on the day of my arrival at your house my eyes were caught by those two cows and three calves, which were like my lifelong friends in the midst of the great city. In those days as a new bride I didn't eat my own food but hid it and fed it to them. When I was older and openly showed my fond-ness for the cows, the relatives made fun of me and began to express doubts about my lineage.

My daughter died soon after birth. Her departure was a summons to me as well. If she had lived, she would have been the greatest thing in my life. She would have brought truth to my life. I would have ascended directly from second daughter-in-law to mother. The mother belongs to the whole world even if she is a member of only one family. I had the pain but not the freedom of becoming a mother.

I recall that the English doctor who came was astonished by our inner apartments and scolded in annoyance when he saw the room where I lay in labor. It is at the far edge of your little garden. The main house lacks nothing in furnish-ings or accessories. But the women's apartments are like the reverse side of a tapestry. They have no delicacy, no beauty, no decoration. The light burns dimly there, the wind comes in like a thief; no one cares to cart away the trash in the courtyard. There are indelible stains on all the walls and floors.

But the doctor was mistaken. He thought, I suppose, that this constantly bothered us. The reverse was the case: indifference is like ashes that keep the fire smoldering but give no warmth when removed from the hearth. When self-respect declines, disrespect does not seem at all unjust. Therefore it did not bother us. I tell you, that is why a woman is ashamed of feeling sad. A woman must suffer but it does her good to be given as little respect as possible. This was your decision. It is true that love only increases a woman's pain.

I never recall thinking that I was unhappy then. Death came and stood at my head in the labor room; I wasn't at all afraid. What in our life would make me fear death? Those who fend off death are those whose lives have been strongly bound with affection and loving care. If Yama had taken me that day, I would have been uprooted as easily as a piece of turf is pulled up with all its roots from the plowed soil. A Bengali girl dies at every word. But is dying so brave a thing? I am ashamed to die; dying is all too easy for us.

My daughter appeared for a moment, like the evening star, and disappeared. Again I took up my daily routine and looked after the cows and the calves. Life might have gone on thus to its end; there would have been no need to write this letter to you today. But a mild breeze can carry off a seed that sprouts a fig tree in the midst of a house of brick and cement. After that tiny beginning the heart and ribs of wood and brick are finally torn apart. A little substance fell from somewhere into a corner of my life, at the center of my solidly settled world; the crevice was begun.

After her widowed mother died, Bindu came to stay with her older sister at our house in order to escape the tyranny of her cousin-brother. This, you all thought, was another piece of bad luck for me. Tell me what to do about my accursed nature. All of you were inwardly irritated because with all my might I immediately espoused the cause of this homeless girl. She had been begrudgingly sheltered at one house after another; she had been terribly humiliated. She was simply shoved aside by anyone to whom she confided her desperate state.

Then I saw how things were with my elder sister-in-law. She was very sympathetic and had brought Bindu to her own house. But when she saw her husband's reluctance, she began to share it and feel that Bindu seriously inconvenienced her, that she would be relieved if only Bindu could be deposited in some distant spot. She did not have the courage to show open affection toward this unprotected sister. She was devoted to her husband.

My heart ached, too, as I observed Bindu's dilemma. I saw that the elder sister-in-law had bluntly directed everyone to keep a constant eye upon Bindu's food and clothes and directed all the maids in the house to do the same, so that I felt not only sorry but ashamed. She was anxious to prove to everyone that doing anything on the sly in our household would place Bindu in a serious situation. She was given plenty of work, yet she burdened the budget very little.

The greatest thing about our elder sister-in-law was her father's distinguished ancestry; she had neither beauty nor money. You all know how she got married into your family by flattering my father-in-law. She always knew that her marriage had been a serious affront to this ancestry. Therefore, this subject was avoided as much as possible, and she very seldom brought it up.

But her virtuous example caused us great difficulty. I could not abase myself so absurdly before all of you. I speak well of those whom I esteem; it is not my way to shun those of whom I speak ill. You knew this.

I took Bindu in with me. The elder sister said, "Our second daughter-in-law is spoiling that girl who's used to a poor house." She went about complaining to everyone as if I had precipitated a serious calamity. But I knew for certain that in her heart she felt relieved. Now the burden of blame fell upon me. She, who herself could not show affection toward her sister, set her mind at ease by giving that same scrap of affection through me.

My elder sister-in-law tried to subtract from two to four years from Bindu's age. But she was not less than fourteen; it was not wrong to hide this fact. You certainly know that she was so unattractive that if she hit her head against the floor people worried about the floor. Hence, in the absence of her parents no one tried to get a husband for her, and now no one had the moral courage to marry her.

Bindu came to me fearfully. She seemed to feel that she would be scorched by touching my body and I couldn't bear that. It was as if she had never agreed to being born into this world. So she merely slipped aside and kept her eyes averted. At her father's house her cousin-brothers, too, had never allowed her anything except some corner that could be used for something unessential. Space was easily made everywhere for the unnecessary castoffs of the household, but people forgot Bindu. It is difficult, however, to ignore a lone unnecessary woman; there is not even a place for her in the trash can. Although Bindu's cousin-brothers were scarcely the most indispensable individuals in this world, they were getting along very well.

That is why Bindu had misgivings when I brought her to my room. Her heart began to quake. I was very much grieved by her fear. I explained to her very affectionately that I had a little space for her.

But my room was not only mine. Consequently, my undertaking was not easy. She had been with me for only a few days when a bright-red rash broke out on her body. Perhaps it was prickly heat; if not, it would be something of the sort. You all said it was smallpox. Obviously she had those spots. Your neighborhood quack doctor came and said that if no other symptoms showed up, it would amount to nothing. But who waited patiently that day or two? Bindu was about to die of shame because of her illness.

"What if it is smallpox?" I said. "I'll settle her in our labor room at the end of the garden; no one else needs it."

Just when all of you were horrified at me and when Bindu's elder sister, highly annoyed, proposed sending the unfortunate girl to a hospital, the red spots spread out to cover her whole body. When you saw that, you were more upset than ever. You said, "It most certainly has turned out to be smallpox. Obviously, those are the spots."

The person who is brought up with indifference has one great attribute: indifference promptly gives the body an immortal durability. It is never ill; the highroads to death are promptly closed off. Disease taunts it; nothing happens. But there is one great disadvantage: it is the most difficult thing in the whole world to shelter an insignificant person. The more acute the need for shelter, the more severe the obstacles placed in the way.

Bindu had just got over her fear of me when still another misfortune befell her. She began to love me so much that she made me fearful. This kind of love had certainly never been seen in the family. I had read of that other love between man and woman. I was beautiful, but for some reason I had never paid any attention to it; after all this time that beauty attracted this unattractive girl. When she looked at my face, her eyes were no longer hopeless. She would say, "Sister, no one else has a face like yours." On the days I braided up my hair, she was very displeased. She loved to take the weight of my hair in her hands and shake it back and forth. Unless I was invited somewhere, there was no need to dress up. But Bindu made me restless asking me each day to dress up in a new style. The girl had suddenly become mad about me.

In the women's part of the house there was not even one katha of land. Somehow or other, a mangosteen tree had managed to take root on the wall of the north edge of the gutter. The day I saw the ruddy glow of new leaves on that mangosteen tree, I knew that spring had come to the earth. As I went about my housework I thought of this neglected girl who that day had turned the same color from head to foot, and that day I realized that a spring breeze was blowing in the world's heart as well, the breeze that comes from some heaven unknown. It did not come from the blind alleys of the household.

The outpouring of Bindu's affection made me nervous. From time to time I would get angry with her, I admit, but her heartfelt love made me see my true self, of which I had never been aware. This gave me freedom.

On the other hand, caring for a girl like Bindu appeared to you to be excessive fussing. There was no end to the complaints and peevishness on this score. The day a bracelet was stolen from my room, none of you felt ashamed to hint that in some way or other Bindu had committed that theft. When the native police threw the house into an uproar with their search, you found it easy to suspect that Bindu was a planted police spy. There was no evidence for this, either; the only evidence was that she was Bindu.

The maids at your house used to object to working for her; if one of them were ordered to do something, she and the other girls immediately became numb and incapacitated. All this increased my desire to help Bindu. On my own initiative I engaged another maid. None of you liked that. I provided Bindu with all her clothes, and when you noticed this, you were so angry that you cut off my spending money. From that day on, I began to wear coarse, rough-textured, machine-made saris that cost four or five rupees apiece. And when Moti's mother came to take the leftover rice from my plate, I kept her from doing it. I gave it to the calves and scrubbed the utensils myself at the water tap in the court-yard. One day when you suddenly spied that scene, you were not at all pleased. That you hadn't made me happy and that there was no further chance of my making all of you happy had not dawned upon me until then.

And while your resentment of me grew, Bindu was also growing. You became abnormally worried about this normal process. One thing astonished me: why hadn't you forcibly put Bindu out of your house? I knew very well that in your hearts you were all afraid of me. God gave me that intelligence, and showing it disrespect gave you no relief.

Finally, since you couldn't make Bindu leave of her own accord, you resorted to the god of marriage. A bridegroom was procured for Bindu. The elder sister-in-law said, "That's a relief! Mother Kali has rescued the reputation of our family."

I didn't know a thing about the bridegroom. I heard the rest of you say that he was perfectly all right. Bindu clutched my feet and wept. She said, "Sister, why am I getting married?"

I knew very well how she felt, so I said, "Bindu, don't be afraid, I've heard that your groom is a good person."

"If the groom is good," answered Bindu, "how could he be chosen for me?"

The groom's representatives made no mention of coming to see Bindu. The elder sister-in-law was unperturbed.

But Bindu no longer tried to check the tears that flowed day and night. I know how tormented she was. I had fought hard for her, but I did not have the strength to stop her marriage. What right had I? Repeating this fact did not give me courage. What authority did I have? If I died, what would become of Bindu?

In addition to being a girl, she was dark-skinned. Wherever she might go, her situation would be dangerous. The thought made my heart tremble.

"Sister," said Bindu, "the wedding is five days away; won't I die before then?"

I scolded her severely. But God knows I felt that if some easy means of death for Bindu could be found, I would feel relieved.

The day before the wedding Bindu went to her elder sister and said, "Sister, I'll live in your cowshed. I'll do anything you tell me to do. I beg you not to throw me away like this."

For a long time the sister had wept in secret, and that day, too, she wept. But rules as well as a heart had to be considered. She said, "You know very well, Bindi, that when she has a husband at hand, a wife is quite free to move about. If sorrow falls upon you here, no one can save you."

The truth was, there was no way out of it. Bindu would be married, whatever the consequences.

I wanted the wedding to take place at our house. But you all stood firm and said that the bridegroom wanted it to be at his own home; it was the custom of his family.

I realized that if you had to spend a lot of money for Bindu's wedding, that would be an affront to your family deity. So I had to keep silent. But there was one fact none of you knew. I got Bindu dressed up and secretly gave her some of my jewelry; I wanted to tell my sister-in-law about this, but I didn't because she would have been mortally afraid. I felt that my sister-in-law may have noticed and would have stopped me, but she ignored that. For God's sake, forgive me for having done this!

Before leaving, Bindu clung to me and said, "Sister, are you all so terribly anxious to get rid of me?"

"No, Bindi," I replied. "Whatever happens to you, I won't cast you off as long as I live."

Three days passed. The tenants on your property gave you a sheep for a feast, and to spare it the consequences of your hunger, I penned it at one side of the first-floor cowshed. I got up early in the morning and came to feed it myself. For a day or two I had relied upon your servants to do this; they were more interested in eating it than in feeding it.

That morning I saw Bindu sitting curled up in a corner of that shed. As soon as she saw me she fell at my feet, grasped them, and began to cry soundlessly.

Bindu's husband was insane.

"Bindi, are you telling the truth?"

"Could I ever tell you so big a lie as that, sister? He is mad. My father-in-law was not in favor of this marriage, but he fears my mother-in-law as he fears the god of death. He went to Banaras before the wedding. My mother-in-law insisted on her son's marriage."

I sank down upon that coal pile. A woman shows no mercy toward a woman. She says, "She's nothing but a woman. Whether or not the boy is mad, he is a man."

Bindu's husband had not suddenly lost his mind but had been so deranged at intervals that he had been kept in a locked room. On the wedding night all had been well, but late on the second night his mind suddenly gave way as violently as on former occasions. In the afternoon Bindu had sat feeding him from a brass tray. All at once her husband seized the plateful of rice and threw it away. He had a sudden delusion that Bindu was Queen Rashmoni in person; a bearer must have stolen the golden tray and was serving rice to the queen on his own tray.

Bindu was mortally afraid. On the third night, when the mother-in-law told her to go and lie down in the husband's room, Bindu's heart withered. The mother-in-law was furious, incoherent with anger. She too was mad, but because the madness was only partial, it was all the more terrible.

Bindu entered the room. Her husband was calm that night. But Bindu was wooden with fear. When her husband went to sleep very late, she sneaked out and fled. There is no need to elaborate upon this description.

My whole body burned and trembled with horror and anger. I said, "There was never such a fraudulent marriage. Bindu, you stay with me just as you did before. I'll see that someone looks after you."

You all said, "Bindu is lying."

"She has never lied," I answered.

"How do you know?"

"I know it for certain."

You all threatened me. "If the mother-in-law's family makes a police case out of it, there will be trouble."

"She was deceitfully married to an insane bridegroom," I said. "Wouldn't that be brought out in court?"

"Then who would bring this to court? Why, who would want to pay the costs!"

"I can sell my own jewelry to pay them," I replied.

You all said, "Do we have to run to the lawyer?"

There was no answer for this. I could strike my forehead in frustration. What else could I do? In the meantime the brother-in-law made a great fuss after coming from the house of Bindu's father-in-law.

I didn't know what I could do, but the cow that had fled the butcher in fear of its life and sought shelter with me would be sent back again to that butcher under police pressure. I couldn't bear to accept this fact. Defiantly I said, "All right, inform the police."

When I said this, I intended to lock Bindu in my bedroom while there was still time. When the search was made I would say I had not seen her. While you all argued with me, Bindu would slip away to her brother-in-law's. She understood that if she stayed in this house she would cause me serious difficulty.

Bindu's troubles were further increased by her flight. Her mother-in-law argued that her son had not tried to devour Bindu. Instances of bad behavior by husbands were not unknown in the world. Compared with others, her son was a moon of gold.

My elder sister-in-law said, "Her fate is a bad one. What shall I do about it if it gives her trouble? Certainly, he may be mad, he may be a goat, but he's her husband."

The proverbial example of a chaste and loyal wife helping her husband even in his crimes occurred to all of you. To this day you men feel not the least hesitation in publicizing such tales of the vilest cowardice in the world. Therefore, since you are born as men, instead of hanging your heads in shame, you were angered by Bindu's behavior. My heart ached for her, but in your eyes there were no limits to my shame. I am just a village girl; on top of that I ended up at your house, and by some trick God gave me such an intelligence! I just couldn't stand all your pious talk.

I certainly knew that if Bindu were dead, she wouldn't come to our house anymore. But I had encouraged her the day before the wedding by telling her that to the very end I would not cast her off.

My younger brother Sarat was in college in Calcutta. You know very well how by various volunteer projects, such as rat killing in plague areas or Damodar River flood control, he became so involved in his enthusiasms that twice in succession he failed the examination. Such setbacks never daunted him.

I appealed to him, "Sarat, you must see that I get news of Bindu. She won't have the courage to write to me, and if she did I wouldn't get the letter."

If, instead of this, I had asked him to get Bindu by means of armed robbery, or to beat her insane husband over the head, he would have been very pleased.

While Sarat and I discussed this, you came into the room and said, "Are you stirring up a commotion again?"

"Things were stirred to their foundations when I came to your house," I said, "but you are the one responsible for that."

You asked, "Where have you hidden Bindu this time?"

"If Bindu had come I would certainly have hidden her. But she won't come, never fear."

Your suspicions increased when you saw Sarat with me. I knew that you did not care at all to have him coming and going in our house. You were afraid that the police would see him, that some day he would precipitate some civil litigation and would involve and besmirch your good name. Therefore, except for the days when sisters ceremonially marked the brothers' foreheads with sandalwood paste, I didn't invite him to the house.

You informed me that Bindu had run off again, and so her brother-in-law came to look for her at your house. When I heard that, a spear pierced my heart. I knew what unendurable misery the unfortunate girl bore, yet nothing could be done about it.

Sarat rushed off to get some information. He returned in the evening and told me, "Bindu went to the house of her cousin-brother, but they were furious and sent her right back to her father-in-law's. They are still burning over having to pay damages, a fine, and cabfare for her."

Your aunt had come home after a second pilgrimage. I told you that I too would go on a pilgrimage.

You were all so delighted by my sudden piety that there was not the least objection. What I really had in mind was that if I stayed in Calcutta now, I would get into trouble again some day over Bindu. I myself was the cause of grave difficulties.

I was to leave on Wednesday. On Sunday everything was ready. I sent for Sarat and said, "Whatever happens, you must put Bindu on the train for Puri on Wednesday."

Sarat looked cheerful. He said, "Don't worry, sister, I'll have her on the train and go as far as Puri myself. By this trick I'll see the Festival of Jagannath."

That evening Sarat came again. My breath caught in my chest when I saw his face. I said, "What is it, Sarat? Won't it work?"

"No," he replied.

"Couldn't you arrange it?"

"It's no longer necessary," he said. "Last night she committed suicide by setting her clothes on fire. I know a nephew from that family and I heard the news from him. She left a letter addressed to you, but they destroyed it."

That was that. Peace reigned.

The whole population was incensed. People began to say

that girls' setting their clothes on fire had become a fad. You all said, "This is all playacting!"

That may be so. But why this stage stunt should be performed upon the saris of Bengali girls and not upon the dhotis of Bengali heroes is another matter that ought to be explained.

Bindi's fate was a bad one! During her lifetime she was undistinguished by beauty or outstanding qualities; nor should the occasion of her death be lightly considered as so novel a manner of dying that the men of the land will applaud with delight! Yet her dying angered everyone!

Bindu's elder sister hid in her room and wept. But among those tears was one consolation: in spite of what had happened there was still one defense. She had done nothing but die. If she had lived, what would have become of her?

I am on a pilgrimage. There was no further need of Bindu's coming, but I had a great need.

In your family I had none of what is commonly called misery. There was no shortage of food and clothing at your house. Whatever your elder brother's character, you had no defect for which God can be blamed. If you were like your brother, I would still have spent my days as I am now spending them. Like my elder sister-in-law I would have tried to blame God instead of blaming my god-husband. I do not want to bring up all this in order to complain about you; that is not the purpose of this letter.

But I won't return again to that house of yours at 27 Makhan Badal Lane. I have seen Bindu. I have known the status of women in the family. I have no more needs.

Then I saw this, also: though she was created a girl, God had not cast her off. You exerted such power over her, but that power is limited. She is greater than her own unfortunate life. Whatever mode of life you choose, you will eternally trample her life beneath your feet; but your feet do not reach so far. Death is greater than all of you. She has become great by her death. There Bindu is not merely a girl in a Bengali home, not only the sister of a cousin-brother, not only the swindled wife of an unknown, insane husband. There she is everlasting.

The day this brokenhearted girl made death's flute sound in my life on the bank of the Jumna, an arrow seemed at first to pierce my heart. I asked God why the most insignificant things in the world are the most difficult. Why are there such trifling effervescences, such terrible obstacles along the joyless path of our accumulating days? Your world holds the bounty of its seasons; it calls to me. Why can't I reach it for even one moment, crossing the threshold of this inner room? Why does a world like yours take a life like mine, screen it with the planks and bricks of utter trifles, and make it die an inch at a time? How trifling is my daily life! How trifling are the rules and regulations, the bonds of habit, of speech, of all this buffeting—but can the fetters of meanness finally prevail over the blissful world of your own creation?

But the flute of death began to play—where then was the mason's stone wall? Where was the thorny hedge of your dire restrictions? What sorrow, what insults, can keep mankind captive? Life's victory flag flies in the very hand of death! Oh, second daughter-in-law, you have nothing to fear! In the twinkling of an eye the shell of your daughter-in-lawhood can be torn away.

I am no longer afraid of your narrow path. Today the blue ocean is before me. The heaped-up clouds of Ashar are overhead.

I have been kept shrouded in the darkness of your customs. While Bindu was there, I was able to see through an opening in that shroud. By her own death that girl caused my covering to be ripped from top to bottom. Now I see that I have emerged; there is no other space in which to preserve my dignity. He who loves to see beauty unveiled has shown me that beauty in the whole sky.

You are thinking that I intend to die. Don't be afraid, I won't play such an old joke on you. Mirabai was a woman just like me. Her fetters were no less cumbersome; she didn't die to get rid of them. Mirabai said in her song, "Father, reject me, Mother, reject me, reject me whoever will, Mira will still persist! Let her be remembered for that."

> To persist is to live.
> I too will live. I have lived.

> One who has lost your protection,[2]

> Mrinal

1914

[2] The signature in the original text, *Charanatalasrayachchinna*, may be translated literally as: Separated from protection under your feet.

BOSHTAMI

I am a writer, but it is not my pen's job to entertain people; that is why the coloring given me by my readers is invariably black. I hear many things said about myself; unluckily they serve no good purpose and they are certainly not agreeable.

The part of the body that sustains repeated blows may be unimportant, but its pain pervades the whole body. So it is with the person brought up on abuse: his entire nature tends toward one reaction. He rejects his surroundings and thinks only of himself; this is neither pleasant nor desirable. Satisfaction lies in forgetting oneself.

So I frequently have to go in search of solitude. The general damage that the mind suffers from the batterings of other people is repaired by the power of Nature's healing hand.

I have an arrangement for living incognito and alone, far from Calcutta; I vanish there when I am oppressed by self-preoccupation. The people there have not yet reached any conclusion about me. They have seen that I am not a sensualist; I have not contaminated the village night with evil brought from Calcutta. Nor am I a religious ascetic, for what little they see of me from a distance has signs of affluence. I am not a traveler; I wander about the village streets, but I give no hint of arriving at a destination. It would be difficult to state that I am a householder, for there is no evidence of my having a family. So it is a relief to me when the village people, unable to place me in a conventional human category, give up thinking about me.

A few days ago I learned that there is one person in this village who has thought seriously about me, to the extent, at least, of not thinking me a fool.

I met her for the first time on an evening in June. After the cessation of rain, which had begun in the morning, all the foliage, the sky, and the breeze were like eyelashes still wet after weeping. I stood on the high bank of our pond and watched the plump black cows grazing. As I watched the sunlight on their sleek bodies, it occurred to me that civilization had established so many tailoring shops in order to keep the light of the sky off our own bodies and that nowhere is there such a waste as this.

Just then I saw a middle-aged woman prostrate on the ground paying her respects to me. Wrapped in the end of her sari were a few blossoms of oleander, queen of the night, and several other flowers. She put one of these into my hand, folded her hands devoutly, and said, "My respects to my deity." With this she went away.

I was so taken aback that I did not even get a good look at her.

The incident was quite simple, yet it affected me deeply; the sight of the cattle enjoying life, flicking flies off their backs in the dusty twilight and grazing with quiet pleasure in the tender, rain-soaked grass, became very beautiful to me. People may laugh at this, but my heart filled with reverence. I paid my respects to the deity of life's simple joys. I took a branch with leaves and green mangoes from a tree in the grove and fed them to the cattle. I felt that I had pleased my God.

The next year I went there at the end of February. It was still winter. The morning sunlight penetrated the east window and shone on my back; I did not shut it out. I was writing when my servant came up to the second floor and informed me that Anandi Boshtami wished to see me. I didn't know who that might be; absently I said, "All right, bring her here."

Boshtami touched my feet in respect. I saw that it was the woman I had met before. She was past the age for noticing whether or not she was beautiful. She was slender and taller than most women. Her body was pliant with an attitude of constant devotion, yet she had an air of powerful determination. Her eyes were her most striking feature. By some power deep within, those big eyes seemed to bring some distant thing close.

Her eyes seemed to reproach me, and she said, "What a

thing to do. Why bring me to the foot of this throne? I used to see you beneath the trees. That was better."

I realized that she had frequently observed me under the trees, but I had never noticed her. I had caught cold and stopped going out in the garden; from the roof terrace I confronted the evening sky. That was why she had not seen me for several days.

She was silent for a moment and then said, "My master, give me some advice."

I was in difficulty. I said, "I can neither give nor take advice. I am concerned only with whatever I observe in silence. I am seeing you right now, and as I see you I am also listening to you."

Boshtami was overjoyed. "Oh, my teacher," she cried, "God speaks not only with His tongue. He speaks with His whole person."

"By keeping silent with our whole selves, we hear all that He has to say. In order to hear that, I have left the city and come here."

"I understand that," said Boshtami. "That is why I came to you."

When she was ready to leave and touched my feet in respect, I noticed that her hand drew back from my socks, and she seemed to hesitate.

The next morning I was sitting on the roof before sunrise. The fields stretched out endlessly beyond the casuarina groves to the south. To the east the sun rises every day over the edge of the cane field beside the bamboo-girdled village. The village road suddenly emerges from the dense shade of the trees, zigzags through the open fields, and heads toward a row of distant villages.

I did not know whether the sun had risen. A white scarf of fog, like a widow's veil, was drawn across the trees of the village. Through the hazy light of that dawn mist I glimpsed Boshtami like an animated fog-image, playing cymbals, singing the name of God, and going eastward toward the village.

The fog rose somewhat later like eyelids released from sleep, and like a village grandfather the winter sunlight settled comfortably amid all the various activities of field and home.

By that time I was seated at my desk doing some writing that would get the editor's bailiffs off my back. Just then I heard a song and the sound of footsteps on the stairs.

Humming a tune, Boshtami came and touched my feet in respect, then sat down nearby on the floor. I looked up from my writing.

"I received your sacred food offering yesterday," she said.

"What do you mean?" I asked.

"Yesterday evening I was sitting outside the door waiting for you to finish your dinner. When you were through and the servant came out with the plate, I didn't know what was on it, but I ate it."

I was astonished. Everyone knows that I have been in England. It is not hard to guess what I ate or did not eat there, but I have not tasted anything sacred. For some time now I had relished neither fish nor meat, but I have not discussed the caste of my cook in public meeting.[1]

Boshtami saw a shade of surprise on my face and said, "If I could not eat your food, there would be no necessity for my coming to you."

"If people knew about this, they would lose respect for you."

"I have told everyone about it. When they heard it they thought I was really out of my mind."

I got no specific information about Boshtami's family life except the fact that her mother was alive and quite well-to-do. She knew that many people were devoted to her daughter. She wanted her daughter to stay with her, but Anandi would not agree to this.

"How do you get along?" I asked.

She informed me that one of her followers had given her a modest piece of land. Its yield fed her and five others, and there was plenty for everyone. Smiling, she said, "I had everything but renounced all of it, and now I receive things from others for nothing. Tell me why I needed all that I used to have."

If she had asked this question in the city, I wouldn't have let her off so easily. I would have explained how begging injures society. But when I was in this place, all the flames of my bookish knowledge died out. No argument rose to my lips; I kept silent.

Without waiting for my reply, she spoke herself. "No, no, this is fine for me. This food I beg is nectar to me."

I understood the underlying sense of her remark. Daily she remembered God through the food she gathered by

---

[1] Hindu cooks are supposed to be of Brahman caste.

begging. But at home we think we earn and enjoy food by our own right.

I wanted to inquire about her husband, but she did not introduce the subject herself and I did not ask.

Boshtami had no respect for people who live in upper-class neighborhoods. She said they give nothing to God yet take the largest share of His gifts. The poor give Him devotion and die of hunger.

I had heard quite a lot about the misdeeds of this neighborhood, so I said, "Stay among these wicked people and improve them. That would surely be a service to God."

I have listened to plenty of this sort of lofty advice, and I love to give it to others. But it came as no surprise to Boshtami. She looked at me with her shining eyes and said, "You are saying that God is among sinners too and that staying among them is serving Him. Is that it?"

"Yes," I replied.

"Since these people are alive," she said, "isn't He with them too? But what is that to me? I can't worship there; my God is not among them. I go about searching for Him wherever He is."

With these words she touched my feet in respect. Her argument was that mere opinions would do her no good. What she wanted was the truth. It is a fact that God is omnipresent, but for her, truth is wherever she sees Him.

Such patently redundant statements must be made to some people; when Boshtami proposed offering devotion to me, I neither accepted nor rejected it.

The spirit of the times had affected me. I had read the Gita and had sat at the feet of learned men and listened to their subtle explanations of the fundamental truths of religion. I was getting old while doing nothing but listening; I had perceived nothing for myself. Finally I discarded my pride in my own powers of perception and saw the truth through the eyes of this unorthodox woman. What an astonishing approach: to give instruction under the pretext of giving devotion!

The next morning when Boshtami came to pay her respects to me she saw that I had begun to write. She was annoyed and said, "Why is my God making you work so uselessly? Whenever I see you, you are busy writing!"

"The man who is good for nothing is the one God puts to work, lest he get spoiled. All the worthless work is left to him."

She became impatient at seeing me surrounded by so many impediments. If she wanted to see me she had to get permission to come upstairs; the encasing socks repulsed her hand when she touched my feet; a few simple words needed to be spoken and listened to, but I was wrapped up in some writing project.

She folded her hands and said, "My master, as soon as I sat up in bed this morning I took hold of your feet. Ah, those two feet of yours, with no covering, how cool they are! How soft! All that time I held them to my head. That was enough. Is there any need for me to come here anymore? My master, is this only an illusion? Tell me the truth."

The previous day's flowers stood in a vase on the desk. The gardener had come to arrange fresh ones in their place.

Boshtami was hurt and burst out, "That's all? Are these flowers being discarded? Are they of no more use to you? Then give them here, give them to me."

As she said this, she took the flowers between her palms, bowed her head for some time, and gazed at them with deep affection. After a time she looked up and said, "You don't look at them. That is why these flowers become withered for you. When you look at them all your knowledge will come to nothing."

As she spoke, with extreme care she wrapped the flowers in the end of her sari, touched them to her head, and said, "I am taking my God with me."

It wasn't long before I understood that it was no honor to the flowers to be merely stuck into a vase. I felt that I had treated them daily like the unprepared schoolboys whom I had made stand on the benches.

That evening when I was sitting on the roof terrace, Boshtami came and sat at my feet. She said, "This morning I went from house to house distributing your flower offering. Beni Chakravarty observed my devotion and laughed and said, 'You madwoman, whom are you worshiping? Everyone criticizes him.' Is it true? Does everyone criticize you?"

I hesitated for just a moment. Even ink splashes a long way!

"Beni thought that my devotion would be blown out in one puff," said Boshtami. "But this is not an oil lamp. This is a fire! My master, why do they abuse you?"

"Because I deserve it," I replied. "Perhaps I would be

greedy enough some day to steal what was hidden in their minds."

Boshtami said, "You surely saw how much poison there is in men's minds. That desire of yours won't last."

"If there is greed in the mind," I replied, "you expose yourself to criticism. Then one resolves to exterminate the poison himself. Therefore my exorcist has shaken me so harshly in order to free my mind of poison."

"Then the merciful Lord fends off suffering by repeated pain," said Boshtami. "Those who endure to the end are saved."

That night as the evening star rose and set again over the dark roof terrace, Boshtami told me the story of her life.

* * * * *

My husband is a very simple man. Some people thought that his mind was retarded. But I know that with those who are simple, what they can understand, they understand perfectly.

I observed, besides, that he did not cheat those who worked his land. He was orderly in his business and family affairs. He never did any harm by what little business he did in the usual rice and jute, for his desires were modest. He kept an account of what little he needed; he neither understood things beyond his needs nor laid hands upon them.

Before my marriage my father-in-law died, and my mother-in-law died a few days after the wedding. No one was left as head of our household.

My husband could not assume the responsibility that would devolve upon a supervisor. Besides, I am ashamed to say that he adored me as if I knew more than he did, though I was the one who talked more.

He was devoted above all to his guru. It was not only devotion, it was love—there never was such a love.

The guru was somewhat younger than my husband. How beautiful he was!

* * * * *

Boshtami stopped speaking for a time; those far-seeing eyes gazed into the distance, and she hummed a song:

The rays of the sun filtered into delicate nectar—
Thus god created this body.

*   *   *   *   *

My husband had played with this guru when they were children and had given himself over, mind and soul, to him.

At that time the guru would tell my husband what a simple soul he was, and therefore he tyrannized terribly over my husband. The guru joined with other playmates in making fun of him, and there were no limits to his harassment.

When we were married and I came into this family, I did not meet the guru, who was studying in Banaras. My husband was the one who collected money to send him there.

I was about eighteen years old when the guru returned to Bengal.

When I was fifteen, my only son had been born. Because I was very young, I had not learned to care for that child myself, and in those days I craved the companionship of neighborhood friends. Now and then I was angry with the boy because he kept me at home.

Ah well, when the boy arrived and I was confined to being a mother, could there have been a worse calamity! My Gopal came and saw that his butter was still unprepared,[2] and so he went away angry. To this day I have gone about the fields and river landings in search of him.

The boy was the jewel of his father's eyes. My failure to learn how to take care of the child distressed my husband, but his heart was so inarticulate that to this day he cannot speak to anyone else of his sorrow.

He gave the boy a woman's care. If the child cried at night, my husband did not want to disturb my deep, childlike sleep. He got up, warmed the milk, and fed him, and I cannot tell you how often he fell asleep with the child on his lap. He did everything in this quiet manner. When there were dramatic performances or recitations at the zamindar's house during the Puja Festival, he would say, "I can't stay awake at night. You go. I'll stay here." If he didn't stay with the child, I couldn't go. Hence his pretext.

---

[2] The reference is to Lord Krishna and his birth in a cowherd's family; various tales are told of his childhood pranks in the dairy.

It was astonishing that in spite of everything the child loved me most of all. He seemed to realize that if the opportunity ever presented itself, I would go off and leave him; so when he was near me he was always apprehensive. Because he saw very little of me, there was no end to his eagerness to be with me.

When I went to the landing to swim it was a daily irritation to me to have to take him along. I met my friends there and I didn't like having to watch over a child. Therefore, whenever possible, I avoided taking him with me.

That day was a day in August. Now and then thick black clouds suddenly and completely enveloped the afternoon. When it was time for me to bathe, the child burst out crying. Nistarini worked in our kitchen, and I said to her, "Child, watch the boy. I'm going for a swim."

There was no one else at the landing just then. I began to swim while I waited for my friends. The lake was an ancient one; some queen had once had it dug out, and therefore it was called the Queen's Sea. I was the only one among the girls who could swim across this lake and back again. It was the rainy season and the lake was bank-full. When I had gone nearly halfway across, I heard a call behind me, "Mother!"

I looked and saw my son calling me as he descended the landing stairs.

"Don't come any farther!" I shouted. "I'm coming."

He laughed at my warning and came farther down. My arms and legs seemed constricted by fear; I could not make it to the shore. I closed my eyes, afraid of what I would see. At that moment on the slippery landing the child's laughter ceased forever in the waters of the lake. I got to shore, took him from the water, and held in my lap the boy who had yearned for that same mother's lap but who no longer called "Mother!"

For a long time I had made my Gopal weep; all that neglect was now returned and beat upon me. I had rejected him and gone away when he was alive. Now he clings to my thoughts day and night.

Only God knows how much my husband suffered. It would have been a good thing if he had cursed me, but he knew only how to endure, not how to speak.

When I was becoming actually irrational, the guru returned to Bengal. When they were children, my husband had been only his playmate; that was the extent of the relationship. Now when his childhood friend returned as a learned man after the long separation, my husband's devotion to him was sudden and complete. Who could call him a mere playmate? My husband seemed completely unable to say a word in his presence.

My husband requested his guru to console me. The guru began to read the scriptures to me. The words of the Shastras seemed to do little for my state of mind. Whatever value there was for me in all those words lay in him who spoke them. Through the human voice God gives man His nectar to drink; there is no similar cup in God's hand, and He too drinks His own nectar by means of this human voice.

My husband's unremitting devotion to the guru kept our house filled as the interior of a beehive is full of honey. All our daily routine, our transactions with men and with money, were charged with this devotion; there wasn't a gap anywhere. I submerged my entire being in this delight, and I was consoled. So I glimpsed God in the very form of my guru.

He would have his meals with us, and then I would take the sacred food left on his plate; every morning when I awoke this was what I remembered, and I would go to prepare for his meals. As I chopped vegetables for his curry, my fingers vibrated with joy. I am not a Brahman; I could not serve the food to him with my own hands. Therefore the hunger of my heart was not completely satisfied.

He was a self-contained ocean of erudition. I am an ordinary woman; I could please him only through a little food. There too was a great far-reaching gap.

My husband's devotion to me was increased by pleasure as he saw me serving the guru. When he observed the guru's eagerness to explain the scriptures to me, my husband thought that the guru had always looked down upon him because of his own lack of intelligence; now it was his good fortune to have a wife who could please the guru by the depth of her intellect.

Four or five years passed in this fashion, but my eyes were unaware of what was taking place.

I could have spent my whole life this way. But I was unaware that a theft was being committed somewhere in secret. God knew what was going on. Then one day in one minute everything turned upside down.

That April morning I was returning home along a shady

path, dressed in my wet clothes after bathing at the landing.
At a turn in the road I met the guru under a mango tree.
He had a towel over his shoulder and was reciting Sanskrit
verses as he went to bathe.

I was ashamed to meet him in my wet clothes and tried
to pass him by moving a little to one side. At the same time
he called me by name. I shrank within myself and stood with
bowed head. He kept looking at my face and said, "Your
body is beautiful."

The whole community of birds called out from the branches. Every bush beside the path burst into *bhanti* flowers.
The mango trees were in blossom. It seemed that heaven
and the world beneath had fallen into chaotic disorder. How
I got home I don't know. In my wet clothes I went at once
to the worship room. I seemed to see no God there; only
the tinseled light that had appeared on that shady road to
the landing still danced before my eyes.

That day the guru came for his meal. He asked, "Why
isn't Andi here?"

My husband went out to look for me; he found me nowhere.

Ah, the earth was no longer mine. I no longer sought the
sunlight. I called upon my God in the prayer room; He kept
His face averted from me.

I don't know how or where I spent the day. At night I
would have to meet my husband. The night is still and dark.
It is then that my husband seems to say what is on his mind.
Sometimes in that darkness I am suddenly able to understand his half-expressed thoughts; whatever this simple man
comprehends, he comprehends with such ease.

Housework often delayed my coming to bed. He waited
up for me. Almost always our talk had something to do with
the guru.

I was out very late. Then, at three in the morning I came
into the room and saw my husband still not lying on the bed,
but asleep on the floor. Taking utmost care not to make
any noise, I lay down at his feet. In the depths of sleep he
jerked his feet once and struck my breast. Thereby I received his parting gift.

When he awoke the following morning, I was sitting up.
Above the jackfruit tree outside the window, an edge of the
darkness took on a tinge of red. The crows had not yet
begun to call.

I dropped my head to my husband's feet and bowed to

him in respect. He got up quickly and looked at me in surprise.

"I won't lead a family life any longer," I said.

My husband thought he was dreaming. He could not say a word.

"Swear on my life that you will marry another wife after I have left."

"What are you talking about?" my husband said. "Who told you to leave the family?"

"The guru," I replied.

My husband was bewildered. "The guru! When did he say such a thing?"

"This morning," I replied. "I met him as I returned from bathing. That's when he said it."

My husband's voice shook. "Why did he give such an order?"

"I don't know. Ask him. If possible, he will explain it himself."

"Surely one can leave the family even while staying in it," said my husband. "I'll make the guru understand that."

"Perhaps the guru can understand, but my heart does not understand. As of today my world has been erased."

My husband was silent and remained sitting there. When the sky became bright, he said, "Let us go. We'll go to him together."

I folded my hands and said, "I must not see him again."

He looked into my face; I looked down. He said no more.

I know that somehow or other he had looked into my mind.

Two men in the world loved me above all others: my son and my husband. That love is my God, and so it could not endure falsehood. One of them went away and left me; I left the other. Now I am searching for truth. There is no more deception.

* * * * *

With these words she touched the ground at my feet and bowed in respect.

1913

THE DEVOTEE

(Tapashwini)

1

April was nearly over. The early part of the night was sultry; the bamboo foliage was motionless. The stars seemed to throb with pain like that of a headache. At three in the morning a soft breeze arose. Shoroshi lay on the bare floor beneath the open window, a cloth-wrapped tin box as her pillow. It was quite evident that she was a zealous practitioner of religious austerity.

Shoroshi arose daily at four in the morning, bathed, and went to sit in the worship room of the house. The morning would be almost over before she finished her rituals. Then her teacher came; Shoroshi sat in that room with him and read the Gita. She had learned some Sanskrit, and she had vowed to read Sankar's Vedanta and Yogic philosophy in the original texts. She was twenty-three years old.

At that time Shoroshi kept very aloof from housework. The reason for this aloofness occasions this story.

Shoroshi's father-in-law, Makhanbabu, displayed no similarity between his name and his nature.[1] It was very difficult to soften his disposition. He saw to it that his son Baroda lived apart from his wife until he had passed at least the B.A. examinations. But study was not congenial to Baroda's disposition; he was a dandified fellow. His temperament allied him to the bees that collect honey in life's arbor, but the labor necessary for producing the honeycomb he found absolutely intolerable. He had great hopes that once he was married he would relax and live in some comfort, and that that would bring a time when he could smoke cigarettes in public.

[1] Makhanbabu, *makhan* means butter.

151

But after Baroda's marriage, his father conceived an even stronger desire to improve his son.

The schoolteacher nicknamed Baroda after Sage Gotam. Needless to say, this had nothing to do with Baroda's spiritual power as a Brahman. If he could not answer a question, the teacher called him "Sage"; when he did answer, there was always something bovine about his response that, in the teacher's opinion, justified the title Gotam."[2]

Makhan sought out the headmaster and was informed that if two teachers, one at home and one at school, were to be attached like two huge locomotives, one in front and one in the rear, things might turn out happily for Baroda. A variety of renowned teachers who had transported inferior boys across the ocean of examinations began to stay with Baroda until ten and ten-thirty at night.

In the golden days of the past those famous hermits who practiced great austerity to attain ultimate truth did a solitary penance, but this penance that Baroda shared with the tutors was far more difficult. In those days the main warmth during penance came from the fire. Now the principal warmth in this examination-penance was produced by the wrath of the tutors. They made Baroda's life miserable. Therefore, when after so much tribulation he failed the examinations, he was consoled by the fact that he had made the renowned teachers hang their heads in shame.

Even this extraordinary frustration did not make Makhan-babu give up the ship. The second year he engaged another batch of tutors; the arrangement made with them was that if Baroda passed in the first division, a bonus would be added to their fees. This time, too, Baroda would have failed as usual, but this imminent crisis had an interesting variation. The night before the examination, after consultation with the neighborhood Ayurvedic doctor, Baroda took a very strong laxative. Thanks to this, he did not have to go up to the examination hall in order to fail but accomplished that feat to perfection by staying at home. The ailment was regulated with the perfect timing of a most reliable newspaper; Makhan knew that this could not have been done without an editor. Waiving further discussion, he informed Baroda that he must prepare for the examination a third

[2] *Gotam* also means bovine.

time. In other words, his term of rigorous imprisonment
was increased by one more year.

Baroda did not eat for a whole day in order to parade his
wounded feelings. The result was that he had to eat more at
the evening meal. He feared Makhan as he would fear a
tiger, but in desperation he went and told him, "I won't be
able to study if I stay here."

"Where can this impossible thing be accomplished?"
Makhan asked.

"In England," said Baroda.

Makhan tried to make Baroda understand in brief that
his misconception about this matter lay not in geography but
in his brain. Baroda said that in one jump from a third-rank
grade in the entrance exams, one of his classmates had
passed a very important examination in England.

Makhan said that he had no objection to sending Baroda
to England, but first he must earn his bachelor's degree.

This was certainly an enormous hurdle. Baroda had been
born without a B.A. and would die whether or not he had a
B.A. And yet, from somewhere between his birth and his
death, this B.A. degree had risen up like the Vindhya Mountain. Must he run into that every time he tried to make a
move? What did the Sage Agasthya do in the Iron Age? Did
he too divest himself of his matted hair and concentrate on
getting a B.A. degree?

Sighing deeply, Baroda said, "The third try is the last."

When he was just about to get all the pencil-marked books
from the shelf and begin again, he suffered a hard blow.
He looked for the carriage that he had used for school
transportation and learned that Makhan had sold both the
horse and the carriage. "I have lost so much money in
these two years," Makhan argued. "How long can I keep
spending?"

It was not at all difficult for Baroda to walk to school,
but how could he explain this humiliation to others?

At last, after considerable thought, he hit upon a work-
able plan, other than suicide, that did not involve getting
a B.A. degree. For this plan, family, wealth, and society
were absolutely unnecessary. This was nothing else than becoming a holy man. For some days he put much secret
cigarette smoke behind this thought. Then one day the torn
pages of his books were found scattered on the schoolroom
floor like the ruins of an examination fortress; the examinee

had vanished. On the table was a scrap of paper weighted
down by a chipped glass. On the paper was written:

I am a sannyasi—I no longer need a carriage.

Srijukta Barodananda Swami

For a few days Makhan made no search. He thought
that Baroda would have to return of his own accord; there
was no need to make any arrangements other than leaving
the door of the cage open. The door remained open, and
the torn pages of the books were cleared away; everything
else remained as it was. In a corner of the room the glass
with the chipped rim remained upside down on the water
jar. On the hair-oil-stained bedstead and the benches the
marks of termites and hard use were covered by the jacket of an old atlas. At one side was an empty packing box,
on top of which was a tin trunk bearing Baroda's name. On
the bookshelves against the wall were an English-Bengali
dictionary with a torn title page, a few pages from Har-
aprasad Sastri's *History of India,* and a number of exer-
cise books with Queen Victoria's face printed on the cover.
If one took up and shook these notebooks, from most of
them would emerge Ogden Company cigarette-box wrappers
bearing pictures of English dancers. The fact that Baroda
did not take these along as consolation when he sought
refuge in austerity would indicate that he was not in his
right mind.

This was the situation of our hero. Shoroshi, our hero-
ine, was then all of thirteen years old. As long as she lived
at home, everyone called her Khooki, and she had brought
this same reputation for perpetual childlikeness to her father-
in-law's house. Therefore even the maidservants in the house
did not hesitate to criticize Baroda's character to her face.
Her mother-in-law was bedridden; she lacked the strength
to say a word about any of her husband's decisions. Baroda's
paternal aunt had a very sharp tongue; she would berate
Baroda unmercifully, and for a very special reason. Since
the grandfather's time this family had customarily sacrificed
its girls before the god of aristocratic lineage. This aunt
had fallen into the hands of a chronic opium addict. Among
his virtues was the fact that he did not live long. So when
she would compare Shoroshi to a necklace of pearls, God
knew that the regret over the useless pearl necklace was
not aimed at Shoroshi alone.

In this instance everyone had forgotten that the pearl necklace had feelings that could be hurt.

The aunt would say, "I don't see why my brother spends so much on teachers and tutors. I can put it in writing that Baroda will never manage to pass the examinations."

Shoroshi too believed that he would not be able to pass, but she had a secret hope that if by any chance Baroda got through, it would at least put an end to the aunt's tirades. After Baroda's first failure, when Makhan tried to draw up the tutors in battle array for the second time, the aunt said, "I'm amazed at my brother. A man should learn from experience."

Then day and night Shoroshi thought only of the unlikely possibility that Baroda would suddenly display an amazing hidden ability and astonish the cynical world; he would pass in the first division, doing even better than the best student, doing so well that the viceroy himself would send his carriage to summon Baroda to his presence. At that point the unerring pill of the Ayurvedic doctor fell upon the examination day like a bomb. The ruse would have succeeded if people had not been suspicious.

"The boy didn't have enough intelligence, but he does have a devious mind," said the aunt. No summons came from the viceroy; with bowed head Shoroshi bore everyone's ridicule. We cannot be sure that the farce of the timely pill did not arouse suspicion in even her mind.

At this point Baroda ran away. Shoroshi strongly hoped that at the very least the family would consider this a calamity and would feel remorse and repentance. But the family did not even pay the full price for Baroda's departure. Everyone said, "Just wait a bit! He'll appear!" Shoroshi kept telling herself, "Oh, never! Dear God, let what they're saying be false! I hope everyone in the family will live to regret this!"

This time God humored Shoroshi; her wish came true. A month went by; there was no sign of Baroda. But still no one was concerned. Two months went by, and then Makhan became slightly worried, but he showed no outward signs of it. When he came face to face with his daughter-in-law, perhaps a passing cloud of distress appeared on his face, but the face of the aunt was still like the cloudless sky of June. As a result Shoroshi was afraid her husband might return, and she jumped whenever she saw anyone at the outside door.

When the third month passed in this way, the aunt began to complain that the boy was causing everyone in the house needless anxiety. Even this was an improvement; anger is better than indifference.

Gradually the household became clouded by fear and sorrow. When a year had been spent in searching for him, even the aunt began to say that Makhan had treated Baroda with unnecessary harshness. When two years had gone by, even the neighbors began to say that although Baroda hadn't shown an interest in his studies, he was a very nice person. The more Baroda's absence lengthened, the more unshakable became the neighbors' faith that his character was unspotted and that he had never smoked tobacco.

The schoolmaster said that this was the direct result of his calling Baroda the Sage Gautam; from that time onward his intelligence had been suddenly overborne by an indifference to this world. At least once a day the aunt would blame her brother's bullheadedness, asking, "What was the need for Baroda's being so learned? There is no shortage of money. Whatever you say, brother, nothing was wrong with his health. Ah, the boy was as good as gold!"

Shoroshi's heart filled with pride at the thought that her husband was the epitome of piety, and in the midst of all her sorrow she was consoled by the fact that the whole world had wronged him.

On the other hand, all the affection of the father's bleeding heart was doubly lavished upon Shoroshi. Makhan's only concern was to keep his daughter-in-law happy. It was his great desire that Shoroshi would order him to get something really hard to obtain; by undergoing much difficulty, by experiencing loss, he might have the relief of pleasing her a little. He wanted to put everything behind him in such a way as to make this his own atonement.

2

Shoroshi was now fifteen. As she sat alone in her room, now and then her eyes filled with tears. The familiar world seemed to press in upon her from every side; her life was being suffocated. Everything in her room, every railing of her veranda, the few flowering plants in planters along the parapet, which seemed to have stood there forever—all seemed to arouse deep disgust in her. From one moment to the next, the bed in the room, the closet, the safe, discoursed at length upon the emptiness of her life; she was angry with all the furnishings.

The only spot in the house that gave her comfort was in front of this window. That outside world became her very own; because of her, "the home became the outside, and the outside became a home."

At ten o'clock one morning—when in the interior of the house the cups and trays, big and little baskets, mortars and pestles, and boxes of betel nut had proliferated and achieved a great pitch of domestic activity—Shoroshi, aloof from all the household bustle, sat at the window and allowed her vacant mind to roam toward the empty sky. Suddenly, with the shout, "Victory to the Creator!" a sannyasi came from under the pipal tree near their gate. Like the taut strings of a vina, every fiber in Shoroshi's body began to vibrate with the most intense anxiety. She ran to the aunt and said, "Auntie, arrange to feed this sannyasi."

This is how it began. Serving the holy men became the goal of Shoroshi's life. After all this time the daughter-in-law had found the means of demanding something from her father-in-law. Makhan looked enthusiastic and said, "I'd like to open a really nice guesthouse."

Makhan's income had been diminishing for some time, but he took out a loan at twelve percent and began this humanitarian work.

The holy men came in droves. Makhan did not doubt that most of them were not the real thing, but how could he even suggest this to his daughter-in-law! Particularly when the matted-haired holy men swore and cursed the unavoidable shortcomings of their food and accommodations, Makhan occasionally wished that he could throw them out of the house. But when he looked at the face of his daughter-in-law, he could only fall at their feet. This was his harsh atonement.

As soon as a sannyasi arrived, he was summoned at once to the inner rooms. The aunt would have him sit down; Shoroshi would stand and watch from behind the door. This precaution was taken in case the holy man suddenly addressed Shoroshi as "Mother."[3] For who knows! Shoroshi's photograph of Baroda was that of a young lad. It would be hard to say what changes would be wrought in a youthful

---

[3] The term "Mother" is used in regard to his wife by one who renounces the world.

face by the combination of matted hair, beard, and ashes. When she thought of all the faces she had seen so often and of how little about them seemed to stay the same, the blood raced through her heart; then it would become apparent that the voice was not quite the same, the tip of the nose was different.

Thus from a corner of her room Shoroshi felt as if the holy men enabled her to conduct her search in the outside world. Her happiness lay in this search. It was her husband, the fulfillment of her life and her youth. All the arrangements of her world revolved about this quest. When she awoke in the morning, her day began with her charitable work. Heretofore she had never done kitchen chores; now these very chores were her delight. The lamp of hope burned constantly in her mind. Before she went to bed at night, the final thought of her day was: Perhaps tomorrow my guest will arrive. Shoroshi created a glowing image of Baroda in her own mind, assembling it from the best features of many types of holy men. His heart was pure, his body was filled with power, his knowledge was profound, his penance severe. Who could afford to ignore this sannyasi? Among all the holy men, this one sannyasi was the one to be worshiped. Her father-in-law himself would be the chief celebrant at this service of worship. For Shoroshi nothing was a greater source of pride.

But hermits did not turn up every single day. These intervals were really unbearable. Gradually even those gaps were filled. Shoroshi got into the habit of serving the holy men even while staying indoors. She slept on a blanket spread on the floor. She ate once a day, and what she ate was largely fruits and roots. She wore a coarse saffron-colored gown, but to emphasize the fact that she was married it had a broad red border, and she continued to put the wide vermilion mark halfway along the parting of her hair. Furthermore, with the permission of her father-in-law, she began to study Sanskrit. It did not take her many days to memorize the text of *Mugdhabodh*.[4] The teacher said, "This is what is known as learning acquired in a former life."

She had concluded that the farther she advanced along the path of holiness, the closer she would come to a meeting of hearts with the holy men. Her fame began to spread;

[4] *Mugdhabodh*, a famous poem attributed to the Indian sage Sankara, warns people against illusions.

crowds grew as people came to be blessed and to touch the feet of this devoted wife of a pious sannyasi so that even the aunt was silenced by fear and respect.

But Shoroshi knew her own mind. The complexion of her thoughts had not completely assumed the saffron hue of her holy apparel. This morning a cool wind blew softly and seemed to come to her whole being like someone's whispered words. She did not want to get up. She forced herself to rise, forced herself to get to work. She wanted to sit by the window and listen quietly to the tune of that flute that came from the far horizon of her thoughts. Sometimes her whole being became abnormally sensitive, and the sunlight that glistened on the coconut trees seemed to speak within her heart.

The teacher's reading and explication of the Gita became meaningless. Yet at the same time, when the squirrels rustled the dry leaves in the garden outside her window, when the keen cry of the kite pierced the heart of the far-distant sky, when now and then the wind was full of the weary sound of the oxcarts following the pondside path—all of this touched upon her mood and made her unaccountably restless. This certainly could not be called a symptom of unworldliness. The vast world of life and warmth touched her, the world where the warmth of the Creator's own love had filled the primal vapor of the sky. Long before his Vedic formulations Brahma had shaped this reality whose color, sound, and fragrance are part of the life-pulses of every creature, whose thousands and thousands of messengers, great and small, know the secret paths for the comings and goings in the living heart. Shoroshi still could not suppress all of that, even by planting the thorns of penance.

Therefore the shade of saffron had to be made still deeper. Shoroshi demanded of the teacher: "Tell me the rules of Yoga!"

"Mother," said the teacher, "you can't need all this. Attainment of your goal has fallen into your hand like a ripe *amloki.*"

People on every hand observed her pious influence and wondered at it, and to Shoroshi it was an intoxication by praise. There was once a time when even the maidservants in the house had regarded her as an object for pity. Now, therefore, when everyone began praising her as a pious woman, she could quench the thirst of a long-standing pride.

But she could not say that she had attained her goal, so she kept silent before the teacher.

Shoroshi came to Makhan and said, "Father, from whom shall I get instruction in the practice of Yoga?"

"I don't see any particular drawback in not learning that," answered Makhan. "You have progressed so far. How many people can come up to you now?"

No matter what, she must learn Yoga. As ill luck would have it, a teacher turned up for this too. Makhan had believed that most modern Bengalis were pretty much like himself—that is to say, they ate, slept, and except for affairs of scandal, did not believe in the impossible phenomena of the world. But when he was forced by necessity to institute a search it became apparent that there were such people in Bengal and that a person living on the bank of the Bhairava River in Khulna District had discovered the original Naimish Forest. The principal proof for this discovery was the revelation of the secret in a dream at dawn on Krishna-pratipada. Saraswati, the goddess of wisdom, had divulged it herself. If she had appeared in person there would have been room for doubt, but with the amazing whimsicality of a goddess she had shown herself as a magpie. There were only three feathers in the bird's tail. One was white, one was green, the middle one was brick-colored. These three feathers represented existence, activity, darkness; the Rik, Jaju, and Sama Vedas; creation, equilibrium, annihilation; today, tomorrow, and the day after tomorrow showed forth this tripartite magic, and the world was its indubitable outcome.

Ever since this revelation, Naimish Yogis had been in training. Two young men from the M.Sc. class had left college and practiced Yoga here. A subjudge had turned over his entire pension to this Naimish Fund, had engaged his orphaned nephew in the service of these Yogi ascetics, and had gained thereby a wonderful peace of mind.

A teacher of this Naimish Yoga was procured for Shoroshi. As a consequence Makhan had to become the home member of the Naimish Committee. It was the duty of a home member to contribute one sixth of his own income for the maintenance of the sannyasi members. Many a time, according to the measure of the devotion of the home members, this one-sixth portion moved up and down the fixed scale like the mercury in a thermometer. When it came time to settle the account, Makhan too began to make mistakes that inclined toward the lower sum. But whatever harm these errors and omissions did to the Naimish Society, they provided fulfillment for Shoroshi. The very last of her jewelry was gone, and every month her allowance vanished in the same fashion.

The family doctor came and said, "Brother, what are you doing? That girl will die."

"That's right," Makhan replied with a worried look, "but what's to be done?"

He couldn't stand up to Shoroshi. Once he came to her and said very quietly, "Mother, will your health hold up under such a strain?"

Shoroshi smiled slightly. The substance of it was that all such unnecessary worries came naturally to worldly beings.

3

Twelve years had gone by since Baroda's departure. Now Shoroshi was twenty-five. One day she asked her Yoga instructor, "Father, how shall I know whether or not my husband is alive?"

The Yogi, silent, kept his eyes shut for nearly ten minutes. Then he opened his eyes and said, "He is alive."

"How do you know?"

"You don't understand that yet. But you know this for certain: even though you are a woman, you have progressed so far on the course of your meditations because of your husband's extraordinary spiritual power. Even though he is far away, he has made you his coreligionist."

Shoroshi was thrilled in body and soul. She thought of herself as Parvati, saying her prayers on a garland of lotus seeds and awaiting Shiva the lord.

Again Shoroshi asked, "Can I know where he is?"

The Yogi smiled slyly and replied, "Bring a mirror."

Shoroshi brought a mirror and at the Yogi's direction kept gazing into it.

Half an hour later the Yogi inquired, "Do you see anything?"

Shoroshi hesitated. "Yes," she said. "I seem to see something, but I can't make it out clearly."

"Do you see something white?"

"That's right! It is white."

"Is it like snow on a mountaintop?"

"It's certainly snow! I've never seen a mountain. That's why it was hazy for so long."

By such mysterious means it was gradually revealed that Baroda was sitting unclothed in the snow on Longchu Mountain, an exceedingly inaccessible spot in the Himalayas. From thence the might of his meditations came forth to touch Shoroshi. This was an astonishing phenomenon.

That day, as she sat alone in the room, Shoroshi began to tremble all over. The fact that her husband's meditations constantly surrounded her, the fact that if she had stayed close to him she could have been separated from him now and then and that there had been no such separation, filled her with joy. She thought that she desired a much sterner austerity. One winter day she discarded the blanket she had been using and her body shook with the cold. Shoroshi felt that the wind from that Longchu Mountain had blown over her. She sat with folded hands and closed eyes, and tears began to flow.

On the afternoon of that same day Makhan called for Shoroshi and said with great hesitation, "Mother, for a long time I haven't mentioned this to you. I thought it would not be necessary, but it can't go on any longer. My debt is now much bigger than my assets. I can't say how long my property will hold out."

Shoroshi's face was alight with joy. She had no doubt that this was all her husband's doing. Her husband had made her his coreligionist without reservation, and now he was obviously obliterating what little barrier remained between them in the form of property. Not only the north wind but this indebtedness as well had come from the Longchu Mountain. This was the touch of her husband's right hand.

She laughed and said, "Why be afraid, Father?"

"Where shall we go?" Makhan asked.

"We'll go to the Naimish Forest and build a hut." Makhan realized that it was useless to discuss money matters with her. He left the room and smoked in silence.

Just then an automobile stopped at the door. A young man in Western clothes jumped from the car, came to Makhan's room, tried in an extremely inept fashion to fold his hands in greeting, and said, "Can't you recognize me?"

"What's this? This can't be Baroda!"

Baroda had gone to America as a crewman on a steamer. Now, after twelve years, he was back as the traveling salesman for a washing-machine company.

"If you need a washing machine," he said to his father, "I can get you one very cheaply."

He thereupon produced from his pocket an illustrated catalog.

1916

BRIDE AND BRIDEGROOM
(Patra O Patri)

1

It is true that I have not been conscripted by the god of marriage, but when I was sixteen he did engage my thoughts. The result in later years was that I became like a person who cannot go back to sleep once his first sound sleep is disturbed. Various friends and relatives managed the rank of a second marriage and were even promoted to a third; I spent my time on the back bench of bachelorhood, counting the rafters of my empty world.

In those days there was no minimum age limit for marriage or for taking the college entrance examinations, and I passed the latter at fourteen. I never crammed; therefore neither my physical nor my mental digestion was out of order. From childhood onward I was like a mouse that sinks its teeth into an object and tears it apart, whether it is edible or inedible; it was my nature to read whatever printed words met my eye. Our world presents us with many more books unassigned than assigned, so that fourteen revolutions of the sun in my literary solar system had provided more of extracurricular than of academic reading. Nevertheless, despite the dire predictions of my Sanskrit tutor, I passed the examination.

My father was a deputy magistrate. In those days we were at Satkshira or Jahanabad or some other such place. It seems desirable to state clearly at the outset that the time, the place, and the people mentioned in this history are all fictional; readers with more curiosity than literary sense will be disappointed.

At the time this account begins, my father was out on a tour of investigation. My mother was performing some sort of religious vow; she needed a Brahman to arrange for the cooking and for distribution of the fees.[1] Our family pundit was her chief ally in arranging for this sort of spiritual welfare. My mother was especially grateful to him on this account, although my father felt just the opposite.

Now I too was on the inventory of sacrificial offering. This was the nub of the current discussions. It was time for me to go to Calcutta to college. Under such circumstances it was necessary to devise something to keep my mother happy in the face of this separation. If a child-bride were left at home in my mother's lap, she could then spend her days raising her and caring for her. The pundit's daughter, Kashiswari, was the ideal choice because she was a child and was also well behaved, and our stars matched exactly. Besides, if you relieved a Brahman of his daughter, there was a further desirable gain in spiritual benefits.

My mother was moved by this. As soon as it was hinted that it was necessary to see the girl, the pundit said that his wife had just arrived with the daughter. My mother wasted no time in making a choice, and why not? Personal taste was very easily counterbalanced by the girl's virtue.

"She shows auspicious signs," said my mother. "I mean to say, if she were not pretty enough, that would be a compensating factor."

I heard such talk through various channels. That the very pundit whose grammar I had always dreaded should allude to my marriage with his daughter was an incongruity that strongly attracted me at first. As in a fairy story, it suddenly seemed as if all the most difficult things were swept away, at one stroke revealing the princess.

One morning my mother called me to her room and said, "Shanu, these mangoes and sweets have come from the pundit's house. Have some."

Mother knew that if she fed me twenty-five mangoes and if another twenty-five were added, I would be pleased. So she enticed my heart by way of the moist road of the tongue. My mother had Kashiswari on her lap. Memory

---

[1] A Brahman was needed to supervise the cooking of the food in the orthodox manner.

has become very dim, but I think there was tinsel twisted into the knot of Kashiswari's hair, and she wore a satin jacket from a Calcutta shop; it gave a delirious impression of red and blue and lace and ribbons. What I recall most clearly is that her complexion was dark. Her eyebrows were very thick, and her eyes looked out unabashed like those of a tame animal, gazing without shyness. I don't remember anything about the rest of her face; it seemed that its form had never been completely finished in God's workshop and was only roughly sketched in. Anyway, she looked like a nice person.

I was bursting with pride. I said to myself, "This tinsel-pigtailed, jacketed object is my exclusive acquisition. I am its lord, I am its god." One must work hard for all other rare objects but not for this thing. All I had to do was to move one finger; God was coaxing me to accept this boon. I had always observed my mother; I knew what it was to have a wife. I had noticed that my father was irritated by all other religious rituals, but when it came to Savitri's ancient vow, he secretly felt that it was rather a pleasant thing. I know that my mother certainly loved him, but when my father was angry about anything, when anything annoyed him, my mother was extremely frightened, and this small satisfaction gave my father the maximum enjoyment of his manliness. Being worshiped doesn't seem to matter to the gods, because that is their due. But for men it is an undue claim, and so their desire for it is increasingly disproportionate. That day the attractions of that girl had not impressed me, but the fact that at the age of fourteen I would have a worshiper of my manliness set my blood to boiling. That day I ate the mangoes with much pride, so proudly that three mangoes remained on the plate, something that had never before happened in my life. And because of that the whole afternoon became an occasion for regret.

That day Kashiswari had not yet been informed about her relationship with me, but it seems that she was told about it as soon as she got home. After that, whenever I saw her she became very flustered and would try to hide. Her shyness before me pleased me very much. That my presence on the earth at a certain spot in a certain form created a commotion was a fact of life I found very agreeable. That someone was frightened or bashful in my presence, or that such a thing would happen, was very unexpected. By running away Kashiswari was letting me know that she considered me the most special, the most complete, and the most mysterious thing in the world.

To step suddenly, in one moment, from a long-standing insignificance to such dignity made the blood pound in my head. Just as my father always got annoyed with my mother over shortcomings in her routine duties or cooking or planning, I too began in my own mind to create my own version of the picture. When Father succeeded in discovering evidence of some deficiency and Mother would recoup her efforts with varied precautions and a charming skill, in imagination I saw Kashiswari following that same course. I pictured myself giving her occasional gifts, casually and unexpectedly, ranging from high-figure bank notes to diamond jewelry. On a day when she didn't eat at dinner, she sat by the window wiping away tears with the end of her sari: I saw this touching scene too in my mind's eye, and I can't say that it even seemed very sad to me.

My father took extreme care with regard to his young son's self-reliance. I had to keep my own room in order, I had to look after my clothes, I had to do everything for myself. But I came to have a distinct mental picture of housework, which I am now putting down on paper. Needless to say, the same thing had happened to my father; there was no originality in my imagination. This was the scene: after the noonday meal on Sunday I propped my head with a pillow on a cot, crossed my legs, and, half-reclining, read the paper. I held a hookah, but I was drowsy, and the pipe slipped down.

On the veranda Kashiswari was giving clothes to the laundryman; I called to her. She quickly came running and put the pipe in my hand. I said to her, "Look here, there is a thick English book with a blue cover on the left side of the third shelf in my study. Get that and bring it here."

Kashi brought a blue book.

"Ach!" I said. "Not this one. It's thicker than this, and the title is written in gold letters on its spine."

This time she brought a green book; I became angry and threw it on the floor with a thud. Then Kashi's face fell and her eyes swam with tears. I went and saw that the book was not on the third shelf; it was on the fifth shelf. Book in hand, I lay down silently on the bed, but not a word did I say to Kashi about my mistake. She hung her head in shame, dejectedly began to give the clothes to the laundryman, and could not forget her crime of disturbing her husband's rest by the sin of stupidity.

Thus imagination helped to pass my time. Father was away investigating a burglary. With respect to me, the pundit's behavior and language passed in one minute from the active voice to the passive and became a voice of extreme friendliness.

When the burglary investigation was concluded, Father returned home. I knew that Mother was prepared to broach the subject of marriage as she mixed Father's favorite curry: ingredients were to be added a little at a time. Father despised the pundit for his avarice; at first Mother certainly criticized the pundit gently, but she laid a foundation of fulsome praise for his wife and daughter. But unfortunately word of the pundit's overweening delight had spread far and wide. He had not kept from anyone the fact that the marriage was arranged and the day set. He even intended to use the nice brick house of Father's head clerk for a few days at the time of the wedding, and he had introduced the proposal at an opportune time. Everyone did everything to help him as much as possible with the happy occasion. The lawyers at Father's court subscribed to the wedding expenses. The third son of Bireswari, the local high-school secretary, was in the third class; he wrote a wedding poem in *tripadi* full of metaphors about the moon and white water lilies. The secretary carried that poem around with him and forced anyone he met on the street or river landings to listen to it. The village people entertained great expectations for the boy.

Consequently, as soon as Father left the house after his return, he heard the happy tidings. Then came Mother's tears and refusal to eat, a state of alarm throughout the house, senseless penalties for the servants, abrupt termination of court cases and the pronouncement of drastic sentences, dismissal of the pundit, and the disappearance along with him of the tinsel-pigtailed Kushiswari. And before the vacation ended I was separated from my mother and rigorously exiled to Calcutta. My morale collapsed like a punctured football: after riding the wind all over the sky, its frisking came to a sudden end.

2

This was the roadblock at the beginning of my road to marriage. Since then the god of marriage has repeatedly favored me, but in vain. Without going into great detail I shall draw an abbreviated sketch of the history of my frustration.

Before I was twenty years old I had made a supreme effort and passed the M.A. examination, was wearing spectacles, and had grown a moustache. At that time my father was stationed at Rampurhat, or Noakhali, or Barashat, or some such place. I spent all this time churning the sea of words and obtaining the precious jewel of the degree; now it was time to churn the ocean of money. My father reviewed his prominent English patrons. His principal patron had died; a lesser one had been pensioned to England; another was uninfluential and had been transferred to the Punjab; and still another remained in Bengal, held out initial hopes to most of the applicants, but let them down in the end. When my grandfather was a deputy under the raja's patronage, things were not so tight, so that in those days a job produced a pension, and a pension produced a job, and family connections were the only ferry to the opposite shore. Nowadays things are bad, and therefore when my father became concerned about the matter, he thought that his son and heir would have to descend from the lofty cage of a government office to a lowly perch in a business office.

Just then, the only daughter of a wealthy Brahman came to his attention. The Brahman was a contractor; more of his income was invisible underground than evident above ground. On the pretext of Christmas, Father went to a great deal of trouble to present oranges and other gifts accompanied by an appropriate letter. About that time I appeared in that neighborhood.

My father's house was just across from the contractor's. A street separated them. To make a long story short, the M.A. son of the deputy became a very high-interest investment in the transaction of marrying off a daughter. Therefore the contractor was groping in my direction. His well-trained arm very easily reached out to the deputy's heart. But my heart was set on higher things.

I was just past twenty. I coveted no jewel at that time but the genuine jewel of a wife. What was more, my

mind glowed at the very thought. That is, the concept
of a legally wedded wife had a very special meaning for me,
and that meaning was not the commonly accepted one.
The family had entered a general decline in our country;
ideals were very spacious while in practice the family was
becoming very constricted, and in my heart of hearts I found
this unbearable. That the wife whom I would make my companion on the road to my ideal should wear shackles in the
domestic prison and drag behind clanking at every step was
an evil I was unwilling to accept. Actually I was as un-
remittingly up-to-date as those others in our country's comedy
who are fresh out of college and are ridiculed as modern.
In our time this modern faction was larger than it is now.
The amazing thing was that they really abhorred social conformity and believed that progress results from defying the
rules.

I, Sanatkumar, was such a person, and I fell right in front
of the yawning moneybags of an influential Brahman with
a marriageable daughter.

"A good thing should be carried through at once," said
my father.

I kept quiet. I thought to myself, let me wait and see
what comes. I kept my eyes and ears open; little was seen
and much was heard. The girl was like a little doll and
beautiful. She didn't look as if she had been formed according to the rules of nature; it seemed as if someone had
smoothed down each hair, had sketched in her eyebrows,
had molded her by hand. She could recite Sanskrit eulogies
of the Ganges. Her mother always used Ganges water to
wash even the coal used for cooking. She was always worried about contact with the world since Mother Earth ac-
cepts all races; most of her customs involved water because
there are no aquatic creatures of Muslim origin, and onions
do not grow in water.[2] The chief preoccupation of her life
was the purification and cleansing of herself, her house,
clothing, various cooking pots, furniture, and household
utensils. It was nearly two-thirty every day before she finished all this. She had raised her daughter so correctly and
so carefully that the daughter was not troubled by any
opinions or wishes of her own. No matter how inconvenient
any regimen, raising the girl was easy if no one ever told

---

[2] "Onions not growing in water" refers to an orthodox Hindu's
objection to onions as food.

her the exact reason for anything. She never wore good clothes at mealtime, lest food be spilled and the purification ceremony must follow; she was even taught to be concerned about the shadows that fell upon her. She got into a palanquin for a bath in the Ganges and returned home as prescribed in the eighteenth Purana.

My mother too had ample respect for rules and regulations but she could not tolerate anyone else in the house who might outdo her in following traditional customs. So when I said to her, "Mother, I'm not a suitable bridegroom for this girl," she laughed and said, "No, it's hard to get a suitable bridegroom in these bad times."

"In that case," said I, "I'll take my leave."

"Listen to that!" exclaimed my mother. "Wasn't she your choice? Why, isn't the girl good-looking?"

"Mother, a wife is meant not merely to be looked at. I want her to be intelligent as well."

"How do you know she is less intelligent than others?"

"If a person has intelligence, she can't survive among all these everlasting meaningless trivialities. She would suffocate."

My mother's face became bleak. She knew that my father had made an almost firm commitment to the other party with regard to this marriage. She knew also that my father had almost forgotten the fact that others have wishes of their own. In fact, if my father had not gotten so extremely wrought up and high-handed about it, perhaps in the course of time I too would some day have felt a strong inclination to marry this Purana-quoting doll and could have kept fasting vows and in due course died on the banks of the Ganges.[3]

That is, if responsibility for this marriage rested on Mother, she could take her time about it, recite scripture now and then when things seemed to move slowly, shed occasional tears, and finally get it done. When my father began to do nothing but rage and roar, I plucked up my courage and said, "Since childhood you have advised me to be self-reliant, in eating and sleep, in my comings and goings. Is self-reliance denied only at the time of marriage?"

I have never seen anyone succeed with logic except in logic examinations in college. Arriving at the correct conclusion by means of fallacious logic is never like using water on a fire; it is more like using oil.

Father stuck to his idea that he had made a promise to

[3] Dying on the banks of the Ganges is the goal of a devout Hindu.

another person; there was no better ground for the appropriateness of the marriage. Yet if I reminded him that my mother had also once made a promise to the pundit, and that nevertheless that promise alone had not kept the marriage from falling through and the pundit's employment as our family priest from going up in smoke—then this turned into a criminal case. Purification ceremonies, charms, and rituals were much better than intelligence, judgment, and personal preference. The girl's feeling for poetry was profound and beautiful, her devotion was steadfast, her accomplishments were of the highest order, supremely symbolic and idealistic. Nowadays my father talked and talked to me on this subject, in season and out of season. I held my tongue, but I certainly could not silence my thoughts. What came to the tip of my tongue was "If you really believe in these holy things, why not be a vegetarian?"

Another fact came to mind: if Father suffered any loss or inconvenience due to the rules and regulations regarding the distribution of fees connected with a holy day, he harshly reprimanded my mother about all these useless rituals. Then my mother admitted spending all the money, confessed that a frail female was stupid by her very nature, hung her head in shame, and in a sudden burst of annoyance commenced making arrangements for an even more elaborate feast for the Brahmans. But Brahma had not created man in a strongly logical mold; therefore there is no consistency between a man's words and actions, and he cannot be won over by means of logic; he only becomes enraged. If you resort to logic, it only makes things worse; those who put their faith in political or domestic agitation ought to keep this in mind. When the horse kicks the carriage because he thinks having it behind him is unjust, the injustice remains and only his feet are hurt. The same thing happened to me in my youth, for youth is little inclined toward debate. I got safely beyond the reach of the Purana-quoting girl, but I was also deprived of the money of an up-to-date father.

"Go," said my father. "Be self-reliant."

I touched his feet respectfully and replied, "As you wish." My mother sat there and cried.

My father's right hand had turned against me, but since my mother was in between, I often caught a glimpse of a messenger with a money order. It stopped raining, but in the cool secrecy of the night the dewdrops fell. On the strength of that I got started in a business. The initial capital was exactly seventy-nine rupees. And nowadays, if the capital operating in this business is much less than the figure set by the gossip of the envious, it is no less than twenty lakhs of rupees.

The messengers of the god of marriage returned to follow close behind me. Formerly all doors were closed; now there was no way of keeping them bolted. I remember that once in the irrepressible optimism of youth I was eager to give my heart to a sixteen-year-old girl of my acquaintance, an age feared by the orthodox but tolerable, however, to me, but I had heard and observed that the relatives on her mother's side of the family aimed for a civil servant—at the very least, nothing less than a barrister. I was below the zero point in the mother's interest gauge.

But when I became prosperous, I not only had tea at that house, but ate lunch there, and after dinner in the evening played whist with the daughters and listened to them gossiping in their own distinctive brand of the English language. My difficulty was that I had been trained in English by reading *Rasselas, The Deserted Village,* and Addison and Steele. My achievement was nothing beside these girls'. "Oh, my! Oh dear, oh dear!" and similar elucidations did little to explain things to me. With my limited education, I commanded at the most a grasp of English that enabled me to make market transactions, but if the conversation of love had to be carried on in twentieth-century English, my love would run away.

Yet they spoke a Bengali so famine-stricken that Bankimchandra himself would have been done out of the words for a pleasant conversation. It wouldn't suffice for even one day's work. However that may be, all these English-gilded girls would some day, as far as I was concerned, be easily obtainable.

But through a chink in the closed door I saw a fairyland of which, if the door opened, I had not gotten the address. Then all I could think of was that former devotee who had satisfied her own dulled intellect by going around and around day and night tangled in meaningless rules and ceaseless repetitions. These modern girls too had intelligence and spent their time with tireless ease circling day after day, year after year, all the trivial formalities of Western etiquette. Like the old-fashioned girls who shuddered at the least slip in anything concerning touching and bathing, these girls too were very particular about accent, and if they saw someone make a little slip with spoon and fork they suspected his authenticity as a human being. That other girl was an indigenous doll; these were Anglicized dolls. They didn't operate voluntarily; they breathed by habit, like machines.

The upshot of it was that I conceived a disrespect for all sorts of women. I reckon that when they were less intelligent they tried to survive by means of baths and ritual purification and fasting. I had read that there is one variety of microbe that steadily circulates in the dark. But man does not circulate, he moves ahead. Has God formally decreed man's marriage vows to one of these enlarged versions of that microbe?

The older one grows, the more one wavers with regard to marriage. A man has one age during which he can get married without much thought. If he passes that age he needs a reckless nature to enter into matrimony. I am not one of these daredevils. Besides, why should some sensible girl suddenly marry me? I have heard that love is blind, but at this point nothing depends on the blindness of love. It takes more than two eyes to run a household; when those eyes look in my direction without infatuation, I wonder what they see in me. I have many good qualities, but one cannot know these at a glance. I know that a high level of intelligence compensates for the shortness of my nose, but the nose is plainly outlined, while God has kept intelligence amorphous. However, when I see that some eligible girl notices me and has not the slightest objection to marrying me, my regard for that girl diminishes. If I were a girl, Sanatkumar's snub nose would make me sigh and forget my hope and pride.

Thus my cargoless boat of matrimony had moved by occasional fits and starts, but it had never reached the landing. Except for a wife, the other items of household equipment kept pace with my rise in the business world. I forgot one fact: I was getting older. I was reminded of this by an unexpected incident.

I went to inspect a mica quarry at a city in the Chota-Nagpur area. Our former pundit lived there in a nice little house built on a riverbank in the shade of a grove of sal trees. His son worked there. I had made camp in that sal grove. By now my wealth was renowned throughout the country.

The pundit said he had always known that in the course of time I would become an outstanding man. Maybe so, but he had been remarkably secretive about it. How he knew it,

I don't know. Perhaps outstanding people do not show any grasp of grammatical nuances in their student days.

Kashiswari was at her father-in-law's house, so without embarrassment I became a member of the pundit's family. A few years earlier he had become a widower, but he was surrounded by grandchildren. Not all of these were his own; two of them belonged to his deceased elder brother. By taking charge of them, the old man had considerably livened up the evening of his old age.

I laughed and said, "Pundit, sir, how are things going?"

"My son," he replied, "your English authorities say that Saturn wears the garland of satellites. Those are my satellites."

When I observed the scene in that modest house, it suddenly occurred to me that I was alone. I realized that I was weary of being a burden to myself. The pundit did not know that his old age had come, but I saw clearly that mine had arrived. As I aged, I had told myself that being old meant complete relaxation, but everything had gone slack. Neither money nor fame can redress that slackness. I got no delight from the world, I was only accumulating material things. I had ignored the frustration of this mode of living. But when I saw the pundit's house, I realized that my days were arid, my nights empty.

The pundit concluded correctly that I was a more fortunate man than he. I had to laugh when I thought of this. There is an invisible world of delight around this visible world. If the bond of union between our lives and the world of delight does not hold, we live in a void like King Trishanku. The pundit possessed that bond, I did not; this was the difference.

As I rested in an armchair, my feet up on its arm, I smoked and reflected that man's life has four presiding deities and four stages: the mother during childhood, the wife during youth, the daughter and daughter-in-law during middle age, the granddaughter and the grandson's wife during old age. This fundamental truth was borne in upon me in the rustling sal grove.

In my mind I looked toward the farthest limit of my future old age; viewing that arid waste my heart cried out. I would have to die flat on my face, my shoulders burdened with my acquisitions, going somewhere along this desert road. If I delayed any longer, nothing would happen. I was now forty; fifty waits at the end of the road to take the last penny from the purse of youth; I can see its walking stick from here.

Now the realities of the pocketbook must be shut out and a little attention paid to the realities of youth. The postponed part of youth would certainly not recur, but there was still time for patching up its damages.

For professional reasons I went to a city in western India where my work introduced me to Visvapatibabu, a wealthy Bengali banker. He was a very cautious man; consequently, it took a long time for him to come to a decision. One day when I was telling myself in annoyance, "This person will be of no use to me," and even told the servant to pack up my things, Visvapatibabu came in the evening and said, "You must know a lot of people. If you care to do so, you might save a widow."

This was the gist of it:

Mr. Nandakrishna first came to Bareilli as headmaster of a Bengali-English school. He was very good at his work. Everyone was amazed. Why would such a competent, well-educated man leave Bengal, come so far away, and take a job at an ordinary salary? His good reputation rested not only on the fact that he had passed his examinations; he took a hand in all worthwhile projects. But inevitably it came to be known that although his wife was beautiful, she had no family background; she was a woman of lower caste, so much so that drinking water was contaminated by her touch, and this vitiated her other good qualities. When everyone pressed him about this, he said, "Yes, the ancestry is undistinguished, but she is my wife."

Then the question arose of how such a marriage could be legal. Whoever asked Nandakrishna about this got the reply, "You have married twice by the stone of Shiva,[4] and you are not even happy after your second marriage. You are ample proof of that. I can't speak for the stone of Shiva, but God knows my marriage is more legal than yours, legal every minute of every day. I don't wish to discuss it with you any further."

The individual to whom Nandakrishna would say this was not pleased and had, besides, an unusual capacity for malice. Therefore, Nandakrishna left Bareilli, came to this city, and began to practice law. The man was extremely particular;

---

[4] The stone of Shiva is referred to here as witness of a marriage: this is a custom in orthodox Hindu circles.

even if he went without food he would have nothing to do with an unjust lawsuit. At first this was quite an obstacle for him; finally he began to prosper, for the judges had complete faith in him. He built a house and was settled on his own land when the country was desolated by a great famine. Nandakrishna reported to the magistrate that those responsible for relief were stealing. The magistrate said, "Where can I find an honest man?"

Nandakrishna replied, "If you trust me, I can take on some of this work."

He assumed the responsibility, and while he was fully engaged in carrying it out, he fell dead one midday beneath a tree. The doctor said that he had died of a heart attack.

I already knew this much of the story. When I heard at our club about the high regard for his character, I had said, "Think of the people like this Nandakrishna who die as failures in the world; they have no fame, no wealth. They are God's co-workers and give the world—"

The words were scarcely spoken when, like a boat under full sail that abruptly runs onto a sandbar, I stopped in midsentence because there was among us a man of great wealth and influence who was reading the newspaper; he glared at me over his spectacles and burst out, "Hear, hear!"

So much for that. I was told that Nandakrishna's widow was living in this neighborhood with her only daughter. Because the girl had been born on the night of Diwali, her father had named her Dipali. Since the widow had no place in society, she lived completely alone and raised and educated her daughter. The daughter would soon be fifteen years old. The mother's health was poor, and she was not getting any younger. Some day she would die and there would be no provision for this girl.

Visvapati spoke beseechingly to me. "If you could find a bridegroom for her, that would be an act of virtue."

I had been secretly a little contemptuous of Visvapati, thinking him heartless and selfish. I was touched that he showed this concern for a daughter of a helpless widow. I thought, Seeds have been found buried in the stomachs of prehistoric mammoths, and those seeds have sprouted; thus the humanity of man emerges from the accumulation of death; it absolutely refuses to die.

I said to Visvapati, "I know of a bridegroom, and there's no problem. You all talk it over and settle on a suitable day."

"But without even seeing the girl—"

"It isn't necessary to see her."

"But if the groom is after property, there isn't much of it. If the mother dies, the girl will get only the house. If he gets anything more, it would be trifling."

"The groom has property himself, so that's not a consideration."

"What about his name and qualifications, and so forth—"

"I won't tell you that now; if it's made public, the marriage would fall through."

"Surely the girl's mother has to have a description of him."

"Tell her that the man has faults and virtues like other ordinary men. The faults are not so great that they cannot be borne, and the virtues are not so great that they are to be envied. As far as I know, parents of daughters have chosen him; what the daughters themselves have thought isn't known."

When Visvapati showed such solicitude about this matter, my respect for him rose. I became enthusiastic about that business transaction on which we had not formerly been able to come to terms and which I had put down in the accounts as a loss. As he was leaving he said, "Tell the bridegroom that aside from all other considerations, he cannot find such a virtuous girl anywhere else."

If the girl who has been deprived of society's shelter and deference wins your heart, will she ever be miserly in giving herself? That girl who entertains great hopes is the one with no end to her hopes. But this Dipali's lamp was made of earth; therefore that little flame would be respected in my earthen home.

In the evening the lights were turned on, and I was reading an English newspaper when word arrived that a girl had come to see me. There was no lady of the house, so I was embarrassed. By some quiet expedient the girl had already entered the house; she came and touched my feet in respect. No stranger would believe it, but I am an extremely bashful man. I didn't look at her face, didn't say a word to her.

She said, "My name is Dipali."

Her voice was low and sweet. I ventured a glance in the direction of her face; that face was overlaid with gentleness and intelligence. There was no veil over her head; her sari was plain white, worn in the current fashion. I was wondering what to say when she said, "Don't try to get me married."

A protest from Dipali herself was the last thing I had expected. I had assumed that she would have been filled, body, mind, and heart, with gratitude for a proposal of marriage.

I asked, "Won't you marry anyone, known or unknown?"

"No," she replied. "I won't marry anyone."

Although I had more experience with material things than with psychology, the workings of a woman's mind, in particular, were more difficult to me than Bengali spelling. Still, the obvious meaning of a word did not always appear to me as the actual meaning.

"The bridegroom I chose for you doesn't deserve that much disrespect," I said. I again asked, "You won't marry any groom, known or unknown?" I added, "That man respects you."

"Oh no, don't ask me to marry."

"All right, I'll tell him not to marry you, but isn't there something else I can do for you?"

"It would be a great help if you would take me along when you go to Calcutta and get me a job at some girls' school."

"There are jobs," I said. "I can get you one."

That was not an altogether true statement. What did I know about girls' schools? But it is no sin to establish a school for girls.

"Will you go to our house and discuss this matter with my mother?" Dipali asked.

Dipali left. That ended my newspaper reading. I went out onto the roof terrace and sat on a bench. I asked the stars, "Do you really sit there silently and from millions of miles away, knit together all the actions and relationships of men's lives?"

Without knowing what had happened, Vispapati's second son, Sripati, suddenly came up to the roof terrace. During our conversation I found that this was his secret: In his eagerness to marry Dipali, Sripati was prepared to abandon society. His father said that he would disown him if he did such a wicked thing. Dipali had said that she would not be worth anyone's assuming so much sorrow, humiliation, and ostracism. Besides, Sripati had been brought up from childhood in a wealthy home; Dipali considered herself outcaste and helpless, and he would not be able to bear the hardship of poverty. They debated this but arrived at no final decision. At this very critical moment I had appeared on the scene and had considerably complicated the problem by proposing another bridegroom. Therefore Sripati was telling me to take myself out of this drama like a section deleted from a proof-sheet.

"When I read," I said, "I don't make deletions. Since I have entered, I'm not going to leave. If I go out, I'll sever all ties and be gone."

There was no change in the wedding date. Only the groom was changed. I kept Visvapati's request, but he was not pleased about it. I was not spared the entreaties of Dipali, but it seemed to me that she was pleased. I did not know whether or not there was an opening in a school, but a daughter's place was vacant in my house, and that was filled.

Through Sripati it had been proven that a useless, worthless man like me has real value. Sripati's household lamp burned in my house in Calcutta. I had thought that the postponed marriages would be compensated for by getting married at an unseasonable time, but I saw that a higher authority was pleased to grant a promotion that skipped me several grades. Now at the age of fifty-five I have a house full of granddaughters, and a grandson as well. But my business transaction with Visvapati came to an end because he did not like the bridegroom.

1917

THE REJECTED STORY
(Namanjur Galpa)

Our political party convened during the last days of political conflagration. We were not fully relieved of responsibility for future events and our voices were hoarse with shouting. Otherwise, the game of starting bonfires was over.

The drama of the revolutionaries began on the stage of divided Bengal. Everyone knew that the last act of the play ended at Alipore Prison or in the Andaman Islands penal colonies. I was charged on enough counts to send me on the ocean voyage, but through the good offices of my lucky stars I landed in jail on this side of the water. After my release I bowed in respect to those comrades who were promoted to the highest rank of the gallows, and proceeded to build up a practice in homeopathic medicine in a city of North India.

My father was still living at that time. He held the title Raibahadur and was public prosecutor in a large district of Bengal. He severed my home ties with scant ceremony. God only knows whether my ties to his heart were broken, but he broke the connection with my purse. There was not even a money order to link us together. My mother had died while I was in prison. She got the punishment I deserved.

Many people wondered whether the lady who is known as my paternal aunt is really a paternal relative or is self-acquired, for before I went north my relationship with her was altogether nonexistent. Let the doubt remain as to who she really is, but at that time of anarchy, when relatives turned against me, I would have been in serious distress without her affection. She had spent her whole life in the north; she was married there, and there she became a widow and lived surrounded by all her husband's landed property.

She had still another bond in the girl Amiya. Amiya's mother had been my aunt's young maidservant, a member of the Kahar caste. After my aunt's husband died, she brought Amiya home and raised her; Amiya still does not know that my aunt is not her own mother.

At this point one more bond was added: that was myself. This widow sheltered me in her home and in her heart when my circumstances, after getting out of jail, were extremely straitened. When my father died and we learned that he had not cut me out of his will, my aunt shed tears of joy and of sorrow. She felt that my need for her was gone. But I always needed her affection.

"Son," she said, "wherever you are, my blessings are always with you."

"That will always be so," I replied, "but you must accompany them. Otherwise I can't manage. The mother whom I never saw again after I came out of prison has shown me the path that led to you."

My aunt gave up her longtime home in the north and came with me to Calcutta. I smiled and said, "I have brought the Ganges River of your affection from the north to the east. I am the Bhagirath of the age."

My aunt laughed and wiped away her tears. Some doubt still lingered. She said, "For ever so long I've wanted to make some sort of settlement for this girl and go on a pilgrimage in my last years—but, my boy, now I'm being pulled off in the opposite direction."

"Auntie," I replied, "I myself am your portable place of pilgrimage. Wherever you sacrifice yourself, your God will come there and accept it. That's how good a person you are."

One argument carried more weight with her than all others. She was afraid that my inclinations tended instinctively toward the Andaman Islands; if no one kept an eye on me, I would certainly end up some day in the hands of the police. She intended to see me settled in a grasp much softer, stronger, and more firm; once that was taken care of, she would go off on a pilgrimage. She would not be free until I had been imprisoned.

She miscalculated with respect to my character. My horoscope did not rule out my being left to the final disposition of the vultures, but it said nothing about turning me over to the god of marriage. The parents of daughters were ubiquitous and their instinct was unerring. Everyone knew the enormous extent of my paternal inheritance; therefore, had I so wished, I could probably have run the father of a bride into bankruptcy by merrily collecting, along with the daughter, twenty or twenty-five thousand rupees for wedding entertainment expenses. Let us hope my future biographer will recall that I did not take such a step; this was my twenty- or twenty-five-thousand-rupee sacrifice to the cause of national freedom. My praises on this score should not go unsung only because the figures for debits and credits are written in invisible ink. Here lay the similarity between my sterling character and that of Grandfather Vishnu.

My aunt would not give up hope. At that point the winds of the new era began to blow from many directions in India's political sky. I have already said that we were not the principal actors in this playlet; nevertheless we came and went in the dimness beyond the footlights. My aunt felt quite reassured. She had planned to have protective rites performed for me once and for all before the goddess Kali, but she put it out of her mind because red-capped clouds were then completely absent in the sky of my fate. This was where she erred.

We picketed one day in the Puja Market on behalf of hand-spun khaddar cloth. I had gone as a spectator only; the temperature of my enthusiasm was below ninety-eight degrees; my pulse rate was not particularly rapid. No one but the stars of my horoscope should have felt apprehensive about me that day. Then a police sergeant shoved a Bengali lady demonstrator. In an instant my nonviolent disposition turned into uncontrollable violence. I ended up in short order at police headquarters. I was sent down, as usual, into the dark interior regions of the jail, a morsel coveted by police custody.

I sent word to my aunt: "Now you are free for a while. For the time being I have no lack of conpetent guardians. Amiya lives at the college hostel; there are people to look after the house, so now if you devote yourself wholeheartedly to serving God, neither God nor man will object."

I regarded the prison as a prison. I made no capricious claims there and caused no disturbance. I was not greatly surprised there by the lack of felicity, respect, courtesy, good friends, and good food. I accepted harsh rules in a mood of harshness. I considered it shameful to put up any sort of objection.

I was set free well before the end of my term. There was general applause. The air of Bengal seemed to resound, "Encore! Excellent!" I felt depressed. I thought, the sufferer suffers alone, and others get together to enjoy the benefits. Even that does not last long; the stage curtain falls, the lights go out, then it is time to forget. The only one who remembers forever is he whose wrists were branded by handcuffs.

My aunt was still on her pilgrimage. Nor did I know her address. Meanwhile, the Puja Festival approached. One morning an editor friend arrived. "Say," he said, "I want something written for the Puja edition."

"A poem?" I asked.

"Oh, no! Your autobiography."

"That certainly wouldn't fit into one edition."

"Why one edition? It will come out in installments."

"Sati's dead body was strewn in pieces on the Sudarsan Chakra. My autobiography will be strewn the same way from one edition to another on the editorial circle. This is not what I want. If I write my life story, I'll bring it out in one installment."

"Why not write about some significant incident in your life?"

"What kind of incident?"

"Your most harrowing experience, one with an edge to it."

"What's the point of writing it?"

"People want to know."

"So much curiosity? All right, I'll do it."

"Remember, your most harrowing experience."

"In other words, people are most amused by what hurt me the most. Well, all right. But the names must be greatly changed."

"Definitely! It's very dangerous not to change clues to such serious historical events. I want something sensational. I'll pay you by the page."

"See the writing first, then set a price."

"But you must promise not to give it to anyone else. No matter who offers you what, I'll top it."

"All right, all right, that's how it will be."

Finally he remarked as he was about to leave, "This author you know—you follow me?—I'll not name him—that literary genius of yours—he prides himself on being a great writer, but whatever you say, your style in comparison with his is like Dawson's Boots compared with slippers made on Taltala Street."

I realized that upgrading me was merely incidental; the real object was to downgrade the literary genius.

So much for my preface. Now the story of my most harrowing experience.

From the very day I began to read the newspaper *Sandhya*, I had trouble enjoying food and drink. We called that the rehearsal for the jail drama and became expert at habitually abusing our health. So I was not at all upset by my first imprisonment. When I came out I would not tolerate anyone's pampering or interference. This distressed my aunt. I would say to her, "Auntie, there is freedom in affection, captivity in being waited on. Besides, the imposition of a physical regime upon another is called dyarchy; our noncooperation opposes that."

She would sigh and say, "Very well, my son, I won't bother you about it."

I was foolish enough to think there was no danger.

I had forgotten that affection and service have a secret aspect: one cannot easily escape their influence. When the indigent Shiva with his begging bowl was full of pride at his poverty, he did not know that Lakshmi had already enmeshed him in silks so soft and rich that sun and stars could not compensate for them. When Shiva said, "I am eating what I have begged," he never knew that his wife Annapurna had concocted such a spicy mixture that even Indra, the king of the gods, connived with Nandi to get a share of that sacred food.

That was my situation. Whether I was sleeping, sitting, or eating, my aunt's solicitous hand secretly spread Indra's net over me, wherever I was. I, the nationalist, was too preoccupied to notice and felt positive that my austerity was unaffected. I got a shock when I went to prison. There was a difference between my aunt's and the police's way of running things, and in spite of my singlemindedness, I could not get the two to harmonize. All I could do was begin to recite the Gita to myself: "Be on guard against your own nature."

Alas for the ascetic, I never knew that my aunt's mixture of virtues had gone beyond the heart and suddenly entered the stomach. That region began to feel distress now that I was in jail.

As a result, the body that only a thunderbolt would have daunted fell ill. The term of prison ailments did not end even after the warden released me. Sometimes my head ached, I had digestive troubles, and I ran a temperature in the evenings. The ache of these afflictions stayed very much alive while the congratulatory garlands and applause gradually faded away.

I thought to myself, My aunt is away and can't look after me, but doesn't Amiya have any sense?

But whose fault was that? My aunt had often encouraged her to look after me when I was sick. I had objected, saying, "I won't have it."

"I'm telling Amiya this in order to teach her, not to please you," said my aunt.

"Why doesn't she take up hospital-nursing?" I replied.

My aunt was angry and didn't answer.

Now I lay there and thought, Does she have to keep it up just because I put her off once? In this age of destruction, such devotion to the orders of one's elders!

Major and minor household details were usually kept out of the patriot's sight. But now that I was ill, my vision had sharpened. I noticed that Amiya's patriotism had grown considerably stronger during my absence. My example and indoctrination had never before achieved such unexpected improvement. Now she sacrificed college to the irresistible momentum of the noncooperation movement; nor did her heart miss a beat as she stood up to address the crowds. She went to the houses of strangers to beg contributions for refugee shelters.

I noticed, furthermore, that her friend Anil watched her dogged perseverance and worshiped her like a goddess. He reached such a pitch of emotion on her birthday that he expressed these feelings in an ode written in broken rhythms and printed in gold ink.

I would have to adopt a similar approach or I would have trouble. Under my aunt's supervision the servants worked according to a fixed routine; no one interfered with anyone else's work. Now if I needed a glass of water, I would wait around like a swallow, hoping for water from an unexpected cloud. My own forgetful mind was the only reminder of the time to take medicine.

Contrary to my own unshakable principles, I called Amiya a time or two to attend my sickbed. But I noticed that if quiet footsteps were heard, she looked quickly toward the door, then just sat there fidgeting. I felt sorry for her. I said, "Amiya, you must have one of your meetings today."

"That doesn't matter, brother," she replied. "There's plenty of time."

"No, no," I would say. "That's no way to do things. Duty comes before everything else."

But many times I noticed that Anil was placed considerably before duty. The wind seemed to blow erratically on the sail of Amiya's sense of duty; I didn't have to say much about it.

Other extremely zealous young school-deserters besides Anil congregated on the first floor of my house to imbibe tea and inspiration in the evenings. Every one of them addressed Amiya as if she were the Lakshmi of the century. There is one kind of title, such as Raibahadur, that is carried casually on the shoulders like a pleated chador. There is another kind of title, and he who is lucky enough to acquire it lives in daily misery and uneasiness attempting to measure up to it. It was clear to me that this was Amiya's situation. She could not keep going without the spur of a glowing enthusiasm. She missed meals and sleep with great ceremony; her fame spread from our neighborhood to others. When someone asked her how her health could stand it, she laughed a little, a laugh of amazement.

The devotees said, "You get a little rest. We'll carry on the work somehow."

At that she would be hurt—was it so important to keep her from getting tired? It was no small thing to be deprived of the privilege of bearing afflictions. I too was put on her list of self-denials. I, her older brother, who had served so much time in jail; whose position was that of a heavenly luminary along with the heroes Ullashkar, Kanai, Barin, and Upendra;[1] who had read through the second chapter of the Gita and had set his sights on continuing to the last chapter—she hadn't a convenient time for him, either. What a great sacrifice!

One day for some reason her group had dwindled. In order to maintain the heat of her enthusiasm, I said, "Amiya, there's no such thing for you as individuals; for you it's a present generation." She received my remark silently and soberly. Since going to jail my sense of humor had flowed inward; those who did not know me thought from my outward behavior that I was very stuffy.

I lay alone in bed, looked at the ceiling, and thought, I'm through with unreliable friends.

All at once I remembered a stray dog that had appeared from somewhere and sought shelter in a corner of my veranda. His body was shaggy; beneath his ancient hide there was no meat on his bones; he was half dead. With extreme loathing I chased him away. Now I wondered why I had regarded him with such strong feelings. Not because he was a stray dog, but because from head to tail he had the look of being at death's door. His presence was a sour note in the chorus of life; his illness was an impertinence. It occurred to me that he and I were similar. The stream of life flowed by on all sides, and my incapacitation was something that stood still, damming up the current. I was demanding, "Sit down beside me and keep quiet." Life demanded, "Get out into the middle of things." The illness that incapacitated me was trying to make a captive of a healthy individual; this was a crime.

[1] Martyrs of the Independence Movement.

Therefore I decided that then and there I would relinquish my claims upon this world, and I opened up the Gita. No sooner had I reached the point of the higher poise, my mind having abandoned the conflict between illness and health, than I perceived that someone was touching my feet in respect. My eyes turned from the Gita, and I saw a girl who was one of the country cousins adopted by my aunt. I knew that I had seen her from afar and remembered her as quite ordinary. I didn't know anything specific about her; I didn't even know her name. With her veil over her head, she began slowly to stroke my feet.

Then I recalled that now and then she came like a shadow to the corner of my doorway and then went away. I suppose she lacked courage to enter the room. When I had had a slight headache, when my body ached, she had been well aware of it from afar. Now she had cast shame aside, had come in the room, and sat there touching my feet in respect. I had once assumed sufferings and offered them up to womanhood in general to save one woman from humiliation; perhaps this girl came in behalf of all Bengali women to offer oblation at my feet. I had been garlanded by many organizations when I got out of jail, but today I received this tribute from an unknown hand in an isolated room. The gesture went straight to my heart. Although I aspired to the highest level of detachment,[2] the long-dry eyes of this jail-hardened man began to fill with tears. I have already said that I was not in the habit of being waited upon. I sharply rebuked anyone who, with the best of intentions, began to massage my feet. Now I didn't even have the courage to refuse this service.

Cousins like this girl were my aunt's colleagues in her daily work and worship. Without them she could not have discharged all her various religious duties. Amiya was in charge of everything in this house except the worship room. She neither knew nor tried to learn its procedure. My aunt thought that when Amiya became well educated she would be married into a family that did not observe strict orthodox customs, from which Brahmans returned empty-handed and unrevered. Amiya's situation was regrettable but what else could she do? Who would completely redeem the daughter from the father's sin? Therefore, my aunt did not prevent

[2] Referred to in the Gita.

Amiya's steering a leisurely course across to the shore of modern unconventionality.

Amiya had always stood first in her class in mathematics and in English. For years she had come from the missionary school wearing frocks, her braided hair swinging, and carrying off four or five prizes. If she ever came out second in the examinations, she would go back to her bedroom, close the door, and weep copious tears. What was more, she would go on a hunger strike. Soliciting success from the god of examinations, she was absorbed for a considerable time in her own form of worship. Finally, she became dedicated to the creed of a noncooperator and passed over into the first class of those who forsook the god of examinations. As she had once collected passing grades, she was now unsurpassed in collecting failing grades. She had been famous for her academic record; when she gave up academic efforts her fame increased. Now all those prizes she collected moved, spoke, wept, and wrote poetry.

Needless to say, Amiya had little respect for my aunt's adopted village girls. At that time the refugee home was more in need of inmates than of contributions, and Amiya constantly asked my aunt to send these girls there.

My aunt said, "What a way to talk. They aren't waifs. What am I here for? Whether they are orphans or not, girls want a home. Why keep them in a house where they're packed up in bales with labels on them? If you're so full of compassion why not give up your room?"

At any rate, when this girl lowered her head and massaged my feet, I was bashful and flustered, kept a newspaper in front of my face, and ran my eyes over the advertisements. Just then Amiya suddenly and inopportunely arrived; she had written a new commentary appropriate in a new era to the ceremony of the anointing of brothers' foreheads. She wanted to circulate that in English. Naturally, she came to me for help. The circle of devotees was very excited over this original idea for a composition; they were preparing to celebrate it with great pomp.

As soon as she saw the girl engaged in waiting on me, Amiya's expression became very grim. If her nationally renowned big brother was rather like a god, was there any lack of people to serve him? There were so many others around, so how could this . . .

She couldn't stand it. She said, "Brother, did you ask Harimati——"

Before she finished the question I tossed back, "There's a bad pain in my feet."

I had gone to jail to save a girl from a police sergeant's insult. Now I was telling a lie in order to protect one girl from the wrath of another. And this time also retribution began. Amiya sat down near my feet. Harimati spoke to her in a soft, hesitant voice; Amiya contorted her face maliciously and did not reply. Harimati quietly got up and left. Then Amiya took charge of my feet. What a mess I was in! How could I say, "It's not necessary. I don't like it!" The complete autonomy that I had always maintained with regard to my feet now seemed to collapse.

Wriggling in my seat, I said, "Amiya, give me what you've written. I'll translate that."

"Never mind now, brother. Your feet are aching. Don't you want them massaged a little?"

"No, why would my feet ache? Yes, yes, they do ache a little. Certainly, look here, Ami, your brothers' ceremony idea is really amazing. I can't imagine how you thought it up. What you have written is that the foreheads of brothers in the present age have become so immense, spreading through all Bengal, that they are no longer confined within the home—a very momentous statement. Give it here, I'll write it: 'With the advent of the present age, brother's brow, waiting for its auspicious anointment from the sisters of Bengal, has grown immensely beyond the narrowness of domestic privacy, beyond the boundaries of the individual home.' A pen would run mad with such an idea."

All at once Amiya stopped massaging my feet. I had a headache; I didn't feel like writing anymore; still, I took an aspirin and began to write.

The next afternoon when my servant, Jaladhara, was asleep; when the doorman at the portico was reading Tulsidas' *Ramayana;* when the little drum of the man with the dancing bear sounded from the intersection of the lane; when the tireless Amiya, the Lakshmi of the age, was out and about on her round of duty, a timid shadow appeared alone outside the doorway to the veranda. That girl wavered there, suddenly took a fan, sat down near my head, and began to fan me. The look on Amiya's face yesterday seemed to deprive her of courage to touch my feet today. For some time now a meeting had been in session to deal with homage to the brothers of the new Bengal. Amiya would be busy. Therefore I thought of saying that my feet

ached badly. It was good that I did not. While this lie
flickered through my mind, Amiya entered carrying the
quarterly report of the refugee home. Harimati's fan-wielding
came to a sudden stop; it was not hard to guess the
reason for the pounding of her heart and the pallor of her
pretty face. Her fan became very still in fear of this secretary
of the refugee home.

Amiya sat on one edge of the bed and spoke very sternly,
"Look here, brother, in our country there is provision
for lots of homeless girls to live with very good families,
yet it's not essential that all of them be placed in wealthy
homes. Poor girls, who are obliged to work in order to eat,
have nothing but trouble in trying to earn a living. If they
do respectable work, such as the work in our refugee home,
then——"

I realized that this hailstorm of a lecture aimed at me
was for the benefit of Harimati. I said, "In other words,
you'll conform to your own hobby, and the homeless girls
will conform to your orders. You'll be secretary of the
refugee home, and they will be its nurses! It would be better
to do the nursing yourself; you'll realize that that work
is beyond your capacity. It's easy to harry the orphans; it
is not easy to serve them. Demand of yourself, not of others."

I have the nature of a Kshatriya; sometimes I forget that
the way to conquer anger is not to get angry. The result
was that Amiya brought in Prasanna, another girl from my
aunt's group. Amiya placed her at my feet and said, "Brother's
feet ache, you massage them."

Prasanna began to massage my feet with befitting perseverance.
Was this wretched brother now to say candidly
that there was nothing wrong with his feet? How could he
admit that all this massaging only embarrassed him? I knew
in my heart that I would no longer be a bedridden invalid.
Better yet, I was made the chairman of the committee for
homage to brothers in the new age. The breeze from the
fan slowly died. Harimati clearly perceived that the weapon
was aimed at her. Using Prasanna to get rid of her was
an approach known as "picking one thorn with another."
Soon she laid down the fan and arose. The head that had
been near my feet bowed in respect and went away.

Again I opened the Gita. Still, between stanzas I peeped
toward the crack in the door, but that fleeting shadow was
gone. Prasanna now came regularly, and after her came

the other girls who had gathered to wait upon Amiya's renowned patriot brother. Amiya had arranged for them to
take turns at my constant nursing. One day I heard that
Harimati, without a word to anyone, left Calcutta and went
to her own village home.

On the twelfth of the month my editor friend came and
said, "What's going on? Surely you're not joking? Is this
your harrowing experience?"

I laughed and replied, "Won't it do for Puja?"

"Certainly not! This is mighty flimsy stuff."

The editor was not to blame. Since I had been in prison
my tears flow inward. People who do not know me think
I am rather flippant.

The story was returned to me.

Just then, along came Anil. He said, "I won't be able to
tell you this. Read this letter."

The letter was to Amiya, his goddess, the Lakshmi of
the age, and it informed her that he wished to marry her.
It also said that Amiya was not averse to the proposal.

Then I had to tell him the facts about Amiya's birth.
This was not easy, but I knew that Anil always professed
compassion and complete respect for casteless persons.

"The sin of the ancestor was removed when she was
born," I told him. "You all see that plainly in Amiya's life.
She is like a lotus. There is no touch of mud anywhere."

The society for homage to the brothers of the new Bengal
met no more. The homage was ready, but the forehead had
run away. I was told, furthermore, that Anil had left Calcutta and had gone to Comilla to do propaganda work for
the Independence Movement.

Amiya is preparing to reenter college. In the meantime,
my aunt has returned from the pilgrimage, and my feet are
released from the multiple bonds of service.

1925

BALAI

Human life is said to be a culmination in the history of living beings. Hidden traces of the nature of various animals appear in humans. In fact, we call that element human that has integrated all our animal instincts; it puts our tigers and cows in the same pen, our snakes and mongooses are caged together. A musical structure called a *ragini,* for instance, transforms its single notes into harmony. Thenceforth, they are no longer chaotic. But a certain note predominates in the song; sometimes it is the fourth, sometimes the sharp third note, sometimes the fifth.

My nephew Balai—the notes of nature somehow have become predominant in his makeup. From early childhood it was his habit to stare silently, observing, motionless. When black clouds piled in layers in the eastern sky, the moist wind seemed to bring alive in his whole being the smell of the forest in July. When the rain fell heavily, his whole body listened to the sound. In the evening, when the sun's rays began to slant, he went to the rooftop terrace and walked about, his body naked; he seemed to gather something in from the whole sky. When the mango trees budded in late February, a deep delight, as of some unexpressed memory, stirred in his blood. In March, his inmost being expanded in every direction like the blossoming sal forest, filled to the brim and touched with vivid color. Then, sitting alone, he would be moved to talk to himself, somehow patching together all the stories he had heard. The same pair of birds had lived for years in the hollow of an ancient banyan tree; he made a story out of that. Big eyes constantly staring, the boy could not express his feelings. Therefore, he thought much more than he spoke.

Once I took him to the mountains. He was overjoyed to see that the thick green grass in front of our house flowed down to the foot of the hill. To him the covering of grass did not seem static; it was a tumbling game, continually rolling. He himself used to go rolling down over the grass; with his whole being he became part of it. As he rolled, the grass-blades tickled the back of his neck and he would burst into laughter.

After it had rained in the night the unripened gold of the morning sunlight filtered among the mountain peaks and fell upon the pine trees. Without letting anyone know, he would walk slowly beneath the still shadows of those pines, standing alone and wondering. He was filled with a sense of eeriness, as if he could see men who lived inside those huge trees. They said nothing, but they seemed to know everything. They were like the grandfathers of all time: "Once upon a time there was a king. . . ." They belonged to that time.

His dreamy eyes not only turned upward; many a time I saw him wandering about in my garden, searching for something on the ground. He had an endless curiosity about the new sprouts that thrust their heads toward the light. Every day he bent low over them as if asking, "What next? What next? What next?" They were his ever-unconcluded stories. How could he ever describe his rapport with the tender, newly sprung leaves? Perhaps they also were anxious to ask him questions. Perhaps they said, "What is your name?" Perhaps they said, "Where has your mother gone?" Balai answered himself, "I have no mother."

It hurt him deeply if someone picked the flowers. He understood that no one else would understand this hesitancy of his. Therefore, he tried to hide his distress. Boys of his age threw stones at the trees to bring down the plums, but as he could not say a word in protest, he turned his face away. His friends teased him by running about inside the garden and hitting the trees with sticks; all at once they would snap a branch from the bakula tree; he felt ashamed to weep lest someone think he was crazy.

His most trying day was the day when the grass cutter came to work, for Balai walked about daily in the grass, looking it over. There were a few small creepers with nameless purple and yellow flowers, extremely tiny; here and there was a nightshade plant, in the heart of its blue, blue flower a tiny golden drop; elsewhere, close to the fence, was a *kalmegh* shrub; somewhere else, some herb plants; there were beautiful leaves on the plants sprouted from the *neem-*

fruit seeds discarded by the birds. Every scrap of this was ruthlessly weeded out. These were not the cultivated garden plants; no one listened to their complaint.

Sometimes Balai came and sat on his aunt's lap, threw his arms around her neck, and said, "Please ask that grass cutter not to cut my plants."

His aunt would reply, "Balai, what a silly thing to say. That is all a jungle, how can we let it go?"

For a long time Balai had been able to understand that some of this sorrow was his alone; it was shared by none of his fellow humans.

The day that the newborn soil came forth from the ocean's womb, when the future forests of the world uttered their first cry, this boy's real age was ten million years. On that day there were no beasts, no birds, none of the tumult of life. Stone and mud and water were everywhere.

The tree came first along the road of time. Saluting the sun with joined hands, it said, "I will stay. I will survive. I am the eternal traveler. I will be the pilgrim to the endless blossoming of life, from one death to another, in sunshine and rain, by day and by night."

This cry of the trees still surges from forest to forest, on the mountains, on the plains. In their very branches and leaves the earth's life-force keeps saying, "I will stay, I will stay." This mute nurse of all life has milked the heavens from time immemorial, gathering vigor, delight, and beauty for the world's storehouse. Night and day she proclaims skyward the earth's eager message, "I will stay, I will stay." Somehow or other Balai had managed to feel in his blood this message of life. So we often smiled over it.

One morning when I was absorbed in reading the newspaper, Balai hastily pulled me out to the garden. He showed me a certain plant and said, "Uncle, what plant is this?"

I saw a tiny cottonwood seedling that had sprouted in the middle of the garden path.

Alas, Balai made a great mistake in showing it to me. This seedling had caught Balai's attention when it was ever so small, as with the first babbling of a child. From then on, he watered it daily, deliberately, from his own hand. Morning and evening, regularly and unfailingly, he examined it for signs of growth. The cottonwood tree grows rapidly, but it could not compete with Balai's eagerness. Seeing its lush foliage when it was about two feet tall, he thought that this was a remarkable tree, just as the child's first sign of intelligence makes the mother think that the child is re-markable. Balai thought that he would astonish me with it.

I said, "I must tell the gardener to pull this out."

Balai was startled. What a terrible thing to say! He said, "No, Uncle, I beg you, don't cut it down."

"What you are saying doesn't make sense," I replied. "This is growing right in the middle of the path. When it gets big, the cotton will fly about and make everyone un-comfortable."

This motherless child went to his aunt when he couldn't argue with me. He sat on her lap, put his arms around her neck, and sobbed, "Auntie, you tell Uncle not to cut down the tree!"

He had hit upon the right approach. His aunt called to me, "Listen, my dear, why don't you keep his tree?"

I kept it. If Balai had not shown me the seedling, per-haps I would not have noticed it. But now I noticed it every day. In a year's time the tree grew shamelessly tall. As for Balai, he poured out more affection on this tree than on any other.

The tree looked more ridiculous every day. Standing where it had no business to be, in utter disregard it drew itself up to its full height. Whoever saw it wondered why it was there. Several more times its death sentence was pronounced. I tempted Balai by offering to give him in ex-change several fine young rosebushes.

"Really," I said, "if you are so fond of the cottonwood tree, I'll have another seedling planted by the fence. It would look lovely."

But at any mention of cutting, Balai would start in alarm and his aunt would say, "It doesn't look as bad as all that."

At this point my older brother returned after nearly ten years in England, where he had gone, impelled, I think, by the death of my sister-in-law, to study engineering. He left Balai to grow up in my childless home. Now he took his son away in order to educate him after the British fashion. First he went to Simla; then he considered taking Balai to England.

Balai, in tears, left his aunt's care. Our house became empty.

Two years went by. Balai's aunt shed tears in secret and went into Balai's empty bedroom to arrange and rearrange a torn slipper, his cracked rubber ball, his animal picture-storybook. She would sit thinking that Balai must have out-grown all these mementos by now.

One day I noticed that the wretched cottonwood tree had grown bigger and bigger; its unreasonableness could be tolerated no longer. I had it cut down.

Just about that time Balai wrote to his aunt from Simla: "Auntie, please send me a photograph of my cottonwood tree."

He had planned to come and see us before he left for England, but that had not been possible. So Balai wanted the picture of his friend.

His aunt called me and said, "Listen, my dear, bring a photographer."

"Why?" I asked.

She showed me the letter written in Balai's immature hand.

I said, "That tree has just been cut down."

Balai's aunt did not eat anything for two days and for many days she did not speak a word to me. When Balai's father took him away from her, it was like ripping away the cord. Now his uncle had removed forever her Balai's beloved tree. Her whole household was stricken and a wound cut deep into her heart.

That tree was the very image of Balai, the boon companion of his soul.

1928

THE ARTIST

(Chitrakar)

Govinda came to Calcutta after graduation from high school in Mymensingh. His widowed mother's savings were meager, but his own unwavering determination was his greatest resource. "I *will* make money," he vowed, "even if I have to give my whole life to it." In his terminology, wealth was always referred to as *pice*. In other words he had in mind a very concrete image of something that could be seen, touched, and smelled; he was not greatly fascinated with fame, only with the very ordinary *pice*, eroded by circulation from market to market, from hand to hand, the tarnished *pice*, the *pice* that smells of copper, the original form of Kuvera, who assumes the assorted guises of silver, gold, securities, and wills, and keeps men's minds in a turmoil.

After traveling many tortuous roads and getting muddied repeatedly in the process, Govinda had now arrived upon the solidly paved embankment of his wide and free-flowing stream of money. He was firmly seated in the manager's chair at the MacDougal Gunnysack Company. Everyone called him MacDulal.[1]

When Govinda's lawyer-brother, Mukunda, died, he left behind a wife, a four-year-old son, a house in Calcutta, and some cash savings. In addition to this property there was some debt; therefore, provision for his family's needs depended upon frugality. Thus his son, Chunilal, was brought up in circumstances that were undistinguished in comparison with those of the neighbors.

Mukunda's will gave Govinda entire responsibility for this family. Ever since Chunilal was a baby, Govinda had bestowed spiritual initiation upon his nephew with the sacred words: "Make money."

The main obstacle to the boy's initiation was his mother, Satyabati. She said nothing outright; her opposition showed in her behavior. Art had always been her hobby. There was no limit to her enthusiasm for creating all sorts of original and decorative things from flowers, fruits and leaves, even foodstuffs, from paper and cloth cutouts, from clay and flour, from berry juices and the juices of other fruits, from *jaba*- and *shiuli*-flower stems. This activity brought her considerable grief, because anything unessential or irrational has the character of flash floods in July: it has considerable mobility, but in relation to the utilitarian concerns of life it is like a stalled ferry. Sometimes there were invitations to visit relatives; Satyabati forgot them and spent the time in her bedroom with the door shut, kneading a lump of clay. The relatives said, "She's terribly stuck-up." There was no satisfactory reply to this. Mukunda had known, even on

---

[1] A play on *dulal*, which can mean darling and spoiled child.

the basis of his bookish knowledge, that value judgments can be made about art too. He had been thrilled by the noble connotations of the word "art," but he could not conceive of its having any connection with the work of his own wife.

This man's nature had been very equable. When his wife squandered time on unessential whims, he had smiled at it with affectionate delight. If anyone in the household made a slighting remark, he had protested immediately. There had been a singular self-contradiction in Mukunda's makeup; he had been an expert in the practice of law, but it must be conceded that he had had no worldly wisdom with regard to his household affairs. Plenty of money had passed through his hands, but since it had not preoccupied his thoughts, it had left his mind free. Nor could he have tyrannized over his dependents in order to get his own way. His living habits had been very simple; he had never made any unreasonable demands for the attention or services of his relatives.

Mukunda had immediately silenced anyone in the household who cast an aspersion upon Satyabati's disinterest in housework. Now and then, on his way home from court, he would stop at Radhabazar to buy some paints, some colored silk and colored pencils, and stealthily he would go and arrange them on the wooden chest in his wife's bedroom. Sometimes, picking up one of Satyabati's drawings, he would say, "Well, this one is certainly very beautiful."

One day he had held up a picture of a man, and since he had it upside down, he had decided that the legs must be a bird's head. He had said, "Satu, this should be framed —what a marvelous picture of a stork!" Mukunda had gotten a certain delight out of thinking of his wife's art work as child's play, and the wife had taken a similar pleasure in her husband's judgment of art. Satyabati had known perfectly well that she could not hope for so much patience, so much indulgence, from any other family in Bengal. No other family would have made way so lovingly for her overpowering devotion to art. So, whenever her husband had made extravagant remarks about her painting, Satyabati could scarcely restrain her tears.

One day Satyabati lost even this rare good fortune. Before his death her husband had realized one thing quite clearly: the responsibility for his debt-ridden property must be left in the hands of someone astute enough to skillfully steer even a leaky boat to the other shore. This is how Satyabati and her son came to be placed completely under Govinda's care. From the very first day Govinda made it plain to her that the *pice* was the first and foremost thing in life. There was such profound degradation in his advice that Satyabati would shrink with shame.

Nevertheless, the worship of money continued in diverse forms in their daily life. If there had been some modesty about it, instead of such constant discussion, it wouldn't have been so bad. Satyabati knew in her heart that all of this lowered her son's standard of values, but there was nothing to do but endure it. Since those delicate emotions endowed with uncommon dignity are the most vulnerable, they are very easily hurt or ridiculed by rude or insensitive people.

The study of art requires all sorts of supplies. Satyabati had received these for so long without even asking that she had felt no reticence with regard to them. Amid the new circumstances in the family she felt terribly ashamed to charge all these unessential items to the housekeeping budget. So she would save money by economizing on her own food and have the supplies purchased and brought in secretly. Whatever work she did was done furtively, behind closed doors. She was not afraid of a scolding, but the stares of insensitive observers embarrassed her.

Now Chuni was the only spectator and critic of her artistic activity. Gradually he became a participant. He began to feel its intoxication. The child's offense could not be concealed, since it overflowed the pages of his notebook onto the walls of the house. There were stains on his face, on his hands, on the cuffs of his shirt. Indra, the king of the gods, does not spare even the soul of a little boy in the effort to tempt him away from the worship of money.

On the one hand the restraint increased, on the other hand the mother collaborated in the violations. Occasionally the head of the company would take his office manager, Govinda, along on business trips out of town. Then the mother and son would get together in unrestrained joy. This was the absolute extreme of childishness! They drew pictures of animals that God has yet to create. The likeness of the dog would get mixed up with that of the cat. It was difficult to distinguish between fish and fowl. There was no way to preserve all these creations; their traces had to be thoroughly obliterated before the head of the house returned. Only Brahma, the Creator, and Rudra, the Destroyer, witnessed the creative delight of these two persons; Vishnu, the heavenly Preserver, never arrived.

The compulsion for artistic creation ran strong in Satyabati's family. There was an older nephew, Rangalal, who rose overnight to fame as an artist. That is to say, the connoisseurs of the land roared with laughter at the unorthodoxy of his art. Since their stamp of imagination did not coincide with his, they had a violent scorn for his talent. But curiously enough, his reputation thrived upon disdain and flourished in this atmosphere of opposition and mockery. Those who imitated him most took it upon themselves to prove that the man was a hoax as an artist, that there were obvious defects even in his technique.

This much-maligned artist came to his aunt's home one day, at a time when the office manager was absent. After persistent knocking and shoving at the door he finally got inside and found that there was nowhere to set foot on the floor. The cat was out of the bag.

"It is obvious," said Rangalal, "that the image of creation has emerged anew from the soul of the artist; this is not random scribbling. He and that god who creates form are the same age. Get out all the drawings and show them to me."

Where should they get the drawings? That artist who draws pictures all over the sky in myriad colors, in light and shadow, calmly discards his mists and mirages. Their creations had gone the same way. With an oath Rangalal said to his aunt, "From now on, I'll come and get whatever you make."

There came another day when the office manager had not returned. Since morning the sky had brooded in the shadows of July; it was raining. No one monitored the hands of the clock and no one wanted to know about them. Today Chuni began to draw a picture of a sailing boat while his mother was in the prayer room. The waves of the river looked like a flock of hungry seals just on the point of swallowing the boat. The clouds seemed to cheer them on and float their shawls overhead, but the seals were not conventional seals, and it would be no exaggeration to say of the clouds: "Light and mist merge in the watery waste." In the interests of truth it must be said that if boats were built like this one, insurance companies would never assume such risks. Thus the painting continued; the sky-artist drew fanciful pictures, and inside the room the wide-eyed boy did the same.

No one realized that the door was open. The office manager appeared. He roared in a thunderous voice, "What's going on?"

The boy's heart jumped and his face grew pale. Now Govinda perceived the real reason for Chunilal's examination errors in historical dates. Meanwhile the crime became all the more evident as Chunilal tried unsuccessfully to hide the drawing under his shirt. As Govinda snatched the picture away, the design he saw on it further astonished him. Errors in historical dates would be preferable to this. He tore the picture to pieces. Chunilal burst out crying.

From the prayer room Satyabati heard the boy's weeping, and she came running. Both Chunilal and the torn pieces of the picture were on the floor. Govinda went on enumerating the reasons for his nephew's failure in the history examination and suggesting dire remedies.

Satyabati had never said a word about Govinda's behavior toward them. She had quietly endured everything, remembering that this was the person on whom her husband had relied. Now her eyes were wet with tears, and shaking with anger, she said hoarsely, "Why did you tear up Chuni's picture?"

Govinda said, "Doesn't he have to study? What will become of him in the future?"

"Even if he becomes a beggar in the street," answered Satyabati, "he'll be better off in the future. But I hope he'll never be like you. May his pride in his God-given talent be more than your pride in *pices*. This is my blessing for him, a mother's blessing."

"I can't neglect my responsibility," said Govinda. "I will not tolerate this. Tomorrow I'll send him to a boarding school; otherwise, you'll ruin him."

The office manager returned to the office. The rain fell in torrents and the streets flowed with water.

Holding her son's hand, Satyabati said, "Let's go, dear."

Chuni said, "Go where, Mother?"

"Let's get out of this place."

The water was knee-deep at Rangalal's door. Satyabati came in with Chunilal. She said, "My dear boy, you take charge of him. Keep him from the worship of money."

1929

SCANDAL
(Badnam)

1

Kring, kring, kring! rang the bicycle bell. Inspector Vijaya jumped off the bicycle at the front door. He was dressed in a short jacket and shorts with a belted waist, and he had the quick gait of a busy man. He banged the knocker, and the lady of the house opened the door.

He had scarcely entered the room when she shouted, "I can't stand any more of this! Night after night I keep your dinner warm for hours. You've caught so many thieves and robbers—you even pick up the honest and the innocent—and you spend all your time chasing after this Anil Mitter. He appears right in front of you, thumbs his nose at you, and disappears no one knows where. The whole country is laughing at you, as if this were a circus."

"What luck that he keeps me under surveillance!" said the inspector. "I know he's on bail, but he has no permit to go anywhere else without reporting to the police. So the other day he informed me by letter: 'Inspector, Sir: Don't be afraid. I'll return as soon as the meeting is over.' No one knows where the meeting is being held. He's playing a trick on the police."

Soudamini, the inspector's wife, replied, "Then listen to what I have to tell you tonight; you'll be stunned to hear this. What defiance, what bravado this fellow has!

"It was two o'clock in the morning; I was still keeping your meal warm and was feeling drowsy. Suddenly startled, I find your criminal Anil before me. He touched my feet in respect and said, 'Sister, today is the day of the Brothers' Ceremony,[1] do you remember? I have come for the anoint-

---

[1] The Brothers' Ceremony, a family festival in Bengal. Sisters, on this day, put an "auspicious mark" on their brothers' forehead to signify welfare.

ment. My own sister is now in Chittagong, engaged in some sort of conspiracy. But I must have my anointment. I won't give it up. Here I sit.'

"To tell you the truth, my heart was filling with affection. It seemed to me that for one night I had found my brother. He continued, 'Sister, the last three days I have been wandering in the forests, half fed. Today I'll have your anointment and food cooked by your hand, and then I'll disappear.'

"I gladly fed him the meal I had saved for you. I told him, 'Get out of here right now; it's time for him to come.' The fellow said, 'Don't be afraid, he has gone to look for me at Chitalbede. It will be at least three A.M. before he returns. I can sit and take your blessings before I leave.' As he said this he took the *pan* that I had prepared for you and popped it into his mouth and even added, 'The inspector smokes Havana cigars, so let me have one of those. I'll smoke it on my way to meet the party members; they are holding a meeting tonight.' And then that criminal of yours, easily, fearlessly, gave me the name of the place."

"May I know that name?" asked the inspector.

"Your asking me such a question," answered Sodu, "proves that your criminal understands me better than you do. Anyway, I gave him one of your favorite Havana cigars. He lit it and calmly took my blessings and went away puffing."

Vijaya had been sitting. Now he jumped up and said, "Tell me which direction he went! Where are they holding their meeting?"

Sodu got up and said, "What! How can you ask such a thing? I am your wife, but is that any reason why I should act as a spy? If I lose my integrity in your own home, then how can you trust me anymore?"

The inspector knew his wife well. She was a very stubborn woman; she would not give in. He heaved a deep sigh, sat down, and said resignedly, "Alas, I've even lost this good chance." He sat twirling his princely moustache, and from time to time he muttered with impatience. The meal was prepared a second time; it was a dish of rice and lentils that he did not relish.

2

"What's the matter?" Sodu asked her husband a few days

later. "You're doing a victory dance! Today your feet barely touch the ground. Have you won over the District Superintendent of Police?"

"I certainly have."

"Let me hear about it."

"Our own spy, Nitai Chakravarty, is assigned to that group
of rebels. Today he let us know that they will have a big
meeting in the Mochkathi Forest. We're arranging to sur-
round it. It's a deep forest, but we've already secretly sent
an inspector and had it thoroughly searched. There will be
no more hidden loopholes for escape."

"There will be big loopholes in your strategy. You have
often made people laugh, why do it again? Why don't you
give up?"

"What a thing to say, Sodu. I'll never get such a chance
again."

"I tell you, listen to me, all that talk about the Mochkathi
Forest is nonsense. He's roaming around your own area.
He'll snap his fingers in your face and disappear. I tell
you this for a fact."

"Of course, if you inform him secretly about our plans,
then everything is possible."

"Look, don't try to be so clever. You've done it many
times, but if you want to be that way with your own wife—"

The rest of the sentence was cut off as she covered her
eyes with the end of her sari.

"Sodu," said the inspector, "I've noticed that you can't
take even the least little joke on this topic."

"That's true. The policeman's humor seems to have a
sharp edge. Now why don't you eat something?"

"Yes, I will. There's time. The strategy has been fixed."

"Look, I'll tell you the truth. If I knew what your policemen whisper together, I'd consider it my duty to tell him."

"Terrible! Have you heard anything?"

"One must keep one's eyes and ears open, and information does get in."

"Where does it go from there?"

"It follows the poet Chandidas: 'Entering by the ears, it
touches the secret heart and sets it aflutter.' "

"You seem to win with your wits, but it's hard to get
your real intentions."

"If you had that much imagination, you wouldn't be a
police inspector. The government would have appointed you

a world benefactor to spread the net of your lectures from coast to coast."

"Good heavens, the woman about whom we've heard rumors is right inside my own house."

"Listen, the dog is yelping outside. Let me go and calm him down with food."

The inspector became very angry. "I'll go out and shoot that dog at once."

Sodu pulled at her husband's coat. "No, I won't let you go."

"Why?"

"The moment you step out, the dog will fly at your throat. It's a very fierce dog. It obeys only me."

"We have heard, Sodu, that that fellow Anil is a ventriloquist. He can imitate the sound of any animal. How do I know that it isn't he who calls you at two A.M. every night?"

Sodu blazed up. "And now you're suspecting me! Here's your household; I'm going to my sister's house."

As she said this she got up.

"Where are you going? What a problem! So I'm not allowed to joke with my own wife. What other woman can I joke with? And how could I keep peace if I did?"

With this he forced her to sit down. Sodu began to wipe her eyes.

"Ah, why are you crying?" he asked. "And all because of a simple joke!"

"I can't stand these jokes of yours, I tell you."

"All right, all right, that's enough. Now you can relax and feed your dog. This dog eats nothing but cutlets, and it isn't satisfied without a dish of pudding. I can never understand, Sodu, why you make so much fuss over an ordinary dog."

"You menfolk wouldn't understand," she replied. "A childless woman will love any living creature. If I don't see the dog for a day, I'm afraid someone has stolen it. That's why I guard it so carefully."

"But I tell you, Sodu, no animal can survive so much pampering."

"But let it live happily as long as it's alive."

Vijaya settled for a nap. Later, the police assembled and went toward the Mochkathi Forest, each following a separate road. It was a long journey, and it took them all night to go there and return.

The next morning at seven the inspector returned from the forest looking tired and sat down heavily on the sofa. "Sodu," he said, "they have given us the slip. You were right. The police surrounded the forest, but there wasn't a soul in it. They set up a hue and cry and shouted, 'Come out wherever you are; otherwise we'll shoot.' They fired many blanks, but there was no response. They entered the forest very carefully and searched it thoroughly. By then the sun was coming up. They yelled, 'Get hold of Nitai, that scoundrel!' Nitai simply was not there. A letter was found with only these words: 'The criminal is safe. Give my respects to Sister. Anil.' There's no end to his mischief! Why involve you in it? The next time——"

"What next time? What do you mean by 'next'? Can't the wife of a policeman also be the sister of the accused? Must all the relationships in this world bear the stamp of government approval? I won't say any more. Now lie down a little and get some sleep."

It was two o'clock in the afternoon when he awoke. After bathing and eating his midday meal, Vijaya chewed his *pan* and said, "What shall I say about that fellow's tricks? He and his followers have spread the rumor that he practices Kumbhak Yoga late at night and sits in midair. Many people are said to have seen it with their own eyes. The villagers believe he is a successful saint and bears the sign of the god Bholanath himself. No Hindu dares lay hands on him. Food is left on the doorsills for him, a regular offering.

"He doesn't show up in the morning anymore. A Hindu policeman won't even approach him. A subinspector captured him after that riot at Hijlakandi. Within a week the officer's wife died of smallpox. As far as they were concerned, that settled it. So this time, when there was no trace of him in Mochkathi, the policemen decided that he could make himself invisible at will. He left one bit of evidence in a marshy spot: footprints two feet apart and a foot and a half long. The Hindu policemen were practically ready to bow down and worship those footprints!

"It is difficult to get this man. I want to enlist Muslim policemen, but it would be fatal to infect the Muslims, too, with this fanaticism. The newspapers have sent reporters to Mochkathi. There's a great debate as to who left those large footprints. Now, what can we do about this fellow? He seems to have used his release on bail to dope everyone.

"All this time stories spread about curious shadows seen in different places. Somewhere they found a tuft of hair belonging to the great god Mahadeva, and my devout constables are all agog. No one has the courage to admit that it was only a few strands of fiber. A regular storm of rumors developed. A rich Marwari gave thirty thousand rupees to build a temple at the site of those footprints. A former district judge turned up as a disciple. The criminal Anil sat with him and began a scriptural discourse; the fellow is a real scholar. So the cult keeps growing. Once his bail expires it will be difficult to get witnesses to speak against him. This is our big problem.

"That's not all, Sodu. There's another crisis. My cousin Girish, who is police inspector in Hatibandha District, had to arrest and handcuff a Kulin Brahman's son. Since then, the villagers have been trying to make Girish an outcaste. His daughter will soon be old enough to marry. When a suitor appears, the villagers break up the match. If a groom is found, then no priest is available. A priest from a distant village was engaged, but he suddenly ran away. This time they've hit on a solution. A holy man from Vrindavan turned up and settled in the house of my head constable. We all try to please this holy man by feeding worthy Brahmans,[2] and he has agreed to perform the ceremony. Now we have to save him from the villagers. Sodu, you give us a hand in this matter."

"Of course I shall!" Sodu replied. "That's only my duty. Ah, our own Girish's daughter, our Minu, she has done no harm. She ought to be married off. Bring your holy man from Vrindavan. I know how to take good care of these swamis."

The holy man from Vrindavan arrived. His white beard flowed down to his chest like that of the saint Narada. Sodu bowed at his feet; the neighbors could scarcely keep from laughing at this show of devotion. An elderly woman neighbor smiled ironically and said, "Why this sudden respect for holiness?"

Sodu laughed and replied, "Devotion surges up whenever there is need for it. These holy men almost melt when you

---

[2] The feeding of Brahmans is considered to be an auspicious act.

touch their feet with respect. I must keep up this reverence until Minu's marriage."

The sound of conch shells and the wedding cry of "Ulu!"[3] accompanied the bridegroom. The married women neighbors brought in the bride, who was dressed up like a doll bundled in a silken sari. The ceremony went through without a hitch. The bride and bridegroom touched the feet of the holy man, got up, and were ready to go into the inner courtyard; the holy man blessed Vijaya and the other members of the assemblage and said, "Sirs, now let me give you my news. I am not really a priest. My real profession is well known to all your police and constables. Now is the time for you to give me the priest's fee, but I can't wait. So before you bid me farewell, I'll take my leave."

The holy man removed his beard and moustache in the presence of everyone and in three jumps crossed the courtyard wall and disappeared.

The whole assembly stared. Vijaya was speechless.

After the marriage feast, when the neighbors had gone home and the bride and groom had retired to the bridal chamber, Sodu said to her husband, "Why are you upset? No matter how the situation was handled, the holy man has made it easier for you by disappearing. Now we have to prepare for the second part of the marriage ceremony. Don't waste your time pursuing thieves and criminals. But did you get any clues on that woman accomplice?"

"If only one woman was my problem! Instead at least fifty women gather at my station every morning with offerings of rice and bananas. It's difficult to find out who all these women are."

"What! It doesn't look right to have so many women at your very door. Have you taken over the role of the holy man?"

"No, you'll be amazed at what he's done now. One day a policeman named Kishanlal came and announced that a stone had appeared on the road in front of the office. The women of the neighborhood were anointing that stone with vermilion and rubbing it with sandalwood. Some hoped for a child, some wished for a husband, some for my downfall. If we try to clear out this crowd, all the newspapers will yell that Hinduism is threatened. My Hindu policemen, too,

---

[3] Conch shells and the cry "Ulu!" are customary in a Hindu marriage.

are giving the stone five silver coins as an offering. Business was fine!

"At last people began asking who was pocketing the money. One day it was discovered that both the stone and the bag of coins had vanished. And that half-mad fellow had changed his costume and gone into hiding somewhere. The air is thick with rumors.

"Now my Hindu policemen are threatening us with a hunger strike. If there's any fresh breach of the peace over this, I will have to answer for it to everyone. That will finish me. What shall I take care of first?

"And that's not all. The other day Chhedilal came crashing into the police station. He wailed and declared that the one-armed deity had come roaring like a bull and chased him. So he gave up his job and became a holy man. He is sitting under a tree smoking hashish. How can we cope with a criminal when the women are all for him? He has convinced every last one."

Sodu laughed and said, "The more I hear of this story, the more it upsets me."

"Look here, don't you create fresh trouble."

"No, you needn't be afraid. I'm not so fortunate. Women have to be good housekeepers, and if their skill could be used for the good of the nation, it could be one hundred percent effective. Men are foolish. They call us women simple, guileless; we practice our womanly virtues under the cloak of such terms, and these fathers of infants are bewitched by our display. We are weak and guileless; we carry this reputation like the chain around the dog's neck, and you drag us along behind you. Why not tell the whole truth: when opportunity offers, we know how to be as tricky as you. We are not foolish enough to get cheated and not cheat in return.

"Old ladies say, 'Sodu is so good.' All they mean is, Sodu never gets tired of cooking, cleaning, running the house. We women enjoy our reputation only within these limits. Our countrymen are starving to death and the real men are being handcuffed, but we women go on practicing our great virtue of domesticity by cooking and washing up the utensils. I tell you, the only thing that will save us is becoming less pious and doing something worthwhile. Perhaps you will find some imperfections under our disguise, but these are the same imperfections left on a cooking utensil scorched by fire. These marks don't come from playing the game of comfort. We have hurt others, but we have been victims for a long time. Women have come into the world to deal with suffering, I can't treat it through housework. I'd like to burn all the heaped-up rubbish of our country with the fire of suffering. People will call us wicked instead of chaste and virtuous. That scandal will mark the forehead of your Sodu, and if you are a real man you will understand her pride."

"I've heard all this from you before," said the inspector. "Then the world goes on in the old way. Sometimes it is necessary to unburden the mind, so I listen and puff on my Havana cigar."

"Whatever happens, I know you'll forgive me, and that forgiveness is true manliness. It is like the footprint of Bhrigu on the chest of Krishna. I have surrendered to your power of forgiveness. I'm not flattering you; you have endless cares in your job as police inspector but you have always trusted me with your eyes closed, although I didn't always deserve it. Therefore I respect you; my respect is not built according to scripture."

"Enough, Sodu, you've said all you wanted to say. Now go and feed your dog; it's yelping and it won't let me sleep. I think I'll have to apply for a leave of absence from the office."

Smiling, Sodu said, "You can give up your inspectorship and become a holy man sitting under a tree. That will bring a big increase in your income, and I'll also get a share."

"You take everything so seriously. I don't like it."

"That's my nature. I can't worry about your criminals and robbers. My day is taken up with worrying about you. What else can I do? Shall I join in the laughter of the whole country? My countrymen have shed plenty of tears in your police station. At least now they have something to laugh at. And that's why everyone is blessing Anil with uplifted hands—everyone except you. Tell me how I can pretend to be worried."

3

A little later the inspector approached his wife again. "Look, Sodu, this time I need your help."

"When didn't you need my help?" asked Sodu. "That's why people call you henpecked. There are two kinds of henpecked husbands. The cowards can't stand up to their wives. The real men accept defeat without embarrassment. They don't know how to distrust, because they are above all that. Look at my advantage: I can trick you whenever and however I like, and you accept everything with closed eyes."

"Sodu, how candid you are!"

"It is all due to you, all due to you."

"Now then, listen to this important business; those other discussions can come later. This time I need your help in an official matter, or I won't be able to show my face. The police have learned for a fact that there is a woman nearby who is helping the revolutionaries in this area. Somehow she obtains information and forewarns Anil. She is quite a woman! They say that she is a widow in our neighborhood. No matter how, you must somehow find out who she is and make friends with her."

"So," replied Sodu, "at last you'll use me, too, for a spy. All right, that's how it will be. A woman may be used to capture another woman. Otherwise you'll lose face. I take this responsibility. In two days the whole mystery will be solved."

"Day after tomorrow will be the night of Shiva's worship," the inspector continued. "I have heard that Anil will spend the whole night in prayer and penance in the temple of Siddheswari. He is fearless, but also so religious that this woman couldn't possibly have stayed with him as a companion without some sort of Tantrik marriage."

"You and your policemen," said Sodu, "can stay in the background; I'll capture him. But don't go there before one A.M. If you do it too hurriedly, the whole thing will misfire."

When the clock struck one in the dark of the moon, two men were walking about barefooted in the silence. Vijaya stood at the door of the temple.

One man beckoned to him and whispered, "An old lady has gone inside the temple now. No doubt about it, she's the famous female yogi, Bhairavi. You can't see her by daylight. We've heard that after one o'clock at night she joins in the dance of Nataraja. A man who happened to see this has been mad ever since. Sir, we can't go in and arrest her. We won't even try to see her, we tell you. We've decided to go back to the barracks. Whatever you want to do, you have to do alone."

They left, one at a time. Then there was deep silence. However modern Vijaya might have been, we cannot say that he was not afraid. His heart began to flutter. From the door the hum of a female voice could be heard reciting a mantra: "I am worshiping him, the great god who is like a mountain of salvation, who is descended from the brilliant moon."

Vijaya's hair stood on end. He wondered what to do. After a while he plucked up his courage and pushed the broken door open. An earthen lamp flickered inside the temple. He saw his wife sitting with folded hands in front of Shiva's stone and Anil standing at one side like a stone statue. When Vijaya saw his wife he felt braver and burst out, "Sodu, so this is what you've been up to!"

"Yes, I am that woman whom you've been seeking for so long. I've come here tonight to reveal my identity. You know that once in a long while a real man appears in our country. Your one aim is to render such persons ineffective. Shame on our womanhood if the women of Bengal can't protect all these good sons of the country with our own lives.

"I've been pulling all these tricks behind your back for a long time. There is one whose command I have never been able to ignore; today, too, in this most difficult hour I must obey that command. I'll hand over this god to you and step aside. He has a protector greater than me. I know scandal about me will be all over the place in a few days. I'll bear that humiliation. Don't think you can get your wife off and send this man to jail by a separate indictment. I will back him up to the very end and accept the final penalty. You can live in peace. Don't worry. If you want, you can easily get another wife. Whatever else you do, don't pity me. You have never pitied those who are far greater than me. I will share that cruelty and take leave of you with my head high. With all my life I've served you and loved you. With all my life I've deceived you out of a sense of duty. I want you to know this. Perhaps I won't have another chance to say it."

Anil interrupted Sodu. "Vijayababu, today I have come to surrender to you. My revolutionary work is done. Don't be upset by what Sodu says. She is an extraordinary girl, born into our chaotic society. I have known her well, and that is why I tell you she is completely blameless. Our stern commitment to duty leaves no room for love, only for self-sacrifice. The rest of the world will know nothing about

Sodu, you can rest assured of that. You go home with her, and use the tunnel under the temple; I'll go from the other direction and give myself up to the police.

"There's one thing I'd like you to know: it's beyond your powers to confine me. I've memorized a song by Rabi Tagore:

> 'Have you the bond to bind me,
> To tie me down!' "

He sang this quickly in a foreign accent; the temple's foundations vibrated to the sound of his voice. The inspector was stunned.

"I've sung this song many times. I'll sing it again, and then I'll head for Afghanistan. I'll find the road, no matter what. I want you to know this. After a fortnight the newspapers will print in bold type: 'Anil the revolutionary escapes.'

"Now I pay you my respects."

Vijaya's hand trembled, the flashlight fell to the ground. He pressed his hands to his face and sat down in the dark. A gust of wind had extinguished the lamp.

1941

CONSEQUENCES

(Karmaphal)

1

Satish's aunt and uncle, Sukumari and Sashadhar, arrive. Satish's mother, Bidhukumari, scurries about welcoming them.

Bidhu: Come in, sister, and make yourself comfortable. What good deeds have I done to earn this chance to see Mr. Ray today? There is no way to get you here unless my sister comes.

Sashadhar: This simply shows how strict your sister's discipline is. She keeps an eye on me day and night.

Sukumari: That's right. Bidhu, you can't even sleep peacefully with such a jewel in the house.

Bidhu: That's because he snores!

Satish enters.

Sukumari: Shame on you, Satish, what kind of clothes are you wearing? Surely you don't go to school in a dhoti like this? Bidhu, what became of the suit I bought for him?

Bidhu: Oh, he tore that long ago.

Sukumari: Well, it would get torn. How long can one suit last when you're young? But is that any reason not to get new clothes? Everything is so peculiar at your house.

215

Bidhu: You know why, sister. It burns him up to see decent clothes on this boy. I think that if it weren't for me he would have sent the boy to school in a shawl and a waistband. Good heavens! I've never seen anyone with such outlandish taste!

Sukumari: You're quite right. Satish is the only son. Doesn't his father want to dress him up a little? I've never seen such a father. Satish, the day after tomorrow is Sunday. You come to our house; I'll get you some cloth from Rowley's for a suit. Ah, can't the young man want *something?*

Satish: What good will it do me, Auntie? Mr. Bhaduri's son goes to school with me and he has invited me to their house to play table tennis, but I don't have the right kind of clothes for that.

Sashadhar: It might be wise not to accept invitations to such places, Satish.

Sukumari: All right, all right, you needn't deliver a lecture. When he's your age——

Sashadhar: Then there will be someone else to lecture him. He won't have a chance to listen to the advice of an old uncle.

Sukumari: Well, sir, I can see what a fix you'd be in if you couldn't find anyone else to lecture.

Sashadhar: Why talk about it? It's better to leave that situation to the imagination.

Satish (looking offstage): No, no. You don't have to bring it here. I'm coming.

Satish exits.

Sukumari: Bidhu, why did Satish run off in such a hurry?

Bidhu: His food was being served on a brass dish. That's why the boy was embarrassed in front of you.

Sukumari: Well, the poor boy might well feel upset by such old-fashioned ways. Oh, Satish, listen, listen—your uncle will take you to Paleti's for ice cream. You go with him. My dear, why don't you go and get the boy some——

Satish (returning): Auntie, what could I wear to go there?

Bidhu: Why, you have a *chapkan*.

Satish: That's awful.

Sukumari: You may say what you like, Bidhu, it's a blessing that your son wasn't fated to inherit his father's taste. It's true; the *chapkan* always reminds me of a butler or an actor on a stage. There's no dress more uncivilized-looking.

Sashadhar: All this talk——

Sukumari: Should be whispered? Whom do we have to fear? Manmatha dresses his son according to his own taste, and we can't say a word!

Sashadhar: Confound it! I didn't say, stop talking. But all this discussion in front of Satish——

Sukumari: All right, all right. You go and take him to Paleti's.

Satish: No, Auntie, I can't go there wearing a *chapkan*.

Sukumari: There's Manmathababu. He'll start scolding Satish right away and get him all upset. The boy doesn't get a moment's peace from his father's nagging. Oh, Satish, you come with me, let's get away.

Sukumari and Satish exit.

Manmatha enters.

Bidhu (addressing Manmatha): Satish has been pestering me for several days about a watch. My sister gave him a silver one. I'm letting you know about it right now; you'll be angry if you hear about it later.

Bidhu goes out.

Manmatha: I'll be angry if I hear it beforehand. Sashadhar, you must take that watch back.

Sashadhar: You're quite a person. If I take it back, who'll answer for it when I get home?

Manmatha: No, Sashadhar, it's not a joke. I don't like all this.

Sashadhar: You don't like it! But you have put up with it. The laws of the universe are not made just for you.

Manmatha: If this concerned only myself I'd have put up with it without a word. But I can't spoil my son. The boy who gets things before he wants them, whose needs are met before he needs anything, is unfortunate. Who ever learns to be happy unless his desires are disciplined? That's why I want the boy to learn to keep his composure, even when he has to go without things. I don't want to load him down with watches and watch chains.

Sashadhar: That sounds fine, but all the world's obstacles won't crumble into dust immediately just because you wish it. If everyone had your wisdom, then there would be no problem. Even the loftiest resolutions can't be rammed through by brute strength. We need patience. Go against a woman's wishes and you'll have plenty of trouble. If you circle around a bit instead, expediently, you may get results. When the breeze shifts, the ship must trim its sails. That's how it is!

Manmatha: That's why you agree with everything your wife says. Coward!

Sashadhar: I'm not foolhardy like you. Whom shall I fear if not the person who rules the house where I have to live twenty-four hours a day? What's the good of acting heroic in front of your own wife? If it hurts to strike out at someone, it also hurts to be struck. If you get into a controversy, accept the wife's argument; when it is time to act, do what you really want. Why be obstinate and get into trouble?

Manmatha: If life were long enough one could go slowly and calmly as you do, but life is short.

Sashadhar: Brother, that's precisely why one must proceed with caution. If you bypass a stone that is in the way and shortcut by jumping over it, you're sure to be delayed. But it's no use telling you all this, you bump into it every day and you still don't learn. So there's no point in my giving advice. You think you'd like to live as if your wife didn't exist, but I see no reason for you to doubt her presence.

2

[*The small things create the big fuss: so say the scriptures about domestic quarrels. But married couples who most ignore this precept are those who know it best and would deny it least. Sometimes, when Manmatha bandied words with his wife, it was certainly a quarrel, although its beginning was neither serious nor trivial.*]

Manmatha: You've started dressing your son in Western clothes. I don't like it.

Bidhu: You think you're the only person who understands taste. These days everyone's children wear English clothes.

Manmatha (laughing): If you're going to live according to

everyone's wishes, why did you leave everyone and marry
me?

Bidhu: If you were going to live only according to your
own wishes, why didn't you stay single?

Manmatha: One needs help.

Bidhu: The washerman needs the donkey to carry his load,
but I'm certainly not——

Manmatha (bites his tongue): Oh, Lord, you are the Ara-
bian horse of my desert world. But let's not argue about
the animal world. Don't make a sahib out of your son.

Bidhu: Why not? Shall I make him a farmer?

[*With this Bidhu leaves the room. Her widowed
sister-in-law sits in the next room, sighs, and
thinks, husband and wife have had a private love
chat.*]

3

Manmatha: Hey, what are you smearing on your son?

Bidhu: Don't rub it off. It's nothing terrible, only a little
cologne. That's not English, it's Indian-made.

Manmatha: I've told you again and again, boys shouldn't
use all these sissy things.

Bidhu: All right, if it's any comfort to you, tomorrow I'll
put kerosene and castor oil on him.

Manmatha: That would be a waste of money too. Why de-
pend on things that you can do without? Smearing kerosene *or* castor oil on one's head and shoulders is equally
unnecessary.

Bidhu: I don't know just how many things you find necessary.
It looks as if you should have excluded me right at the
start.

Manmatha: Excluding you would eliminate the arguments.
It would be unbearable to suddenly cut off an old habit
at my age. Now listen, I'm repeating what I've told you
before: don't make the boy into a sahib, or a nabob,
or a sahib-nabob hodgepodge—not while I pay the bills.
What he'll get after I'm dead won't be enough to support
his fads.

Bidhu: I know that. If I relied on your money I'd dress
the boy regularly in a loincloth.

*Manmatha (cut to the quick by Bidhu's resentful words and
taking a moment to recover):* I know that too. You're

depending on Sashadhar. Since he has no heir, it will be just the thing for him to will everything to your son. So you dress the boy like an Anglo-Indian, smear him all over with perfumed stuff, and send him out to grab his uncle's affection. I could very easily bear the shame of poverty, but I won't bear the shame of begging for the affection of rich relatives.

[*Manmatha had not so far expressed his harsh thoughts; he had kept them to himself. Since the community of husbands doesn't know wifely psychology, decided Bidhu, he could not divine her secret wishes. But now Bidhu cannot face the fact that patient Manmatha had known her motives all along.*]

Bidhu (her face flushed): You can't stand having the boy go to his aunt's. I didn't know there was such a proud man in the house.

Bidhu's widowed sister-in-law enters.

Sister-in-law: Sister, my respects. After seventeen years you haven't gotten through talking. It isn't enough to go on all night, you two have to get together and whisper all day too. I wonder how God gets his daily supply of honey for the tips of your tongues. Don't be angry, brother-in-law. I won't interfere with your pleasant conversation. I've only come for two minutes to have a look at my sister's sewing patterns.

4

Satish: Auntie?
Aunt: What is it, dear?
Satish: Mother's having Mr. Bhaduri's son to tea today. Don't you go crashing in there.
Aunt: Why would I need to go there, Satish?
Satish: If you did, those clothes you're wearing wouldn't be right at all. You'll have to——
Aunt: Satish, you have nothing to worry about. I'll stay in this room. As long as your friend is having tea, I won't come out.
Satish: Auntie, I think I'll arrange for him to have tea in

this room of yours. Our house is so overcrowded; there's not an empty room fit for serving tea or dinner. There are so many chests and boxes in Mother's room. I'd be ashamed to take anyone there.

Aunt: My things are here, too.

Satish: These will have to be put outside for the day. Especially those fish knives and baskets and trays of yours have to be hidden somewhere.

Aunt: My dear, why are you so ashamed of those? How do vegetables get chopped if there are none of those in the house?

Satish: I don't know about that, Auntie, but it isn't proper to have tea with those things in the room. If Naren Bhaduri saw all this he'd surely laugh and tell his sister about it when he got home.

Aunt: Now listen to this boy! Fish knives and baskets have always been in houses. I've certainly never heard a story about that.

Satish: You'll have to do something more, Auntie. Keep our servant away somehow or other. He wouldn't listen to me and would appear without his shirt.

Aunt: I might be able to stop Nanda, but when your father appears without a shirt——

Satish: I've already gone to my aunt about that. She invited Father to have pancakes there today. Father won't know a thing about it.

Aunt: Satish, my dear, do as you please, but these parties of yours in my room——

Satish: I'll get it cleaned up properly right now.

5

Satish: Mother, this just isn't right.

Bidhu: Why, what's happened?

Satish: I'm ashamed to go out in a ready-made suit. When the Bhaduris had that evening party, all but a few of the men wore tuxedos. I was terribly embarrassed there in these clothes. Father gives me so little money for clothes that I can't even keep myself decent.

Bidhu: You know perfectly well, Satish, that he won't give in a bit on what he believes. Listen, how much would it cost for the clothes you want?

Satish: A morning suit and a sport jacket would take about a hundred rupees. A passable tuxedo wouldn't be a bit under a hundred and fifty.

Bidhu: What are you talking about, Satish! This would be close to three hundred rupees. So much money——

Satish: Mother, this is your trouble. If you want to live like a monk, that's all right, but if you want to go out in civilized society, that sort of corner-cutting won't do. To be civilized will be expensive, there's just no other way. Why don't you send me out to the forests to live? Tuxedos aren't necessary there.

Bidhu: I certainly know that, but— All right, your uncle is sure to give you a birthday gift. This one time, why don't you suggest that he give it to you early? Give your aunt a hint.

Satish: That's easy enough, but if Father hears that I wangled a suit from my uncle, I'll be in trouble.

Bidhu: All right, I can take care of that.

Satish goes out.

If it could be arranged somehow for Satish to marry the Bhaduris' daughter, I'd have nothing to worry about. Mr. Bhaduri is a barrister and earns plenty. Satish has been coming and going at their house since he was a little boy. The girl's not exactly a clod, and she must like my Satish. Satish's father has never once thought about all this; the mention of it would set him on fire. I'm the one who has to do all the worrying about the boy's future.

6

On the Bhaduris' tennis court.

Nalini: Say, Satish, where are you running off to?

Satish: I didn't know you were having a tennis party. I haven't worn tennis clothes.

Nalini: Not all cows have hides the same color. Maybe you'd become famous for originality. All right, I'll let you have it your way. Mr. Nandi, do me a favor.

Nandi: Why a favor? Why not an order? I'm at your service.

Nalini: If it isn't inconvenient to do it just for the day, pardon Satish; he hasn't worn tennis clothes. What a terrible calamity!

Nandi: If you were a lawyer pleading a case for murder, fraud, or house-breaking, I could pardon him. If you're so merciful to someone who comes without tennis clothes, I'll give mine to Mr. Satish as a gift. What do you say to that? What's this you're wearing, Satish? Why not call this a patchwork suit? I'll come here every day in this patchwork suit of yours. Even if I stopped the sun and moon and stars, I wouldn't be ashamed. Satish, if you have any objection to a gift of clothes, give me the address of your tailor. Miss Bhaduri's favor is much more precious than a fashionable suit.

Nalini: Listen, Satish, now listen hard. It's not only style in dress but style in pleasant conversation that you can learn from Mr. Nandi. You can't find a better example. In England he talked with no one but dukes and duchesses. Mr. Nandi, what Bengali students were in England when you were there?

Nandi: I didn't mix with Bengalis there.

Nalini: Are you listening, Satish? One must take great pains to become really civilized. You might manage it if you try. You have such subtle spiritual notions about tennis clothes that I have hope for you.

She goes aside.

Satish (sighs): I still can't understand Nalini. She always seems to laugh at me. My trouble is that I can't relax when I come here. I always seem to feel as if my tie is crooked over my collar or my trousers are twisted halfway up my leg. When I can be as self-confident as Nandi—

Nalini (returning): Well, Satish, your troubles still aren't over. Your soul was torn up in that bad business on the tennis court. Alas, where in the world is consolation for the soul without a coat—except at the tailor's!

Satish: If you have any notions about my soul, you won't talk like that anymore, Neli.

Nalini (clapping her hands): Bravo! In following Mr. Nandi's footsteps you've already begun to import sweet words. With indulgence, there's every hope for you. Come on, come and have a little cake. Sweets are the reward for sweet words.

Satish: No, I won't eat any more today. I don't feel——

Nalini: Satish, listen to me. Don't ruin your health grieving over tennis clothes. There's no sense in giving up eating altogether. Clothes certainly are among the best things in the world, but without the unimpressive human frame, there's nothing to hang them on!

7

Sashadhar: Look, Manmatha, you're entirely too harsh with Satish. He's grown up now and it's not good to restrict him so much!

Bidhu: Well said, Mr. Ray! I've never been able to make him see it.

Manmatha: Two false accusations in one minute! One person says heartless, the other says fool. I'll take anything from the one to whom I'm a fool. I won't complain even if her sister says something of the sort, but I've no patience with her sister's husband. How am I strict?

Sashadhar: Poor Satish is fond of good clothes. He has begun going to all sorts of places. Take him to the shops.

Manmatha: I didn't ask him to wear clothes from the shops. European clothes are poison to me. He'll never need be ashamed in dhoti and chador, *chapkan* and *choga*.

Sashadhar: Look here, Manmatha, if Satish can't get this craze out of his system at this age, who knows what strange things he'll do in your old age; that will look even worse. And consider—how will you stop the onslaught of something that we've been told since childhood is civilization?

Manmatha: He who becomes civilized must pay its price. The culture you speak of and the money haven't come from the same source. Instead, the money's flowing from here to there.

Bidhu: Mr. Ray, you can't argue with him. It's hard to stop him once he starts talking about India.

Sashadhar: Brother Manmatha, I understand everything you've said. But we can't shrug off the boy's childish whims. When Satish goes around with the crowd at Mr. Bhaduri's without the right kind of clothes, the poor fellow will have a very bad time of it. I'll get him something from Rankin's.

A servant enters.

Servant: These clothes came from an English shop.

Manmatha: Take all this back! Take it back right now!

Bidhu leaves.

Look, if I see Satish wearing these clothes, I won't let him stay in the house. I'll send him to his uncle. He can manage there any way he wishes.

Exits quickly.

Sashadhar: Amazing!

Bidhu (reenters, weeping angrily): Mr. Ray, what shall I say? I can't enjoy anything. Has anyone ever seen a father treat his own son that way?

Sashadhar: His treatment of me doesn't seem fair either. I think Manmatha has indigestion. Take my advice. Don't give him the same old rice and lentils every day. He can talk as he pleases, but food isn't good without spices now and then; it isn't digestible, either. Feed him well for a couple of days; then you'll find that he listens to everything you say. Your sister understands all this better than you do.

Sashadhar leaves. Bidhu cries.

Sister-in-law (enters speaking to herself): Sometimes crying, sometimes smiling—there are so many kinds of affection. She's really happy. *(Sighs.)* Sister, you've got the sulks! Shall I call my brother-in-law? Let's have the reconciliation scene now.

8

Nalini: Satish, I'll tell you why I sent for you. Don't be angry.

Satish: Is my disposition so bad that your invitation would make me angry?

Nalini: Never mind that. Don't be Nandi's disciple all the time. Look here, why did you get such an expensive thing for my birthday?

Satish: I gave it to someone with whom the most expensive thing can't be compared.

Nalini: You're being Nandi's carbon copy again.

Satish: I wish I were Nandi's carbon copy! When a particular person is so partial toward him——

Nalini: Go on, then, I won't talk to you anymore.

Satish: All right, forgive me. I'll keep quiet and listen.

Nalini: Look, Satish, like a fool Mr. Nandi sent me an expensive bracelet. Why do you want to be just as foolish by sending me an even more expensive necklace?

Satish: Neli, you're angry because you haven't experienced the state of mind in which people lose the ability to think.

Nalini: I never want such an experience. But I'll have to return this necklace to you.

Satish: Return it?

Nalini: I'm giving it back. There's no value in this because you've really given it only to show off.

Satish: You're being unfair, Neli.

Nalini: I'm not at all unfair. If you had given me a flower, I'd have been much happier. You've been sending me all sorts of valuable things so often. I haven't said anything because I knew you'd be hurt. But this is going too far. I mustn't keep quiet anymore. Here is your necklace.

Satish: You can throw this necklace out to be run over in the street, but I simply won't take it.

Nalini: Very well, Satish. I've known you since you were a little boy. You don't fool me. Tell the truth, haven't you gone quite a bit into debt?

Satish: Who told you? Does Naren know?

Nalini: No one told me. I can see it in your face. Why are you being so unfair because of me?

Satish: A man may want to give his life to a certain person at a certain time. These days there are few chances to offer one's life. Won't you let me at least have the fun of getting into debt? Whatever is impossible for me—that's what I want to do for you, Neli. If you call this being Nandi's carbon copy, it really hurts me.

Nalini: Well, you've done it your own way. I accept your little self-sacrifice. Now you take back this thing.

Satish: If I take that back, it would be better for me to die with this necklace as a noose around my neck.

Nalini: How will you pay the debt?

Satish: I'll get the money from my mother.

Nalini: Shame on you. She'll think that her son is getting into debt just because of me.

Satish: She'll never think that. She has known her son too long.

Nalini: All right, let it be. Promise that you won't give me such an expensive thing again. You can't give me anything more expensive than a bunch of flowers.

Satish: All right, I promise that.

Nalini: Fine. Now, then, let's get started on Professor Nandi's course of study. Let's see how far you've progressed in the

art of flattery. Well, tell me what you can about my earlobe.
I'll give you five minutes.

Satish: What I'd say would make that ear blush.

Nalini: Fine, fine! That's not a bad preface. That's enough
for today, we'll have the rest another day. My ears are
burning already.

9

Bidhu: You can be angry with me for what's been done.
Don't be angry with the boy. I beg you to pay his debt this
time.

Manmatha: I'm not getting angry. I must do my duty as I
see it. I've told Satish repeatedly that I won't take on his
debts. I won't do anything that contradicts what I've said
in the past.

Bidhu: My dear, you can't live in this world like Juddhisthir.
Satish is grown up now. If your allowance won't cover his
debt, what will he do?

Manmatha: If a person wants to live beyond his means, there's
no way to make ends meet. Neither the beggar nor the
emperor can do it.

Bidhu: Then will the boy have to go to jail?

Manmatha: If he's prepared to go and if all of you help him
along, how can I prevent it?

Manmatha exits.

Sashadhar enters.

Sashadhar: Manmatha hates to see me here. He thinks I've
come with a tape to measure his son for a tuxedo. So I
haven't come for several days. When your sister Suku got
your letter today, she wept and wailed and put me out of
the house.

Bidhu: My sister hasn't come?

Sashadhar: She'll come soon. What's the matter?

Bidhu: You've heard the whole story. He won't rest now
unless he sends the boy to jail. He didn't like the suits
from Rankin and from Harman. It seems he thinks that a
jail uniform is more civilized.

Sashadhar: No matter what you say, I can't go and make
Manmatha understand. I don't understand him, he doesn't
understand me, and then——

Bidhu: Don't I know that? You're not his wife, who has to

take all this with bowed head. But how shall I stop this catastrophe?

Sashadhar: Haven't you anything on hand?

Bidhu: Nothing. It took nearly all my jewelry to pay off Satish's last debt. I've only a pair of bangles left.

Satish enters.

Sashadhar: Well, Satish, you spent a lot of money without thinking and look what a fix you're in.

Satish: I don't see any fix.

Sashadhar: Then you've got something tucked away and haven't told anyone about it.

Satish: Certainly I have something.

Sashadhar: How much?

Satish: Enough to buy opium.

Bidhu (starting to cry): Satish, what kind of talk is that? I'm so miserable, don't make me feel any worse.

Sashadhar: Shame on you, Satish. Even if you think such things, is that the way to talk to your mother? It's very unfair.

Sukumari enters.

Bidhu: Sister, help Satish. I'm always afraid of what he'll do some day. Just to hear him talk about it makes me tremble.

Sukumari: What does he say?

Bidhu: He says he'll go and buy opium!

Sukumari: What a mess! Satish, give me your hand and promise you won't ever think of it again. Why don't you say something? My dear boy! Think of your mother and your aunt.

Satish: It's better to brush it off by thinking of silly things outside of jail than to be thinking in jail.

Sukumari: We're all here—who will take you to jail?

Satish: The bailiff.

Sukumari: Well, we'll see about the bailiff. *(To Sashadhar.)* My dear, why don't you put up this money? Why give the boy so much trouble?

Sashadhar: I can put up the money, but Manmatha would put up a brick at my head!

Satish: Uncle, that brick won't reach your head. It will fall on my neck. I've failed one of my examinations.

On top of that I'm in debt. On top of that, if I miss this golden opportunity of going to jail, Father will never forgive me.

Bidhu: It's true, sister. If he heard that Satish had taken his uncle's money, he'd surely put him out of the house.

Sukumari: Let him do that. It isn't as if Satish has nowhere to go. Oh, Bidhu, why don't you let Satish come to me? I have no children. Why don't I bring him up myself? *(To her husband.)* What do you say, dear?

Sashadhar: An excellent idea. But Satish is such a tiger cub, if you want to pull him over to our side it will be hard to stay clear of his teeth.

Sukumari: The senior tiger has handed the boy over to the bailiff at the jail. He can't say anything if we take Satish now.

Sashadhar: What does the tigress say? What does the cub have to say about it?

Sukumari: I know what they say. Don't ask any more. Now you can pay off the debt.

Bidhu: Sister——

Sukumari: No more of this crying and "Sister, sister." Steady, now let me put up your hair. Aren't you ashamed to appear like that in front of your brother-in-law?

All exit except Sashudhar.

Manmatha enters.

Sashadhar: Manmatha, brother, why don't you reconsider——

Manmatha: I don't do anything without considering it thoroughly.

Sashadhar: Then, heaven help you! Be more modest. What's the idea of letting the boy go to jail? What good would come of that?

Manmatha: No one can foresee good or bad. If a person behaves unreasonably after repeated warnings, no one should contrive to save him from the consequences. If we had not jumped in and ruined the process, Nature's hard knocks would have made men into real human beings.

Sashadhar: If Nature's hard lessons were the only lessons, God would not have put love into the hearts of parents. Manmatha, I don't believe so implicitly in the consequences that worry you day and night. Nature may want to collect the results of our actions, but the Lord who is above Nature intervenes and forgives most of them. Other-

wise, paying every bit of the debt for our actions woul
make life not worth living. Consequences are very real fo
science, but there is a wisdom higher than science. Th
record kept by love is so different. Nature demands conse
quences that humanity can transcend.

Manmatha: He who doesn't believe in natural law may d
whatever he wishes. I am a very ordinary man who be
lieves in such a law and its effects, and I shall believe in
to the very end.

Sashadhar: All right, if I get Satish off by paying his debt
what will you do?

Manmatha: I'll wash my hands of him. Look here, from th
very beginning you've interfered with my way of bringing
up Satish. Restriction on one hand and indulgence on th
other—this has ruined him. If he gets alms day after day
what happens to his self-respect or sense of responsibility
Your interference keeps him from learning the result
of his behavior; I have no hope for him. Bring him up
according to your rules: his trouble comes of straddling
two boats.

Sashadhar: What are you saying, Manmatha? Your son——

Manmatha: Look, Sashadhar, I only know how to raise my
son according to my own nature and beliefs. I know of no
other method. When I see that it can't be done by any
means whatsoever, I'll give up the responsibility of a
father. I can't do any more.

Manmatha leaves.

Sashadhar: What's to be done? The boy can't go to jail. No
matter how bad the deed, jail is worse.

10

Mrs. Bhaduri: Have you heard? Satish's father died suddenly.

Mr. Bhaduri: Yes, I heard it.

Mrs. Bhaduri: All his property has been willed to a hospital;
Satish's mother gets a monthly allowance of seventy-five
rupees during her lifetime. What can we do?

Mr. Bhaduri: Why are you so concerned about it?

Mrs. Bhaduri: You're a fine sort of fellow! Your daughter is
in love with Satish. Can't you see that with your own eyes?
You were even prepared to get them married. Now what's
to be done?

Mr. Bhaduri: I certainly wasn't depending on Manmatha's money.

Mrs. Bhaduri: Then were you depending on the boy's good looks? Do you think food and clothing are unnecessary?

Mr. Bhaduri: Quite necessary. Whatever anyone says, there is nothing more necessary than food and clothes. You recall that Satish has an uncle.

Mrs. Bhaduri: Many people have uncles. That doesn't take care of it.

Mr. Bhaduri: That same uncle is my client. His money is inexhaustible, he has no children, and he's getting old. He wants to adopt Satish.

Mrs. Bhaduri: What a fine uncle! Let him do that quickly! Shouldn't you prod him along a bit?

Mr. Bhaduri: I don't have to prod him. There's someone in his own family to do the prodding. Everything is almost settled. There's only one hitch that has come up: whether or not an only son can be adopted by someone else. Besides, Satish isn't a child.

Mrs. Bhaduri: The legal points are up to you. Shut your eyes and give them a decision.

Mr. Bhaduri: Don't get upset. There are other ways besides adoption.

Mrs. Bhaduri: I'm relieved. I was wondering how we could break off Neli's friendship with Satish. Then, too, our Neli is such a stubborn girl that there's no telling what she'd do. But that doesn't mean we have to hand her over to a poor man. Do you know, your daughter has cried her eyes out. She was at dinner yesterday when she heard about Satish's father. She got up and left at once.

Mr. Bhaduri: But it didn't look as if Neli were in love with Satish. She makes his life miserable. I used to think she preferred Nandi.

Mrs. Bhaduri: That's how she is. She torments the very person she loves. Don't you see how she teases the kittens? But the funny thing is, no one wants to leave her.

Nalini enters.

Nalini: Mother, won't you go to Satish's house? His mother must be very upset. Father, I want to go and be with her.

11

Satish: Mother, you can see now how glad I am that I made all that fuss about clothes. But I won't feel easy about it until Uncle adopts me. Your monthly allowance won't help me at all. It's been a long time now, there's been a lot of shilly-shallying, and he still hasn't adopted me. Maybe they still hope for a child of their own.

Bidhu (despairing): Satish, that hope may well come true.

Satish: Hah! Is that so, Mother!

Bidhu: There's every sign that it is.

Satish: You can be mistaken about signs, too.

Bidhu: No, Satish, you're wrong. You're certainly going to have a cousin-brother.

Satish: What are you saying, Mother? No such thing. Who says there'll be a cousin-brother! Maybe it will be a cousin-sister.

Bidhu: From my sister's appearance, I don't think she'll have a girl. It will surely be a boy. Whether a boy or a girl, it's all the same to us.

Satish: A first son after so many years—so much could go wrong in the meantime.

Bidhu: Satish, you try to get a job.

Satish: Impossible. I haven't passed the examinations. Besides, I've never been used to working at a job. But whatever you say, Mother, this is very unfair. By now I would have had my father's property, but I've been cheated of that. Besides——

Bidhu: It's definitely unfair, Satish! On the one hand, your uncle took you into his house; on the other hand, he called in the doctor to treat his wife. In the end, the doctor's treatment worked. Is this the way to behave toward his own nephew? Don't be upset, Satish. Keep praying to God. No doctor can compete with Him. If He——

Satish: Aha, if even *He,* there's still time. Mother, we should be grateful to them, but it's rather hard to remember that after such a shabby treatment. We can't keep praying for a calamity. May God mercifully——

Bidhu: Ah, let that be so. Otherwise, I wonder what will happen to you. Oh, God, may You——

Satish: If this doesn't work out, I won't believe in God any-more. I'll preach atheism in the papers.

Bidhu: Oh, hush, hush, don't say such things. He is merci-

ful. What can't He do if He wants to? Satish, you're so
dressed up today. Where are you going? Your collar makes
your head look as if it's aimed at the sky! How will you
ever bend down?

Satish: I'll try to hold my head up with the help of a collar
as long as I can. When the day comes to bend my neck
I'll get rid of these collars. I have something very important
to see to, Mother. I'm going. We'll discuss all this later.

He leaves.

Bidhu: I know where the important business is. Heavens,
this boy seems to have no patience. The marriage will go
through. I know my Satish's fate isn't a bad one. No matter
how many troubles there seem to be at first, it will turn
out well for him in the end. I've always known that. I
don't know why it shouldn't be so. I haven't knowingly
committed any sin. I was a faithful wife, so I'm really
confident that sister will have a——

12

Sukumari: Satish!

Satish: What, Auntie?

Sukumari: Yesterday I asked you to get some clothes for your
cousin. Did that offend you?

Satish: Why should I feel offended, Auntie? Yesterday I was
invited to Mr. Bhaduri's, that's why——

Sukumari: I can't for the life of me see why you have to get
so thick with the Bhaduris. They're Westernized people.
In your circumstances it isn't proper to be friendly with
them. I've heard that they don't care a thing about you,
but I see that you still dress like an Englishman and keep
going there with tie clasps on colored neckties. If you had
any self-respect, you'd have tried to get a job instead of
lying around here. And if someone asks you to run an
errand, you're angry for fear you'll be mistaken for a
delivery boy. But even the delivery boy is better; he lives
on his own earnings.

Satish: Auntie, maybe I could have done the same, but you——

Sukumari: So that's it. I knew it would end up as my fault.
Now I see that your father was strict with you because
he knew you very well. I was more easygoing, I took you
and saved you from jail, and now it's all my fault. This
is gratitude! Well, even if I was at fault, can't you do a

thing or two during the days you have to eat here? Is it so unheard of? Does it insult you terribly?

Satish: Not at all. Tell me what to do. I'll do it right away.

Sukumari: I want seven and a half yards of rainbow silk and a sailor suit for the boy.

Satish is about to go.

Oh, listen, I want shoes for him. Measure his foot.

Satish is still at the door.

What's your hurry? Listen to all of it. I think you're still hurrying off for the Bhaduris' cake and cookies. Bring a straw hat for the boy. I need a dozen handkerchiefs too.

Satish goes out. She calls him back again.

Listen, Satish, there's something more. I heard that you took money for a new suit from your uncle without telling me. When you can afford it, get as Westernized as you like, but don't bankrupt your uncle trying to impress Mr. Bhaduri on someone else's money. Give that money back to me. These are hard times for us.

Satish: I'll go and get it.

Sukumari: Go to the store now, buy the things with that money, and return the change. Don't forget to keep an account.

Satish is about to go.

Listen, Satish, don't spend two and a half rupees on taxi fare when you go for these things. That's why I dread asking you to get anything. If you have to walk a few steps you're terribly upset. A man can't survive if he's so fastidious. Your father used to go to the New Market himself every morning to buy fish, do you remember? He didn't spend a penny on a delivery boy.

Satish: I'll remember your advice. I won't pay them, either. From now on I'll always see to it that the delivery boy and the orderly get as little as possible.

13

Haren enters.

Haren: Cousin, what have been writing for so long? To whom are you writing?

Satish: Go away, go away, it's none of your business. Go and play.

Haren: Show me. I can read now.

Satish: Haren, I tell you, don't bother me. Go away.

Haren: L-O-V-E, love. Cousin, tell me what you're writing about love. I think you love green guavas. I love them too.

Satish: Oh, Haren, don't shout. I didn't write about love.

Haren: What? You're lying. I just read L-O-V-E, love. Let me call my mother and show it to her.

Satish: No, no. You don't need to call your mother. Please go and play somewhere else. Let me finish this.

Haren: What's this, cousin? Oh, a bunch of flowers. I want it.

Satish: Don't touch those flowers. Get your hands off them, you'll ruin them.

Haren: No, I won't. Give them to me.

Satish: Sonny, I'll bring you lots of bouquets tomorrow. Let this one alone.

Haren: Cousin, this is beautiful. I want this one!

Satish: No, this belongs to someone else. I can't give it to you.

Haren: What a lie! I told you to bring candy and you used that money to buy flowers. Now you're saying they belong to someone else.

Satish: Haren, my little cousin, calm down a bit. Let me finish this letter. I'll get you lots of candy tomorrow.

Haren: All right! Show me what you're writing.

Satish: All right! I'll show you. Let me finish this letter.

Haren: Well, I'll write too, then. (*Writes on a slate, reciting loudly.*) L-O-V-E, love!

Satish: Hush, hush! Don't shout so much! Shut up!

Haren: Then give that bouquet.

Satish: All right, take it. But be careful, don't tear it up. Look what you're doing, just what I told you not to do. You tore it apart. I've never seen such a pesky boy. (*Snatches away the bouquet, slaps Haren's face.*) Naughty boy! Get out of here! Go on!

Haren cries and Satish leaves.

Bidhu enters, worried.

Bidhu: Satish must have made Haren cry. If my sister hears him it will be a disaster. Haren, my boy, don't cry. Oh, you sweet boy, you darling!

Haren (sniffling): My cousin slapped me.

Bidhu: All right, all right, hush up now. I'll give your cousin a good slap.

Haren: My cousin took the flowers away from me.

Bidhu: All right, I'll get them from him for you.

Haren cries.

I've never seen such a crybaby. My sister is spoiling this boy. When he wants something, he must have it right away. Look at this; the clothing stores are cleaned out for him as if he were a prince. What a shame! How can a person spoil her own child this way? Haren, quiet down. There comes the bogeyman.

Sukumari enters.

Sukumari: Bidhu, what's going on? Are you scaring my son with ghost stories? I've forbidden all the servants to do this. None of them would dare and his own aunt does it. Why, Bidhu, what has my son done to you? Obviously, you can't stand the sight of him. I reared your son as my very own, and now you're taking this revenge on me.

Bidhu (weeping): Sister, don't say such things. What difference is there to me between my Satish and your Haren?

Haren: Mother, my cousin slapped me.

Bidhu: Shame on you, Haren, that's not true. Your cousin wasn't here. How could he have slapped you?

Haren: Huh! He sat right here writing a letter, and in that letter there was L-O-V-E, love. Mother, you asked him to get some candy for me, and he bought a bunch of flowers instead. He slapped me because I just touched that bouquet.

Sukumari: Both you and Satish have it in for my son. You'd be better off if he were out of the way. I tell you, that's why he takes medicine by the bottleful and still gets thinner every day. Now I see it all.

14

Satish: Neli, I've come to say good-bye.

Nalini: Why, where are you going?

Satish: To hell!

Nalini: In that case, why say good-bye? The person who knows the way can go there sitting in his own home. Why are you in such a bad mood today? Is your collar on crooked?

Satish: Do you think I always think about collars?

Nalini: So it seems. That's why you look so thoughtful all of a sudden.

Satish: Don't make fun of me, Neli. If you could only see my heart today.

Nalini: Then I'd be able to see the flowers on the fig tree or the fifth foot on the snake.

Satish: You're making fun of me again. You're heartless. I'm telling you the truth, Neli. I've come to say good-bye.

Nalini: Are you going shopping?

Satish: I beg you, Neli, don't scorch me with your jokes. I'm saying good-bye for good today.

Nalini: Why are you suddenly so anxious to do that?

Satish: I'll tell you the truth. You don't know how poor I am.

Nalini: Why are you afraid of that? I didn't ask for a loan.

Satish: There was talk of our marriage.

Nalini: Is that why you're running away? Would marriage give you a heart attack?

Satish: Your father broke off the marriage arrangements when he found out about my financial position.

Nalini: So that insult makes you run away? No one should go near anybody so touchy. You think I laugh at your loving words for no good reason.

Satish: Neli, do you still want me to have hopes?

Nalini: For heaven's sake, Satish, don't talk like a novel. You make me laugh. Why should I ask you to have hopes? He who has hopes has them on his own initiative, not because others advise him to.

Satish: That's right. I want to know whether you hate poverty.

Nalini: Certainly I do, if that poverty wants to hide behind shame.

Satish: Neli, would you ever be able to give up the luxuries you're used to and become the daughter-in-law in a poor home?

Nalini: If I caught the disease we read about in novels, then luxury would go out the window.

Satish: Does this disease have a name?

Nalini: You've never been able to pass a single exam. Even Mr. Nandi wouldn't have raised such a question! People like you shouldn't be tolerated for a minute.

Satish: I still don't understand you, Neli.

Nalini: How could you understand me? I'm not your fashionable tie or collar. You don't understand anything except what you think about all day long.

Satish: I beg you with folded hands, Neli, and ask you not to say these things to me. You know very well what I think about.

Nalini: Don't be so certain that my insight about you is so sharp. Father's coming. He'd be angry if he saw me here. I'd better go.

                                             She goes out.

                    Mr. Bhaduri enters.

Satish: Mr. Bhaduri, I've come to say good-bye.

Mr. Bhaduri: Very well, then.

Satish: But I have something to say before I leave.

Mr. Bhaduri: But there's no time now. I'm going out for a walk.

Satish: May I come with you for a little way?

Mr. Bhaduri: There's no doubt you can, but I don't think I could. I'm not so eager for companionship these days.

                             15

Sashadhar: Ach! What are you saying? Are you out of your mind?

Sukumari: Am I out of my mind or are you blind?

Sashadhar: Neither would surprise me. Both are quite possible, but——

Sukumari: Haven't you noticed how long their faces have been ever since our Haren was born? Don't you see through Satish's reactions?

Sashadhar: You know I'm not a mind reader. The mind's mystery has been dinned into me since childhood. I understand a little if I see something happen.

Sukumari: Satish spanks your son whenever he gets a chance.

And then Bidhu comes along and scares him with ghost stories.

Sashadhar: There you go, making a mountain out of a molehill. Even if Satish sometimes——

Sukumari: Maybe you can take that, but I can't. You didn't bear the child.

Sashadhar: I can't deny that. What do you want done now?

Sukumari: You talk big about discipline. Why don't you stop and think? We want to raise Haren a particular way and his aunt teaches him differently. And look what an example Satish is for him.

Sashadhar: Since you're doing so much thinking, I see no reason to do any myself. What's he done now?

Sukumari: I think you'd better tell Satish to look for a job and stay with his mother. It doesn't look right for a young man to be fashionable on someone else's money.

Sashadhar: How will Satish support himself on his mother's money?

Sukumari: Why, they don't have to pay rent. Seventy-five rupees isn't bad.

Sashadhar: The way Satish has been going, he'd blow away seventy-five rupees on the tip of a cigarette. His mother's jewelry went long ago. How will she pay his debts?

Sukumari: People with limited ability should live modestly.

Sashadhar: That's what Manmatha used to say. We taught Satish differently. Can we blame him now?

Sukumari: No. How can it be his fault? Everything is my fault. You don't see anyone else's faults. Your power of vision increases when it focuses on me.

Sashadhar: My dear, why are you so angry? I'm responsible too.

Sukumari: That's possible. You know about yourself. But I've never told him to sit in his uncle's room with his feet up, twirling his moustache and looking daggers at my little boy.

Sashadhar: No, you didn't make him promise to do just that. Therefore I can't blame you. Tell me what I have to do now.

Sukumari: Do whatever you think best, but as long as Satish is around, I daren't send my son outdoors. The doctor prescribed fresh air, but when Satish gets him alone out there—even the thought of that upsets me. He's my own sister's son, but I don't trust him for a second. I'm making no bones about this.

Satish enters.

Satish: Whom don't you trust, Auntie, me? Are you afraid I'll strangle your son? Is that it? But if I do, will it do him more harm than you've done to your own sister's son? Who has made me into a royal fashion plate since I was a kid and now turns me out into the street like a beggar? Who shielded me from my father's discipline and brought me down in the world? Who has——

Sukumari: Do you hear that? Can he insult me like that right in front of you? Didn't he say himself that he'll strangle my son! Oh, heavens! What will happen? I've raised a snake on milk and honey!

Satish: There was milk and honey in my home too, but that milk and honey wouldn't have turned my blood to poison. You deprived me of that for good, and your milk and honey has made me dangerous. You're right. You should be afraid of me now. Now I can bite.

Bidhu enters.

Bidhu: What's wrong, Satish? You look so terrible! Why are you staring like that? Don't you recognize me? I'm your mother, Satish.

Satish: Mother! How can you call yourself mother? If you're my mother, why did you cheat me of my father's discipline? Why did you keep me out of jail? Was it any worse than my aunt's house? You people regard God as a mother. If He's a mother like you, then I don't want His love. He may send me to hell.

Sashadhar: Ach, Satish! Come off it, you're talking nonsense. Stop it! Come along to my room.

16

Sashadhar: Satish, calm down a bit. Do you think I don't realize you've been treated very unfairly? Your Auntie said something in anger; you shouldn't take it so to heart. Mistakes made in the past can be partly rectified now, rest assured.

Satish: Uncle, this can't be rectified. As things stand now between my aunt and me, I couldn't eat a bite here. I won't rest even after I'm dead unless I can repay every cent I've made you spend. If anything is to be rectified, I must do it. How can you make it right?

Sashadhar: No. Listen, Satish, calm down a little. Worry about your duties later. I must atone for the wrongs we've done you. Look here, I'll sign over a part of my property to you, and don't consider that a gift. That's coming to you. I've gotten everything set up. Day after tomorrow—Friday —I'll register it.

Satish (touching his uncle's feet): Uncle, what can I say? Your love——

Sashadhar: All right, that's enough. I don't understand all that love. I know I must do this duty somehow. You said you were going to the theater. It's eight-thirty now. One thing Satish, Mr. Bhaduri drew up my will and appeared very pleased about it. It didn't seem to me that he dislikes you. When I was leaving, he even said, "Why doesn't Satish come to see us these days?"

Satish leaves.

Oh, Ramcharan! Call your mistress here.

Sukumari enters.

Sukumari: What did you decide?

Sashadhar: I've decided on a marvelous plan.

Sukumari: I know how marvelous your plan will be. Anyway, I hope you're getting rid of Satish.

Sashadhar: If I don't do that, what is the point of planning? I've decided to sign our Manipur property over to Satish. Then he'll be able to live in his own house at his own expense. He won't bother you anymore.

Sukumari: Oh, what a marvelous plan that is! I'm absolutely enchanted by your ingenuity. No, no, I tell you, you can't do such a crazy thing!

Sashadhar: Look, once we thought of giving him all our property.

Sukumari: My Haren hadn't been born then. Besides, do you think you won't have any more children?

Sashadhar: Suku, think how unfair we're being. Why don't you try to think that you have two sons?

Sukumari: That's too much for me to understand. If you do such a thing I'll put a rope around my neck.

Sukumari leaves.

Satish enters.

Sashadhar: Well, Satish? Didn't you go to the theater?

Satish: No, Uncle, not today. Look here, look here. After all this time, an invitation from Mr. Bhaduri. See what your will has done. I'm beginning to hate this world, Uncle, I can't take your property.

Sashadhar: Why, Satish?

Satish: I won't enjoy things under false pretenses. I'll enjoy only what little I'm worth, and not a penny more. Besides, if you want to give me a part of your property, have you gotten Auntie's permission?

Sashadhar: No. That is, she—in other words, we'll manage that. She might not agree right away, but——

Satish: Have you told her?

Sashadhar: Of course! She knows enough. If I didn't tell her, what else——

Satish: Did she agree?

Sashadhar: I wouldn't call it agreement, but if I explain it nicely——

Satish: It's no use, Uncle. I don't want to take your property if she's unwilling. You tell her that after today I won't feel easy until I've repaid her with interest.

Sashadhar: That's not necessary, Satish. I'd rather give you some cash secretly.

Satish: No, Uncle, I won't increase my debt. I have one request: get me that office job with your British friend.

Sashadhar: Can you do it?

Satish: If I can't, my only punishment will be to eat my aunt's food again.

17

Sukumari: Look at that! Satish is really working hard now. Look at that Westernized fellow going regularly to the office in a tattered chador and an old black alpaca *chapkan.*

Sashadhar: His boss praises him very highly.

Sukumari: See, if you had set him up as a landlord, he would have put the property up for auction to buy ties and collars and walking sticks and such. It's a lucky thing you took my advice, and now Satish acts like a human being.

Sashadhar: God hasn't given us men intelligence, but He has given us wives, and He has given you the brains, as well as the job of looking after the foolish husbands. We're the real winners.

Sukumari: That's enough. You needn't make fun of me! If we now had the money you've put on Satish's back——

Sashadhar: Satish said that some day he'll pay off all that debt.

Sukumari: I know how he'll pay off. He always talks big. You're hoping for that, are you?

Sashadhar: I hoped that for a long time, but if you advise me to give it up, I will.

Sukumari: You'll lose less if you do. I've told you so all along. There comes Mr. Satish. He hasn't darkened our doorstep since he's had the job. That's gratitude for you. I'm leaving.

> *Sukumari starts to leave.*

> *Satish enters.*

Satish: Auntie, you don't have to run away. Look, I haven't a single weapon with me, only a few bank notes.

Sashadhar: Well! This is a lot of money! If this belongs to your office, you shouldn't carry it around this way, Satish.

Satish: I won't carry it with me any farther. I'll offer this at my auntie's feet. My respects, Auntie. You've done me many favors. In those days I never thought of keeping accounts, so my arithmetic might be a little off. Count this fifteen thousand rupees. I hope that it didn't cause a shortage of a single grain of rice in your son's kingly fare.

Sashadhar: What's all this, Satish? Where did you get all this money?

Satish: I bought some jute six months ahead of the market. In the meantime the price went up. This is the profit.

Sashadhar: Satish, this is gambling.

Satish: This is the end of the game. I won't do it again.

Sashadhar: You take back your money. I don't want it.

Satish: I didn't give it to you, Uncle. This is for my aunt. I can never repay your debt.

Sashadhar: What, Suku, all this money—

Sukumari: Count it and give it to the cashier. Would you let it lie around here?

Sashadhar: Satish, have you eaten?

Satish: I'll eat at home.

Sashadhar: Oh, what a thing to say! It's so late; eat here today.

Satish: I won't eat here anymore, Uncle. I've just paid off one debt. I can't start another.

Satish leaves.

Sukumari: I shielded him from his father's harshness and fed and clothed him. Look at him as soon as he gets a little money! What ingratitude! It's a shame.

18

Satish: I thought I'd get the jute money before the boss looks at the accounts tomorrow, but the market fell. Now there's nothing but jail. I've been headed there since I was a kid.

But I'll cheat my fate. This pistol has two bullets; that's plenty. Neli—no, even if she had loved me, I've spoiled it. I've told her everything in my letter. Now this pistol is the only thing on earth that loves me. I'll die with its kiss on my forehead.

I really made this garden of my uncle's and collected all those rare trees. I thought it would be mine some day. My fate didn't tell me whose these trees would be—well, let it go. I'll possess this garden by dying beside this pond among the English stephanotis. No one will ever again be brave enough to come out here for fresh air.

Who's there? It's Haren! He's slipped out to steal green guavas. All his wants have bloomed on that low branch. What's he worth? His life is as immature as the guava. If I tore him away now, who can tell how many of life's disappointments I'd save him? And Auntie—oh, she'd be wild!

It's the right time, the right place, the right person. I can't control my hand! What shall I do? What shall I do?

Satish takes a stick and begins to beat the trees one after another. This increases his excitement. Finally he beats his own hand, but feels nothing. He takes the pistol from his pocket and rushes toward Haren.

Haren (startled): What's this? Is it my cousin? Please, please, don't tell my father.

Satish (shouting): Uncle, Uncle, help! Help! Hurry! Save your son!

Sashadhar (running): What's wrong, Satish, what's wrong?

Sukumari (running): What's happened to my son?

Haren: Nothing, Mother, nothing. Cousin's teasing me.

Sukumari: What a terrible joke! Shame! It's fantastic! Look at that! My heart is still pounding. I think Satish is drunk!

Satish: Get away. Take your son and run right away if you want to save him.

> *Sukumari takes Haren and leaves.*

Sashadhar: Satish, don't be so upset. Tell me what's going on. From whom did you want me to save Haren?

Satish: From myself. *(Shows the pistol.)* Look at that, Uncle.

> *Bidhu enters.*

Bidhu: Satish, what are you up to? Your boss and the police searched our house. If you must run, run right now. Oh, God! I never committed any sin. Why am I so unlucky?

Satish: Don't worry. I have an escape right in my hand.

Sashadhur: What are you——

Satish: That's it, Uncle, just what you suspected. I stole to pay off my debt to my aunt. I'm a thief. Mother, you'll be happy to know that I'm a thief and a murderer. Now you needn't cry anymore. Go away, get out of my sight. I can't stand it anymore.

Sashadhar: Satish, you owe me a debt too. Now pay it.

Satish: Tell me how. What can I give you? What do you want?

Sashadhar: Give me this pistol.

Satish: Take it. I'll go to jail. Otherwise, I'll never be able to discharge the debt of my sins.

Sashadhar: Sin's debt isn't paid by punishment, Satish, but by your actions. You know very well that if I make an appeal, your boss won't send you to jail. From now on, stay alive and make something of yourself.

Satish: Uncle, you don't know how hard it is for me to stay alive now. I threw away my last hope of happiness when I knew I was going to die. What shall I live for now?

Sashadhar: Still, you must live to pay my debt. You can't run off and cheat me.

Satish: If that's what you want, all right.

Sashadhar: Listen to another request: forgive your mother and aunt with all your heart.

Satish: If you can forgive me, there's no one in this world

I can't forgive. *(He touches his uncle's feet in respect.)* Mother, bless me so that I can face everything. You've accepted me with all my faults and virtues. I want to accept this world in the same way.

Bidhu: My dear boy, what more can I say? Being a mother, all I could do was love you. May God take care of you. Let me go to my sister and beg her forgiveness for you.

Bidhu leaves.

Sashadhar: Come on, then, Satish. You'll eat at my house today.

Nalini enters quickly.

Nalini: Satish!

Satish: What! Nalini!

Nalini: What's this all about? Why did you write me that letter?

Satish: You understand it very well. I didn't write it to deceive you, but everything turned topsy-turvy. You can think I wanted to arouse your sympathy, but my uncle will testify that I wasn't playacting. Still, if you don't believe me, there's time for me to keep my promise.

Nalini: Why do you keep raving like an idiot? What did I do to you that you act so harsh?

Satish: Nalini, that promise—it was no secret. Do you respect me at all?

Nalini: Respect! Satish, this is just why I get angry with you. Respect! Shame on you. Many people respect many others in this world. I've done just what you did. I've left no distinction between us. Look at this. I've brought all my jewelry. It isn't mine yet; it's my parents'. I took it without telling them. I don't know what it's worth, but won't it help you?

Sashadhar: He'll be all right. You have brought another priceless jewel to help Satish.

Nalini: Oh, Mr. Ray, forgive me. I didn't see you.

Sashadhar: My daughter, why be ashamed? We old people have trouble with our eyes, but at your age the veterans are overlooked. Satish, I see your boss has come. I'll go and talk to him. In the meantime you entertain my guest. Daughter, this pistol can now be placed in your custody.

1902

THE HOUSEWARMING

(Griha-prabesh)

PART ONE

The room next to Jatin's:
Neighbor and Jatin's sister, Himi.

Neighbor: Himi, how is Jatin today?

Himi: Not well, neighbor.

Neighbor: I hope he still has an appetite?

Himi: No, he can't even keep down a spoonful of barley water.

Neighbor: Dear child, why don't you try my suggestion? My son-in-law had the very same trouble. By God's grace he was able to eat. He ate well, and that's what saved him. But if he moved a bit sideways Jatin has the same kind of pain in his ribs——

Himi: No, he doesn't have any such pain.

Neighbor: Maybe not, but my son-in-law was also bedridden like this for quite a few months. That's why I say, child, get some of those medicines from Kapileshwar's temple in Faridpur. If you want, I can have my son, Atul——

Himi: Why don't you speak to my aunt and see if she——

Neighbor: Your aunt? She pays no attention to all this. You think she believes in such things? If she did, do you think she'd be in such a fix? I tell you, Himi, Jatin's wife doesn't even go near his room.

Himi: No, no, once in a while——

Neighbor: Why hide it from me, dear child? You were all so set on bringing a beautiful girl into your family. Now in such dark days what good is her angelic beauty to you? It would be better to have a dark, ugly——

Himi: Don't talk like that, neighbor. Mani is young.

Neighbor: Oh heavens, whom are you calling young? She

was married off by faking her age. Do you think we don't have eyes? Jatin is such a fine young man, and for his fate to have such a— Mani is coming.

Mani enters.

Come, child, come here. Were you on the roof terrace?
Mani: Yes.
Neighbor: Did you go to see the groom leaving the Sils' house? Poor child! How can a little girl spend day and night in a sickroom?
Mani: I went to water my flowerpots.
Neighbor: Oh, good, you reminded me of something important. You must give me a couple of your rose cuttings. Atul is very fond of plants, just like you.
Mani: Surely. I'll give you some.
Neighbor: And listen to me, child. You don't even touch your phonograph anymore nowadays. If you like, maybe I'll get it repaired at my own expense and——
Mani: Why don't you take it?
Neighbor (addressing Himi): Jatin's wife is very openhanded. Why not? She comes from a wealthy home. She is very kind. Oh, there comes your aunt. I'm going. She sits guarding Jatin's door. She can't keep the disease away, but she keeps us out.

She leaves.

Himi: Mani, what are you looking for?
Mani: That saucer I use to give my puppy milk.

Aunt enters.

Aunt: Mani dear, you know that Jatin's listening for the sound of your footsteps. Go in and see him and turn on the light yourself this evening. Cheer him up. What's the matter? Give me an answer.
Mani: Soon our——
Aunt: No matter who comes, I'm not asking you to stay a long time. It's just time for him to take his tonic. I've gotten it all ready for you. Why don't you take the cup and stand by his bedside, add a little honey to it, and feed it to him very slowly? Then as soon as he has taken the medicine, come away.
Mani: I went to his room this afternoon.

Aunt: He was asleep then.

Mani: I'm afraid to go into that room in the evening.

Aunt: Why? What are you afraid of?

Mani: My father-in-law died in that same room. I remember it very well.

Aunt: Is there a single spot in this world where no one has died?

Mani: Don't say that, Auntie, don't say it. I'm telling the truth. I'm so afraid of death.

Aunt: All right. In that case, why don't you go more often in the daytime?

Mani: I have tried to go. But somehow I get all shivery. He stares at my face so that his eyes glitter.

Aunt: What is there to be afraid of?

Mani: He seems to stare at me from far, far away, as if he's not in this world.

Aunt: All right, then. In that case, why don't you prepare his medicine and food outside the room? If he hears that you thought of doing something for him yourself, he'd feel a little——

Mani: Auntie, please, why don't all of you excuse me? I won't be able to handle all this day-and-night nursing.

Aunt: I ask you, then, if you were seriously ill yourself, then——

Mani: I don't recall ever being sick. Once I had a fever when I was at the Konnagar garden house. My mother kept me in a closed room. I sneaked out and took a dip in a pond full of stagnant water. Everyone thought I'd get pneumonia. Nothing happened. That very day my fever broke.

Aunt: Hasn't anyone in your family ever had any misfortune?

Mani: I have never seen any. I saw death for the first time in this house. All I want is to leave, to get away somewhere. When I smell liniment, it seems as if the air is haunted by a ghost from the hospital.

Aunt: If you have such a temperament in this world——

Mani: I don't know about that. Why don't you all make me the gardener? I could do that very well.

Mani leaves quickly.

Himi: Look, Auntie, her nature is such that I can't get mad at her even if I try. It seems that God has sent her into this world without any liabilities. To Him there is no distinction between happiness and sorrow.

Aunt: God put so much care into creating her outer shell that He didn't get time to finish her off inside. She's just like this house of your brother's. He began it with big plans, but by the time the outer shell was built, he was bankrupt. The interior scaffolding never arrived. Now he has to be deceived continually, both about the house and about Mani.

Himi: I can't decide whether we're doing the right thing.

Aunt: You know, Himi, when you face death, whether the house is built or not built is immaterial. That is why I tell him, "What you wanted with all your heart to do has been done." Himi, that is the truth.

Himi: Maybe that is true about the house, but what about Mani?

Aunt: Himi, He who has made Mani beautiful has made her as complete as He intended. That precious jewel, that Mani[1] of eternity, that Mani who is God's own treasure, is like a special gem. There is no touch of incompleteness anywhere. If only Jatin on his deathbed could see that Mani who is the creation of God's will.

Himi: Auntie, when I listen to you, I feel so much better.

Aunt: Himi, I talk, but it doesn't keep me from getting angry with her. I understand it all, yet I can't forgive her. But Himi, you just said you couldn't be angry with Mani. It made me realize that you are truly Jatin's sister. I'd better go to Jatin now.

She leaves.

In the sickroom.

Jatin: Auntie, is all the masonry being set on the second floor of the house?

Aunt: Yes, it was all completed yesterday.

Jatin: Good. It's all finished after all this time. After such a long time my building of this home is done, my longtime dream.

Aunt: So many people are coming to see this house of yours, Jatin.

Jatin: They are seeing it from the outside. What I see on the inside hasn't been finished yet. It will never be finished. To this day what artist ever set the last stone of his creation and said, "Now I am finished!"? The Creator of the

[1] Mani means jewel.

universe hasn't been able to say that. He is still at work too.

Aunt: Jatin, no more of this, dear boy. You'd better try to sleep a little now.

Jatin: No, Auntie, don't tell me to go to sleep so early.

Aunt: But the doctor——

Jatin: Forget the doctor. Today my world has been completed. I'm not going to sleep tonight. Put on all the lights in the house, Auntie. Where is Mani? Have her——

Aunt: I have sent her to that new room on the second floor to arrange flowers.

Jatin: How did you think this up? A grand idea! Have you set up the ceremonial water jars at each side of the door?

Aunt: Oh yes!

Jatin: And the lotus-flower design in rice paste on the floor?

Aunt: It's certainly there.

Jatin: Just this once can't you all carry me there somehow? Just this once I want to see my Mani sitting in the middle of the room that I designed.

Aunt: No, Jatin, that can't be done. The doctor would be very angry.

Jatin: I'm imagining how she looks. Which sari did she wear?

Aunt: That red sari that she wore at her wedding.

Jatin: Do you know what I'll call this house of mine, Auntie?

Aunt: Tell me what.

Jatin: Mani-Mahal.[2]

Aunt: A fine name.

Jatin: You can't understand the whole meaning of this, Auntie.

Aunt: Perhaps I can't understand it all.

Jatin: By "mansion" you shouldn't think of the house alone. There is sweetness in it too.

Aunt: It is there, Jatin. This was not built only with money. You have poured the sweetness of your heart into it.

Jatin: All of you will laugh at this.

Aunt: No, why should we laugh, Jatin? Tell me what you were saying.

Jatin: Today I can understand what consolation Shah Jehan got from completing the Taj Mahal. That consolation superseded his death and even to this day——

Aunt: Don't talk any more, Jatin. Jatin, if you don't want

---

[2] Mani-Mahal means, literally, Mani-Mansion.

to sleep, then don't. Why don't you just think quietly for a bit?

Jatin: Mani has put on her red wedding sari. I'd like to see her just once now.

Aunt: Jatin, the doctor warns that——

Jatin: The doctor is afraid that if you——

Aunt: Not on your account, but for Mani; it is difficult to understand her from outward appearances, but inwardly——

Jatin: She has a weakness. Did the doctor say that?

Aunt: We have all noticed that.

Jatin: Aha! Poor girl, all of you be very careful. It is better this way. She ought to stay far away from the sickroom.

Aunt: She is dying to come, but we——

Jatin: No, no, better not, better not. Auntie, there's an album on that shelf. Can you get it?

> *She brings the album to him.*

I was telling you about the Taj Mahal. Now it seems that what happened to Shah Jehan has happened to me. I am on this fading side of life, she is on the side of perfection—far away. I can't reach her anymore. Just like the Emperor's Mumtaz. I dedicate this house to Mani, this Taj Mahal of mine. She lives in it. She will live here for eternity, and yet she is out of my sight.

Aunt: Oh, Jatin, why do you have to talk anymore? Stop for a moment. I'll get the sleeping medicine.

Jatin: No, Auntie, no. I don't want to sleep tonight. When I stay awake I get something out of it. When I'm asleep everything gets lost. Auntie, I talk to you about nothing but Mani. I hope you don't mind.

Aunt: Not at all, Jatin. I can't say how much I like it. Do you know whom you remind me of?

Jatin: Of whom?

Aunt: Of your mother. Once long ago I had to listen to her inmost thoughts, too. Your father lived at our house then and went to medical school. In those days no one in the house knew your mother's feelings except me. When Father brought another suitor for her, I was the person who told him.

Jatin: You have told me that. Grandfather couldn't convince Mother, and at last he had to let her marry my father. It makes me so happy to imagine those days.

Aunt: Your mother's love was like a penance. For five years that sacred fire burned, and then she received the blessing. Jatin, I see the same fire in you and I am amazed.

Jatin: Mother poured her sacred fire into my bloodstream. I too will receive a blessing at the end of my penance. For some reason, Auntie, I feel that that time is very near. Where is that flute playing?

Aunt: It's a wedding *sanai*. This is an auspicious day for weddings.

Jatin: How surprising! This is the night Mani has also put on the red Banaras sari. The auspicious moment of the wedding recurs many times in life. Auntie, why don't you have all the lights turned on tonight from the courtyard to——

Aunt: Jatin, you couldn't sleep with so much light in your eyes.

Jatin: It wouldn't do any harm. I'll be more at peace awake than asleep. You know, Auntie, the temple is built. Now we'll have the ceremony for consecrating the image of the goddess. I never imagined that all this could be done while I was still alive.

Aunt: You won't stop if I stay in the room. I'm going. If you don't want to sleep, at least lie quietly.

Jatin: All right. Give me the house plan that I drew and my box from the playroom. Speaking of the playroom reminds me of that song. Himi! Himi!

Aunt: Don't get upset, Jatin. I'll send for her.

She leaves.

Himi enters.

Himi: What is it, brother?

Jatin: Sing that song, sister, the one about the playroom.

Himi's Song

I began to build a playhouse
    In my mind.
How shall I tell you of all the nights
    I lay awake?
On the road the traveler passes calling,
Alas! I have no time to reply
That call to the game outside—
    How shall I take part?

What everyone rejects,
    Whatever lies discarded,
The bricks of bygone, broken days—
    I build my house with these.
This is the play-throne for Him
Who is my everlasting treasure.
He will mend what was broken,
With magic of his own.

The Doctor enters.

Doctor: Singing! Fine, fine, very good. Better than medicine. Jatin, stay in a happy frame of mind; everything will be all right. It's a great crime to live to less than ninety-five. It deserves capital punishment.

Jatin: I'm very happy. You know, Doctor, after all this time my house is finished. It's all my own plan.

Doctor: That's the way. If a person lives in his own house, things really come up to the mark. Actually, the father's house is a rented house—not your own. Your father, Kedar, was my school friend; he inherited nothing from his ancestors but his own life. Whatever riches he had, he slowly but surely built up by himself. Did that detract from his pleasure? Since his father-in-law was against his marriage, Kedar was angry and took none of his property. You too have built your own house yourself. That too is something to be happy about.

Jatin: I'm very happy.

Doctor: Fine, fine. Let's have the housewarming. Give us a big feast. You can't stay on in bed like this.

Jatin: Today I feel that there will be a housewarming. I'll check the almanac. On the very first auspicious day, we'll——

Doctor: Good, good! Not the almanac, my boy. Everything depends on your own mind. Whenever the mind says it's an auspicious day, that's when the auspicious day arrives.

Jatin: My mind says the auspicious day has come. That's why I sent for Himi and listened to her song. It seems that the *sanai* for the housewarming begins playing now in the autumn sky.

Doctor: Let it play. In the meantime I'll check your pulse and examine your chest. Let's dispose of all this nonsense before we order sweets and such. What do you say, my son?

Jatin: What does it matter how the pulse is?

Doctor: Nothing at all, nothing at all. We have to do these things to please ourselves. We wear the mask of the cure-all and massage the patient's chest and back and pocket, and Yama sits and laughs. No one but the doctor himself can faze the solemnity of Yama. Himi, dear child, you go to the next room and sing like a bird. I'm writing a book in which I'll explain how waves of singing clear the air of sickness. All diseases are out of tune; they are the most discordant of all discords. They interrupt the harmony of the body. Go, my child, and sing loudly.

Himi: Which song shall I sing brother?

Jatin: The song of the newlyweds.

Doctor: Yes, yes, that would be appropriate. It's an auspicious time today. I was held up by three wedding processions. That's why I was so late.

> *Himi goes to the next room and sings.*

Himi's Song

> Play, flute, play.
> O lovely one, adorn yourself
>   With garlands of sandalwood
> On this auspicious evening.
> Has the restless traveler come
> On this sweet month of Spring?
> Did the champak flower trembling at the
>   touch of the bee
>   Bloom in the courtyard today?
>
> She wears the crimson veil, the crimson
>   flower wristlet.
> In the murmur of ankle-bells,
> In the fragrance-laden breeze,
> The courtyard echoes the welcoming song;
> Come, stay in this garden of joy.

> *In the next room: the Doctor and the Aunt.*

Doctor: It is good to know the truth. It is better to accept the pain that we'll have to stand. We only increase sorrow by trying to save ourselves from it.

Aunt: Doctor, why are you saying all this?

Doctor: I'm saying that you must prepare yourself.

Aunt: Doctor, did you think you would prepare me just by saying these few words? God Himself has been preparing

me since I was eighteen years old, just as bricks are prepared by baking in the kiln. The mold of my misfortunes
was formed long ago. Now only the last little bit of it remains to be done. Whatever God had to say to me, He
has said very directly. Why do you beat around the bush
in telling me?

Doctor: There is no hope for Jatin. Just a few more days.

Aunt: I'll keep that in mind. I'll have to get family affairs
settled in these few days. After that, if God is merciful
He will give me leave and let me go about His own work.

Doctor: I have prescribed a different medicine. Now he should
always be kept in a pleasant frame of mind. There is no
better physician than the mind.

Aunt: The mind! Alas! I'll do whatever I can.

Doctor: You should let Mani go to the patient once in a
while. I have a feeling that you people keep her away a
little too much.

Aunt: After all, she's just a child; she can't be burdened with
nursing the sick.

Doctor: That's not the point. You're being a little unfair to
her too. I've noticed that Mani has great strength of
mind. Such a great strain on her, but she hasn't broken
down.

Aunt: Still, inwardly——

Doctor: We doctors know only the pain of the sick. We don't
concern ourselves with the pain of those who are well.
Better yet, have Mani come to me. I'll tell her myself.

Aunt: No, no, there's no need to do that. I'll tell her.

Doctor: Look here, our profession gives us the great advantage of knowing a lot about human nature. I've been aware
that the mother-in-law bears a natural enmity toward the
daughter-in-law, and this persists even in the darkest days.
The daughter-in-law takes care of the son and wins away
his heart. Nothing is more——

Aunt: What you say is not wrong. There can be some enmity. There is so much sin hidden away in our minds. Who
knows it except the God who dwells within us?

Doctor: Why think only of your nephew? You have a responsibility toward his wife too. Why don't you try to
imagine how she must be feeling? She must be miserable
with waiting to come to his room and look after him.

Aunt: I'm lacking in judgment. I hadn't thought of all that.

Doctor: Look, I'm a blunt person. I don't hold back from
saying what I must say. Don't take offense.

Aunt: Why should I take offense, Doctor? If there is unfairness anywhere, how can it be corrected unless it is criticized? Well, I'll remember what you said. It will be corrected.

The Doctor leaves.

Himi, what are you doing?

Himi: I'm warming some milk for Jatin.

Aunt: Well, I'll warm the milk. Why don't you go and sing to Jatin a little? He might sleep a little while he listens to your songs.

The Neighbor enters.

Neighbor: Sister, how is Jatin today?

Aunt: He's not well, Suro.

Neighbor: Listen to me, sister. Call our Dr. Jogu. My granddaughter was in misery with a swollen nose. At last Dr. Jogu took out a big glass bead from her right nostril. He has a good reputation. My son knows his address.

Aunt: All right. Tell your son to send me his address.

Neighbor: The other day I saw Mani visiting the Alipore Zoo.

Aunt: She is very fond of animals. She goes there quite often.

Neighbor: If she loves animals, is that any reason not to love her husband?

Aunt: Who says she doesn't love her husband! She's a child. How can she stand being with the sick day and night? We ourselves force her to——

Neighbor: Say whatever you like, but all the girls in the neighborhood talk about her.

Aunt: The neighborhood girls aren't married to her, Suro. My Jatin understands her. He has not once——

Neighbor: But, sister, just because he doesn't say anything——

Aunt: He doesn't say anything. She sometimes goes to the museum or goes to see the tigers and the lions. This makes him so happy.

Neighbor: What are you saying, sister? Is nursing——

Aunt: He says this is Mani's way of taking care of him. Jatin himself is tied to the bed. Mani goes here and there and Jatin takes a vacation through her. Is that insignificant to a sick person?

Neighbor: I don't know, sister. We're old-fashioned people and can't understand all that. Anyway, I'll send my son.

He knows Dr. Jogu's address. What harm is there in calling him once?

In the sickroom.

Jatin: There you are, Himi, I'm relieved! I can't find that photograph anywhere. Why don't you look around for it?

Himi: Which photo?

Jatin: That picture of me with Mani at the Botanical Gardens.

Himi: That was in your album.

Jatin: I took it out of the album a little while ago. It must be somewhere in the bed, or maybe it has fallen underneath.

Himi: Here it is, brother, under your pillow.

Jatin: It seems as if this belongs to another life, that spot under the *neem* tree. Mani was wearing a yellow sari. Her hair was wound up low on her neck. Remember, Himi, from somewhere a bird kept calling. The tide had come up in the river; there was such a wind, and how the casuarina branches rustled! Mani picked up the casuarina fruits and peeled them and sniffed them. She said, "I like this smell so much." I don't know what she doesn't like. I have enjoyed many things in this world through her enjoyment. Sing the song you sang that day, Himi. Good girl! Do you remember?

Himi: Yes, I remember.

Himi's Song

In the lake-waters of youth
    The lotus of love
Trembles restlessly on the flood.
    Within its purple shyness
Bloom its secret dreams.
Among its fragrant filaments
    Is one teardrop.
    Gently, gently blow, O breeze,
    Your touch carries pain.
My heart fears
That the stem will break,
And my eyes are filled with tears
Of tenderness unknown.

Jatin: That day the shade of the tree spoke out. Now the whole world is absolutely silent inside these four walls. The walls are like bloodless lips. Himi, turn the light down a little. On our side of the river there were so many shades of green from the trees scattered across the sky, and on the other shore the smoke from the factory chimneys wound toward the sky—even that had such a lovely color and such a beautiful form. Everything seemed so good. And that dog of yours—Mani threw the ball into the river again and again, and the dog would swim and——

Himi: Brother, don't talk anymore.

Jatin: All right, I won't. I'll close my eyes and listen to the rustling of those casuarina branches. But Himi, the song you sang tonight was just like that— Who knows? Let darkness settle a little more. Then I can hear it for myself. "Slowly, slowly blow, O breeze." Well, you'd better go now. Where did I put the picture?

Himi: Right here.

The Aunt and Akhil in the next room.

Akhil: Why did you call me, Auntie?

Aunt: Akhil, you're the lawyer, you'll have to take care of something.

Akhil: No one has any patience; a decree has to be drawn up now, in order to bring it to court——

Aunt: This won't require patience for very long. They're your own clients. Explain it a little. The doctor says ——

Akhil: The doctor said something once before; they won't believe that anymore. Mortgaging one house to build another—what got into Jatin? Where's his intelligence?

Aunt: It's not his fault, not his fault at all. His wife, Mani, sits like the inauspicious Saturn in place of his intelligence. He thought that he would hold onto his Mani, that will-o'-the-wisp of his, by putting a brick wall around her.

Akhil: He had some cash.

Aunt: He has lost everything in his jute business.

Akhil: Jatin's jute business? Tilling the soil with a pen! Shall I laugh or shall I weep?

Aunt: He was ready to spend unbelievable sums of money. He thought he would buy and sell and make a quick profit, but somehow flies smell wounds from the sky and ill advisers flock around from somewhere at the least smell of misfortune.

Akhil: Misfortune! The way the market is now, it doesn't even pay the cultivators to harvest the jute in the fields.

Aunt: That's enough! Enough! Don't say any more. We needn't worry too much. His days are numbered.

Akhil: Auntie, his creditors must have heard about his jute speculation. They realized that a lot of vultures would gather. That's why they've planned to get their own debts cleared quickly.

Aunt: Oh, Akhil, ask them to be patient for a few days. Don't let Yama's messenger and the bailiffs compete. Or take me to your clients. I am a Brahman woman; I'll go and beg at their feet.

Akhil: All right, let me speak to them once more. If necessary, you might have to go with me. Just let me go and have a word with Jatin.

Aunt: No. As soon as he sees you, he'll remember his jute business.

Akhil: Well, he took out a big life-insurance policy in Mani's name. What happened to it?

Aunt: I've put that aside somewhere or other. What little I had is all gone. And these doctor bills! I won't be able to save Jatin, but I have been able to protect that policy of his, and I'll always have this pleasant memory. I recall when once in a while he had to pay a premium for the insurance, what a row there was! For Heaven's sake, Akhil, tell your client——

Akhil: Look here, Aunt, I'll tell him the truth. I haven't a bit of sympathy for Jatin. Such colossal stupidity!

Aunt: But look how much of God's grace has been granted to him. He staked everything he had on building this house. He couldn't finish it, but the Companion in his game is picking up the broken playthings and is taking him along with Him. Who knows what other games he will be invited to share?

Akhil: Aunt, there's nothing written in the law books about your game of Fate. That's why I'm able to earn a living. Otherwise, if the wind of whims had blown this way, I'd be done for.

He leaves.

Mani enters.

Aunt: Mani, have you got any news from your father? I've seen your cousin-brother, Anath.

Mani: Yes, Mother sent the message that my little sister's rice ceremony will be held on this coming Friday. So I thought——

Aunt: Very good, my dear. Why not send a gold necklace? Your mother would be very pleased.

Mani: I think I'll go. I haven't seen my little sister for a good while. I'd like to see her.

Aunt: Oh, Lord, what a thing to say! Would you leave Jatin alone?

Mani: I wouldn't be gone long.

Aunt: Who can say whether or not it would be long, dear child? Can we control time? It can become too late in the twinkling of an eye.

Mani: After three brothers, I'm the first daughter. There will be a great fuss over the rice ceremony. If I don't go, my mother will be very——

Aunt: I can't understand your mother. Your mother belongs to that tribe of mothers whose lives are surrounded by seven seas of tears, yet she doesn't understand another person's great pain and goes on and on asking for you.

Mani: Look here, Auntie, don't make rude remarks about my mother. If you were my real mother-in-law, I could have taken it from you, but——

Aunt: All right, Mani, it was my fault. Forgive me. I'm not speaking to you as a mother-in-law. As an ordinary woman, I beg you, don't leave Jatin just now. I know for certain that if you go, your father will be angry.

Mani: I know that. You must write a line for me, Aunt. Say that it would be fine if I went home sometimes.

Aunt: Don't I know there'd be no great loss if you went? But if I have to write to your father, I'll write just what I think without omitting a thing.

Mani: Very good, you don't have to write. If I go and tell my husband, he'd——

Aunt: Look here, Mani, I've stood enough, but if you take this matter to Jatin, I won't tolerate anything more.

Mani: All right. I don't want your letter. Why such a fuss because I want to see my parents? When my husband wanted to go to Germany to study he needed a passport. Do my parents live in Germany?

Aunt: All right, all right. Don't shout so much. There, he's calling me. I'm coming, Jatin. Who knows whether he heard us?

She leaves.

In Jatin's room.

Aunt: Did you call me, Jatin?

Jatin: Yes, Auntie. I was lying here thinking that I have no way out. I'm a prisoner here, held inside these four walls by the net of sickness. Why should I keep Mani cooped up too?

Aunt: You don't know what you're saying, Jatin. Your life is tied to hers. Even if you wanted to let her go, would her bonds vanish?

Jatin: There was a time when some wives died on their husbands' funeral pyres, but that is no longer in vogue. But for Mani, now, this is dying second by second along with me, dying with her husband while she is still alive. I feel suffocated whenever I think of this. Let her out of this, Auntie, let her out.

Aunt: Why do you suddenly talk like this, Jatin? Did you hear something in another nightmare?

Jatin: No, no, I've thought about it a long time, along with the rustling of the casuarina branches, the tide in the river, the faraway call of the *bou-katha-kao* bird. I remembered Mani wearing her yellow sari, playing with the dog and laughing for no reason at all. Why should her ungovernable heart be shut in by the walls of death? Give her a vacation. It's been a long time since I heard her laugh in this house. She has the current of a fresh tide. Would you dam that up with all these bottles of medicine and invalid diets? I feel strongly that it's unfair, very unfair.

Aunt: It's not at all unfair, not a bit of it. Only she who has life in her can give life. Only heavy clouds give rain. Don't sit up, Jatin, lie down; you shouldn't be so restless. Tell me where you want to send Mani. I've no idea.

Jatin: In that case, why not send her to her parents? I forget where her father is now.

Aunt: Sitarampur.

Jatin: Yes, Sitarampur. That's a healthy place. Send her there.

Aunt: Listen to that! Why would she want to go to her father's and leave you in such a state?

Jatin: What has the doctor said? Has she heard that——

Aunt: She certainly does not know. She sees it with her own eyes. The other day she was upset and cried when I even hinted at her going to her parents.

Jatin: Really, Auntie? She cried? Really? Did you see her cry?

Aunt: Jatin, don't get up, don't get up, lie down. There it goes. I forgot to close the kitchen door and the dog will get in. I'm going. Sleep a little, Jatin.

Jatin: This time I'll surely go to sleep, don't you worry. Just one thing: decide on an auspicious day for the housewarming.

Aunt: What are you saying, Jatin? In your condition——

Jatin: None of you can believe it. I'll be able to go, I'll certainly be able to go. Start getting everything ready right now. Then see that nothing holds it up.

Aunt: There'll be one, there'll be one, don't worry.

Jatin: Let Mani know about it right away. Won't she have work to do too?

Aunt: Definitely, Jatin, she surely has work to do.

Jatin: You will bring blessings to us both. Well, Auntie, I have one question I'm afraid to ask anyone. Can you answer it for me? Did the market price of jute go up?

Aunt: I don't know for certain. Akhil said something about it.

Jatin: What? What? What did he say? I don't want to scare you, but if the market hasn't risen, it's certain.

Aunt: What about it?

Jatin: Then this house of mine—in one moment it will become a mirage. There! There's our warehouse manager. Narahari! Narahari!

Aunt: Jatin, don't shout! You're mistaken. Please lie down. I'm going, I'll have a talk with Akhil.

Jatin: I'm afraid that it seems— Auntie, if the market is in bad shape, ask Akhil for some——

Aunt: All right, I'll talk to Akhil. Now you——

Jatin: Do you know, Auntie? The money that I borrowed was Akhil's money put under another name.

Aunt: I guessed as much.

Jatin: But see here, don't let Narahari come here. I'm afraid he might say something. I wouldn't be able to face it. You take him to Akhil.

Aunt: I'm just going.

Jatin: If you have the almanac, send it in to me.

Aunt: Let the almanac go. You go to sleep.

Jatin: Mani cried when you spoke of her going to her father's? That's very surprising to me.

Aunt: What's there to be so surprised about?

Jatin: She's an Urvasi of that paradise that has no shadow of death. You want to make her a nurse in a private hospital.

Aunt: Jatin, will you keep thinking of her as being like a picture? Would you hang her up on the wall?

Jatin: What's wrong with it? Pictures are very scarce in this world. Is one less lucky for being able to see what he wants to see? Forget it. You said that Mani cried? The goddess Lakshmi sits on the lotus. She too makes the breeze smell sweet when she sighs.

Aunt: If a girl isn't able to make herself useful, then——

Jatin: There were plenty of people to do the work in Shah Jehan's household. He saw only one among them all who didn't demand anything. Otherwise he wouldn't have thought of the Taj Mahal. The Taj Mahal needed nothing. Auntie, when I'm better I'll concentrate on this house again. As long as I live, my only project will be the completion of this house, this Mani-Mahal of mine. I have seen God's dream with my own eyes, and I want to leave that message behind me by reshaping the dream. Auntie, maybe you don't quite understand what I'm saying.

Aunt: That's right, my dear boy. I don't quite understand what you menfolk say.

Jatin: Open this window a bit wider.

> *The Aunt opens the window.*

Look there, look there. In the endless darkness all tears have become stars. Where's Himi, Auntie? Is she sleeping?

Aunt: No, it's not very late. Oh, Himi, come here.

> *Himi enters.*

Jatin: They have forbidden me to sing. That's why I have to send for you so often. Don't be annoyed, sister.

Himi: No, brother, you know very well how much I like to sing. Tell me which song you'd like to hear.

Jatin: That one—"My Mind Looks at Itself."

> *Himi's Song*

My mind looks at itself and sees its own loveliness.
    So, my eyes, do not wander about like beggars.
      The song of the *ektara*

Peers into my heart,
The flute sounds upon the path of my desires,
The formless is rocked by beauty's form.

On some shoreless lake of delight
The rootless flower floats upon the water:
My reaching out for it
Stirs the wave that takes it away;
So I am silent, I do not steal:
That formless beauty is not easily won.

Jatin: Auntie, you have all thought of Mani as always flighty. It seemed that her mind wasn't on this house, but see——

Aunt: No, my boy, I was mistaken. It takes time to know a person.

Jatin: You thought I couldn't be happy with Mani. That's why you were angry with her. But happiness isn't something to be sprinkled over the darkness like stars. Hasn't the light of happiness been lit here and there in our lives? I received all that was coming to me. I have no complaint. But Auntie, she's quite young. What will she live by?

Aunt: Who says she's young? When we were her age, we had begun to do God's work in the world and had taken Him into our hearts. What damage has that done us? That's why I say, why this great obsession with happiness?

Jatin: The moment I heard that Mani cried, I realized that her mind had awakened. Call her in just once, Auntie. One day she came here in the afternoon. It was bright daylight then and all at once it seemed that there was no shadow in her anywhere. Let me see her in this darkness, at dusk. Perhaps I'll be able to see the tears of her heart.

Aunt: She is still shy about unveiling her love before you. That's why she hides all her crying.

Jatin: All right, let it be that way. Let it stay behind a screen. But Auntie, bring me news about that screen, for when it is moved aside, then maybe— But this evening I'm especially anxious to talk to her a little.

Aunt: What is it that you're so anxious to say?

Jatin: My Mani-Mahal has been finished. I want to give her this news myself. The housewarming is on my mind. She'll have to arrange for it. This thing I have created is for her, this is my song played on a *vina* of wood and brick.

Aunt: Do you think she doesn't know that?

Jatin: Still, it must be dedicated to her. I'll ask Himi to stand
outside the door and sing that song:
> "The gift of my life,
> Make it precious by your acceptance."

Go on, Auntie, call her. Auntie! Look there! Narahari
has come to talk to me—my warehouse manager—don't
let him come in here today. No, no, no, I don't want
to know a thing. If he has news, I'll hear it later.

The Aunt leaves.

Himi, listen, listen—

Himi enters.

Listen to a song. You must learn it.
Himi: No, brother, don't sing. The doctor has forbidden it.
Jatin: I'll hum it. After all this time I've remembered our
sister Kuni's song.

> When my heart was unawakened
> The man of my heart came to the door.
> > The sound of his departing
> > Awakened me.
> My sleep was broken in the darkness.
> The wind of his returning
> > Beat its way into my heart.
> Ah, it rouses a storm that wails aloud.

After hearing what Auntie had to say, Himi, I feel sure
that Mani's heart has been awakened. Maybe you can't
understand everything I'm saying. All right, let it go. Have
you seen all of this house?
Himi: It's really beautiful.
Jatin: In the room upstairs where I asked them to set a
stone— Where's the plan? Here it is. I hope the wooden
ceiling covers the beams in this room.
Himi: Yes, every bit of them.
Jatin: Tell me how it's designed.
Himi: There's a wide border done in blue, in the middle
there are red lotuses and white swans in the background.
It's just as you planned it.

Jatin: And on the walls?

Himi: There's a row of cranes on the wall, drawn with inlaid shells.

Jatin: And on the floor?

Himi: The floor has a border of white conch shells. There's a huge lotus set into the center.

Jatin: Did they set the two white marble jars in place beside the doorway?

Himi: Yes, they're there. There are two electric lights inside them—beautiful!

Jatin: Do you know the name of that room?

Himi: I know, the Mani Temple.

Jatin: The other day Akhil came to see Auntie. What did he say? Did you hear any of it? Anything about this house?

Himi: He was saying there wasn't a prettier house in Calcutta.

Jatin: No, no, not that. Did Akhil talk about this house? Let it go, it doesn't matter. Auntie was saying that Mani made the fish gravy this afternoon. It tasted really delicious. Would you——

Himi: I couldn't say that.

Jatin: Shame on you, sister. To this day you can't get along with your sister-in-law. This is my——

Himi: Because I'm a sister-in-law, maybe that's why.

Jatin: That's why you're on good terms at the times prescribed by the scriptures, then get mad again?

Himi: Yes, brother. Haven't you heard that Hindi song, "The sister-in-law stays on guard."

Jatin: You've changed that line a little. You sang, "The sister-in-law stays mad."

Himi: Yes, brother, it doesn't sound bad if you put the tune to it. *(Sings.)* "The sister-in-law stays mad."

Jatin: But don't sing it out of tune, sister.

Himi: How could it be? I learned the tune from you.

Jatin: Look there, look how many workmen have crowded in. Naren Khan's people are milling around the courtyard. Himi, do something for me. Can you get me some bits of information? Today's market—no, no, forget it. Shut that door.

In the next room. Mani and Aunt.

Aunt: What is it, Mani? Are you going somewhere?

Mani: I'm going to Sitarampur.

Aunt: What a thing to say! With whom are you going?

Mani: Anath is taking me.

Aunt: My dear Mani, do go. No one will stop you. But not today.

Mani: I've bought the ticket and made the train reservation. Mother sent the money.

Aunt: Don't worry about that. We don't mind that expense. But in that case why not take the early-morning train tomorrow? Tonight——

Mani: Aunt, I don't believe in your stars and lucky days. What's the harm in going today?

Aunt: Jatin has been asking for you. He wants to tell you something especially important.

Mani: All right, I still have ten minutes. I'll go and talk to him.

Aunt: No, you can't tell him that you're going.

Mani: I won't tell him, but I can't stay too long. The rice ceremony is tomorrow. I must go tonight.

Aunt: I beg you, daughter, pay attention to me this once. Compose yourself and sit by Jatin. Don't hurry.

Mani: What can I do? The train won't sit and wait. Anath had already left. He came back to get me. I must go right now and tell him I'm going.

Aunt: No, then you can't go in there. I won't let you go to him that way. Oh, you unfortunate child, you'll remember this day as long as you live.

Mani: Aunt, I warn you, don't curse me like that.

Aunt: Oh, my dear son, why are you still alive? There's no end to our sorrow. I couldn't hold her any longer.

Mani leaves.

Shaila enters.

Shaila: Auntie, is this any way for your daughter-in-law to behave? What a thing! How can she go to her father's when her husband is in such a condition?

Aunt: She's such a little girl, seems as if made of butter, but what a heart of stone!

Shaila: I've known her for a long time but I never knew that she could go this far. On the other hand, look at all the dogs and cats and monkeys and peacocks and other animals she keeps petting. It doesn't make sense. If anything happened to them she'd create such a scene, yet about her husband— I can't understand her.

Aunt: Jatin understands her. Once Jatin was in bed with a

bad headache, and Mani went to the theater with her friends. I couldn't stand that and went to fan Jatin. He snatched the fan out of my hand and threw it away. I was so upset. The thought of those days breaks my heart.

Shaila: I'm saying this, Auntie: unless the girl is as hard as stone, she can't hold on to the fickle heart of a man. The softer you are, the more they'll slip away.

Aunt: You know, Shaila, maybe this is man's nature. Unless there is something hard in the bond, it's not a bond at all, whether it be men or women. The flowers in the garland of life are amaranth blossoms, but they are strung together with thunder.

Shaila leaves.

The Neighbor enters.

Neighbor: Lord, what an affair! Is it true that Jatin's wife has gone to her father's home?

Aunt: What if she has? Why should it concern you so much?

Neighbor: That's true. How does it concern us? Everyone in the neighborhood loves Jatin, and that's why.

Aunt: Yes, that's why the person Jatin loves is everyone's concern.

Neighbor: All right. In that case, Mani has done something really noble. Very few other girls can do such a fine thing.

Aunt: We call that wife who acts according to her husband's wishes a good wife. Mani is that kind of wife.

Neighbor: Yes, I see that all right.

Aunt: Mani is young. Jatin simply couldn't stand seeing her cooped up with an invalid. Finally, at the doctor's advice, still, he— That's all there is to it. You people go and gossip as much as you can all over the neighborhood. But don't shout any more near Jatin.

Neighbor: Oh, fine! Now we can understand what kind of sorrow makes Mani go to her father's house so often.

She leaves.

The Doctor enters.

Doctor: What's going on? I saw a trunk and a suitcase at the door and Mani in a great rush to get into a cab with her cousin-brother. Where's she gone? When she saw me she didn't stop for a moment. I thought she'd ask something about the patient, but no such thing. Have you quarreled with her?

The Aunt shakes her head.

Look here, you should have cut out your mother-in-law behavior toward the girl for a few days while the patient is in this condition.

Aunt: I never succeeded in doing that, Doctor. Nature doesn't work on you daily, either. If two people live in one house there is bound to be some wrangling.

Doctor: Surely when Mani called the cab you could have stopped her.

The Aunt shakes her head.

Who knows? Maybe you're relieved because she's gone, but I'm telling you very plainly that every minute his wife is banished and Jatin is disappointed only shortens his life. Our prime duty is to the patient. That's precisely why I speak to you this way. Otherwise I have no right to get into your family feud.

Aunt: If I'm to blame, there's no use arguing about it. I can humble myself and write asking her to come back as long as I'm alive to do it, whether you curse me or not. Now can you do something for me, Doctor?

Doctor: What is it?

Aunt: Write a letter now to Mani's father at Sitarampur. Say just what Jatin's condition is. If I know her father as well as I think I do, I'm absolutely certain that when he gets that letter he'll bring her here at once.

Doctor: Very well, I'll write it. But on no account should Jatin be told that his wife has gone to her father's house. I'm making this perfectly plain. There is no medicine that would counteract this news. Himi, dear child, do something while you're sitting there. Sing a song while you sit by his door, that song you like so well. He won't get a chance to ask about his wife. Do you hear me? This is no time for tears. It's a time to sing. Tears will come later. Now, then, the song. Did I tell you that I'm writing a book to show that the vibrations of musical sound waves and the movements of germs are diametrically opposed? Did you know that I'm expecting to collect a Nobel Prize?

He leaves.

Himi's Song

Silently crossing the ocean of death,
You came as a lovely dream.
My tears call to you hour by hour;
Wandering everywhere, everywhere repulsed,
I was sealed in the dark well of this life;
Now you have come as a lovely dream.

Now I see darkness pour down like dark hair,
In its folds gleam the jewels of the evening stars.
Now the sky fills with the pain of song.
And trembles with the hum of crickets underfoot.
You worship with incense from the flowering forest—
Now you have come as a lovely dream.

Himi (looking offstage): I'm coming, brother. I'm coming in.
                                                She leaves.

Akhil enters.

Akhil: Why did you call, Auntie?
Aunt: Since yesterday Jatin has asked me again and again to send for you. I couldn't put him off any longer.
Akhil: About that mortgage?
Aunt: That's quite obviously on his mind, but he doesn't want to ask that question. Whenever that thought gives him a jolt, he shoves it away. Don't you bring that up when you see him. He won't bring it up himself.
Akhil: Then why did he have to call me?
Aunt: To make a will.
Akhil: A will? That's surprising.
Aunt: I know it's unnecessary. But I swear on my life, you must keep this quiet. Whatever he says, possible or impossible, you must write everything down any way he wants it. Don't laugh, don't argue. I know what will happen to that will later.
Akhil: I know very well. I can make Jatin will me all of King George's empire. I don't believe the emperor would lodge a legal complaint of undue influence. But listen, Aunt, let me tell you a few things about this house. My client——
Aunt: Akhil, let's get a few things straight right now. It

only suffocates me to tell lies inside this house. Now listen, you are your own client. I've known it all along.

Akhil: What are you saying, Aunt?

Aunt: That's enough. There's no need to wheedle me. You've done the right thing. I know that you've always kept an eye on me because some day my property would be yours.

Akhil: For shame, what a thing to say!

Aunt: Are you to blame for that, tell me? Both of you are exactly like my own sons. I would have given you everything. But your mother and I were sisters. Our father was angry with her and gave all his property to me. He died before getting over that anger. He's in Heaven, and now his anger is gone. That's why I've poured out all his money for the benefit of his grandson. None of you have missed any of the goddess Lakshmi's blessing.

Akhil: Have I ever said a word to you about that?

Aunt: If one has intelligence, words aren't necessary. Jatin was obsessed with the idea of building a house. You astute lawyers can understand how much unbearable anguish there is in that obsession. I'm a woman, his aunt; my heart felt as if it would break. Where would we get a loan? We had to come to you. You set up a fictitious client——

Himi enters.

Himi: Auntie, the cook has come.

Aunt: Good girl! Ask her to sit and wait a bit. I'll be right there.

Himi leaves.

Akhil: Auntie, how old is this niece of yours?

Aunt: She's just seventeen. She'll take her intermediate exams at the university.

Akhil: She has a very sweet face. I heard her song from outside.

Aunt: This brother and sister are very much alike. The brother built the house, she sings, and both of them play the same tune.

Akhil: About her marrying——

Aunt: No. Since her brother's been sick she doesn't talk to anyone about that; she has given up all her studies and stays here.

Akhil: But I can find her a good husband, Auntie, if ever——

Aunt: The same way you found a client? Is that it?

Akhil: No, Aunt, I'm not joking. I'm thinking that if I sent her a harmonium, would you——

Aunt: No objection, but she doesn't like the harmonium.

Akhil: To accompany her songs?

Aunt: She plays the *esraj* with her singing.

Akhil: In that case, maybe an *esraj*.

Aunt: She has an *esraj*.

Akhil: She'll have one more. Increasing one's property is known as prosperity.

Aunt: Very well, give her an *esraj*. Now listen to me. All the time you've been paying interest to that client, I've been selling my heirloom jewelry. Now and then, whenever the client wrote harsh letters and threatened to ask payment within three days, the rate of interest went up, and now I have nothing left. Thus the aunt's property has ended up in the nephew's safe. My father-in-law's spirit must be gratified, but my father and Jatin's mother—if they are weeping, even in the next world——

Himi enters.

Himi: Auntie, brother is calling you continually. He's very restless and all he does is ask about Mani. I can't give him a straight answer; my voice sticks in my throat.

She puts her hands over her face and cries.

Aunt: Don't cry, dear. I'm going to Jatin.

Akhil: Auntie, if I can do anything, say so. Why don't I go to Jatin?

Aunt: Yes, you'll have to go to him. See him about his will.

She leaves.

In the sickroom. The Aunt and Jatin.

Jatin: Didn't Mani come? What's keeping her so long?

Aunt: Oh, that's a long story. I went and found her crying her eyes out because she had let your milk get scorched. She's a girl from a rich family; she knows how to drink milk, but she never learned how to prepare it. We only let her do it because her heart wants to do something for you. It took a lot of doing to calm her down and then I sent her to bed. Let her sleep a little.

Jatin: Auntie!

Aunt: What, my son?

Jatin: I can tell that my days are coming to an end. But I have no regrets. Don't grieve over me.

Aunt: No, my son, I have no time to weep. God has made me realize that being alive is not necessarily the best thing and death is not necessarily bad.

Jatin: Death strikes me as rather pleasant. I can hear the *sanai* now from across the pond. Himi! Where's Himi?

Aunt: She's standing at the window there.

Himi: Why, brother, what do you want?

Jatin: My dear sister, don't cry behind my back like that. I can hear your tears in my heart. Give me your hand. I'm quite well. Sing that song, sister: "If it is time to part, I'll take my leave."

Himi's Song

If the time for parting has come,
Then give me your last touch.
> Again and again I launch my dreams,
> Toward the distance, floating on my songs,
Look now and again at the empty window—
> That empty window is mine.
What is the secret in the pensive fragrance
Of this *malati* vine at the forest's edge?
> When the bird of another Sravan sits in its
> branches—
> > Will it bring you memories—
> Meeting and parting in the moist shadows of this
> Sravan—
> > Our parting and reunion.

Aunt: Himi, bring a hot-water bottle. I'll have to put it under his feet.

Himi leaves.

Jatin: It's very painful, Auntie, but not nearly as painful as you think. I feel as if there's a gradual separation between my pain and myself. The ship of my life was like a boat moored and loaded with cargo; now the moorings have been cut. I can see it, but it's no longer attached to me. During these three days I haven't seen Mani even once.

Aunt: Dear boy, drink a little pomegranate juice. Your throat is getting dry.

Jatin: My will was written yesterday—did I show it to you? I don't remember clearly.

Aunt: You don't need to show it to me, Jatin.

Jatin: When my mother died, I didn't have a thing. You brought me up and provided for me. That's why I was saying——

Aunt: Are you on that again? I had only this one house and some very ordinary property. You earned all the rest of it yourself.

Jatin: But this house——

Aunt: This house isn't mine. You've added so many rooms to it. You can't even find the little section that used to be mine.

Jatin: In her heart Mani is very——

Aunt: Don't you think I know that, Jatin? Go to sleep now.

Jatin: I have willed everything to Mani, but it's really yours. She'll never go against your wishes.

Aunt: Why are you thinking about it so much, dear child?

Jatin: Your blessing is all that I have. When you see my will some day, don't think that——

Aunt: What a thing to say, Jatin! Would I be upset because you have given Mani something that is your own? Is my disposition as bad as that?

Jatin: But I've also given you——

Aunt: Look here, Jatin, this time I'll be angry. You'll go away and leave me with a lot of money?

Jatin: Auntie, if I could leave you something greater than money——

Aunt: You've already given me plenty, Jatin. You have filled my empty house. This is my great good fortune. All this time what I've received has filled my heart; if it is time now for me to stop receiving, I won't complain. Give it all; will the house, the furniture, the carriage, all the real estate; put it all in Mani's name; I can't carry the burden of all this.

Jatin: You have no liking for luxury, but Mani is young, so——

Aunt: Don't say that. If you want to give her money and property, you may, but to enjoy it——

Jatin: Why wouldn't she enjoy it, Auntie?

Aunt: No, my dear, no, she can't, I tell you. She won't be able to enjoy it. Her throat would be as dry as wood. She won't be able to enjoy anything.

Jatin (lies silent, sighs): I haven't given anything worthwhile.

Aunt: Are you leaving her so little? Don't you think that

some day she'll realize the value of the money and property you're leaving for her?

Jatin: Did Mani come yesterday? I don't remember.

Aunt: She came. You were asleep. She sat by your bed for a long time.

Jatin: Amazing! I was dreaming just then that Mani wanted to come into the room; the door was a little ajar, and she pushed hard at it but couldn't open it the least bit wider. But Auntie, you people are rather overdoing it. Let her see how much like the evening light I am, how easily and slowly——

Aunt: My boy, let me pull this woolen shawl over your legs. The soles of your feet are so cold.

Jatin: No, Auntie. I don't feel like having anything over me.

Aunt: Do you know, Jatin, Mani made this shawl. She sat up night after night making it. She finished it yesterday.

Jatin takes the shawl in his hands and turns it over. His aunt draws it over his feet.

Jatin: I have a feeling that Himi knitted that. Mani doesn't like to knit. Can she do that?

Aunt: Women learn with the strength of love. Himi showed her how to do it. There are lots of mistakes in the stitches.

Jatin: Himi, you needn't fan me anymore, sister. Come and sit near me. I'll check the almanac and tell you just which day will be auspicious for the housewarming.

Himi: Brother, don't talk of all that.

Jatin: I can't be there myself. That's why I thought— I'll be there, sister. I'll be there that day in the very air of this house. You haven't realized it. I've decided just which song you should sing. That one, "Flame of Fire"—let's hear it once.

Himi's Song

Come, O flame of fire,
    Bring, oh, bring the light.
In sorrow, in bliss, light the sacred lamp
    In this empty house.
        Bring strength and brightness,
           Peace and joy,
           Soothing love,
        Bring everlasting good.
Come in the wake of the auspicious day,

Come, happy fulfillment.
Bring sweet sleep,
Bring wakefulness;
Like a mother in the night of sorrow
Awake, unwinking,
Pour your radiance
Over the festive sky.

Jatin: Himi, do you know what festival the song speaks of?

Himi: I don't know.

Jatin: Well, why don't you guess?

Himi: I can't guess.

Jatin: I can. The day you are married, the festivities will begin at dawn.

Himi: That's enough, brother, that's enough.

Jatin: It seems I hear the flute playing Bhairavi. I've written a provision into my will for your wedding expenses.

Himi: Brother, I'll go now.

Jatin: No, no, stay. But on the day of the housewarming you'll have to do everything on my behalf. Remember, get as many white lotuses as you can, have a seat set up in the room, and put my red Banaras chador on it.

Shambhu enters.

Shambhu: The doctor is asking whether you want him to stay tonight.

Aunt: Yes, he'll have to stay.

Shambhu leaves.

Jatin: But I don't want a sleeping pill tonight. That way sleeping and waking get all confused. Auntie, we were married on the night of Vaisakh-Dvadoshi. Tomorrow is that same auspicious day. I want to remind Mani of that. Call her in just for two minutes. Why are you so silent? My mind is trying to tell her something; that's why I haven't slept these two nights. Don't delay any longer. After this I won't get another chance. No, Auntie, I can't stand these tears of yours. You were so calm for so long. Now why——

Aunt: Oh, Jatin, I thought all my tears had been shed; now I can't help it.

Jatin: Why did Himi go away so quickly?

Aunt: She went to get some rest. She'll come back after a while.

Jatin: Call Mani in.

Aunt: I'm going to, my dear. Shambhu will stay at the door. If you need anything, call him.

She leaves.

In the next room. Akhil enters.

Himi (quickly wipes away her tears and stands up): Let me call Auntie.

Akhil: There's no need to do that. It's not that urgent.

Himi: Will you go to my brother's room?

Akhil: No, I'll get news about him right here. How is he?

Himi: The doctor says his condition isn't good now.

Akhil: You've all worked night and day for a long time. I came to give you a little relief. Maybe I could do a little of the nursing.

Himi: No, that can't be done. I'm not at all tired.

Akhil: In that case I'll work along with you.

Himi: All this work!

Akhil: I know, it's much harder than practicing law.

Himi: No, I didn't say that.

Akhil: No, it's true. If I had to prepare barley water I'd probably set the house on fire.

Himi: What a way to talk!

Akhil: I'm exaggerating just a little. It's our habit to set houses afire. Can't you understand? Why don't you see it? You're preparing barley water for Jatin; perhaps I'm preparing something that is not at all suited to our invalid, something difficult for even the well to digest. Why don't you sit down? Let me tell you a few things.

Himi: But this is no time for story-telling.

Akhil: Of course it is! If I could tell stories, I'd give up my profession and become the second Bankim Chatterji. Are you laughing? We have to make up plenty and plenty of stories. I don't like it; if I could really make up stories, I'd quit this business. Perhaps you've started writing stories?

Himi: No.

Akhil: Composed plays?

Himi: No, I can't do that either.

Akhil: How do you know?

Himi: The words don't come.

Akhil: You don't need a lot of words to write plays. You don't need books or papers. Maybe your play has gotten under way right now. Who can tell?

Himi: Let me go and call Auntie.

Akhil: No, that's not necessary. I was talking nonsense. I'll be serious. I thought I'd speak to Jatin. But if he's that bad now——

Himi: He often asks me whether I've heard any rumors about his business. Perhaps you——

Akhil: I know that the business has gone to smash.

Himi: I beg you, don't give him this news. No matter what, this house of his——

Akhil: Has Jatin said anything about the house?

Himi: He talks of only one thing. One of these days there'll be a housewarming, and plans for that——

Akhil: The housewarming preparations were completed.

Himi: How do you know?

Akhil: They were completed at my office. The bailiffs are all dressed up and nearly ready.

Himi: Look here, Akhil, this is no laughing matter.

Akhil: Don't I know that? What's the use of hiding it from you? This house will be put up against the indebtedness.

Himi: No, no, no, that can't be. Akhil, please have mercy.

Akhil: But why are you so worried? You know all about it. Your brother hasn't much longer——

Himi: I know, I know, my brother won't be alive much longer, and that has to be borne, but if this house goes, it will break my heart. It means more to him than his own life.

Akhil: Look, you always made the highest scores in literature, math, logic, but you don't even rate a passing grade in worldliness. There is nothing in the business world called heart, and the rules——

Himi: I don't know about that. I beg you, save his house. At your office——

Akhil: The bailiffs will have to dress as musicians and carry flutes. In law college I learned everything in the books, but I didn't practice up on improvisation. Maybe I could learn that from you.

The Aunt enters.

Aunt: Akhil, what's going on? Why is Himi crying?

Akhil: There's a slight hitch in the housewarming plans, that's why.

Aunt: Why do you have to discuss all that with her?

Akhil: I heard that her brother turned the whole matter of the housewarming over to her. So that there'd be no trouble over it, she came to me about this rather than to anyone else. If you all agree, I can pull in my belt and work on the housewarming too. Do you understand, Auntie?

Aunt: I understand. But you don't want to pull in your belt, you want to tie everything up tighter. This is no time to give advice. Now is the time for you to give Jatin assurances that no one will lay hands on his house.

Akhil: Certainly, you can say the jute market went up. Now tell this lady to wipe her eyes.

The Doctor enters.

Doctor: Oh, the lawyer! Then that's it.

Akhil: Look here, what's the point of arguing with Saturn or with Kali? My business deals with the unextraordinary remains of those few Bengalis who survive after passing through your hands.

Doctor: I haven't noticed that there's much time left for that kind of business in this house.

Akhil: You don't scare me, sir. Your business terminates with death, ours gets going afterward. No, no, let's not talk about all that. Auntie, I'll say this: I'm assuming all the responsibility for the housewarming ceremony; along with it I'll take on something else. I'll be outside. When you need me, call.

He leaves.

Doctor: Jatin's wife hasn't come yet. I know you haven't been to his room for quite some time either.

Aunt: I can't think what answer to give when he asks about Mani. I can't make up any more stories. I'm ashamed of myself. If he falls asleep I'll go in.

Doctor: I'll wait outside. Let me know in a little while how he's doing. In the meantime I'll have to keep the lawyer away. Even under ordinary circumstances, the pulse stops dead if the lawyers show their faces.

He goes out.

PART TWO

Shambhu is near the door of the sickroom. The Neighbor enters.

Neighbor: Say, Shambhu!

Shambhu: Yes?

Neighbor: I'd like to see Jatin just once. Auntie isn't around
for once.

Shambhu: How do you know that?

Neighbor: There's a job open at the estate of the Maharajah
of Natore. I want a letter from Jatin for my son.

Shambhu: Good lady, that positively can't be done. If Auntie
comes to know about it, I'd catch it from her.

Neighbor: How would she know? It'll take me a quick five
minutes.

Shambhu: Forgive me, it just can't be done.

Neighbor: Can't be done! Your mistress thinks her nephew
wouldn't survive coming into contact with us. She doesn't
take herself into consideration. She used up her husband,
her only daughter is dead, her parents are gone, and that
Jatin is the only one left now. When he's gone, only then
she'll budge. If things were otherwise, she'd have nothing
to live for. I tell you, Shambhu, you'll see; once Auntie
has got hold of him, Jatin is done for.

Shambhu: There! He's calling me. You'd better go now.

Neighbor: Don't worry. I'm going.

She leaves.

Shambhu enters the sickroom.

Jatin (startled by the sound of footsteps): Mani!

Shambhu: Master, it's I, Shambhu. Did you call me?

Jatin: Call your mistress, just this once.

Shambhu: Whom?

Jatin: Your mistress.

Shambhu: She hasn't come back yet.

Jatin: Where did she go?

Shambhu: Sitarampur.

Jatin: She went today?

Shambhu: No, three days ago.

Jatin: Who are you? Am I seeing correctly?

Shambhu: I'm Shambhu.

Jatin: Tell me plainly, am I all mixed up?

Shambhu: No, sir.

Jatin: What house am I in? Is this Sitarampur?

Shambhu: No, this is your bedroom in Calcutta.

Jatin: This isn't a lie? All this isn't a lie?

Shambhu: Let me call Auntie.

He leaves.

The Aunt enters.

Jatin: How will I know I haven't died, Auntie? Maybe everything is upside down.

Aunt: Oh, what are you saying, Jatin?

Jatin: You are my aunt, aren't you?

Aunt: What else would I be, Jatin?

Jatin: Why don't you call Himi? Have her sit beside me. Have her stay by me. Don't let her go anywhere now.

Aunt: Himi, come here! Sit right here!

Jatin: Why don't you stop that flute? Did you get it for the housewarming? We don't need it any longer.

Aunt: There's a wedding next door. That flute is playing there.

Jatin: Is that a wedding flute? Why is there so much sorrow in it? Is it the Behag raga? Did I tell you about my dream, Auntie?

Aunt: What dream?

Jatin: It seemed that Mani was pushing at the door of my room, trying to get in. The door wouldn't open the least bit. She kept looking at me from outside. No one could get in at all. I called and called, but she couldn't get into the house. She couldn't, she couldn't, she couldn't—

The Aunt is silent.

I understand, Auntie. I understand. I'm bankrupt, absolutely bankrupt, completely broke. I don't even have this house anymore. Everything has been sold out. I was trying to fool myself.

Aunt: No, Jatin, no. I swear your house is all right. Akhil is here. I'll call him in if you say so.

Jatin: Then the house is intact? It will last? It's not a shadow like me? Let it stand with the door open, year after year. What do you say, Auntie?

Aunt: Yes, it will last, Jatin. It will stay filled with your love.

Jatin: Sister, Himi, you live in my room. I'll know about it. Himi! Himi!

Himi enters.

Himi: What, brother?

Jatin: The responsibility is yours, sister. Remember which song you'll sing?

Himi: I do. "Come, O Flame of Fire."

Jatin: My dear sister, don't be angry with anyone. Forgive everyone. And when you'll think of me, think then, "My brother always loved me and he loves me now." Do you know, Auntie, will Himi be married in my house? In the old wing of the building, where my mother was married? I haven't touched that part.

Aunt: That's where it will be, my son.

Jatin: Auntie, in the next life you'll be born as my daughter, and I'll look after you and bring you up.

Aunt: What are you saying, Jatin? I'd be born again as a woman? Maybe I'll be your son next time. Why not wish for that?

Jatin: No, not a boy. Shame on you! You'll come to my house as a beautiful woman, as beautiful as when you were young. I'll dress you so beautifully.

Aunt: That's enough. Stop a little.

Jatin: I'll call you Lakshmirani—

Aunt: That's not a modern name.

Jatin: No, it's not modern. You always represent the old days for me. You come into my house and fill it with your old-fashioned affection.

Aunt: I won't come to your house bringing the sorrow that a daughter brings. I never want to do that.

Jatin: Do you think I'm weak, Auntie? Do you want to shield me from sorrow?

Aunt: Child, I have the heart of a woman. I'm the one who is weak. That's why I've always been so afraid and have wanted to shield you from every sorrow. But what can I do? I haven't been able to do anything.

Jatin: Auntie, I can say one thing with pride. I never snatched at what I didn't get. All my life I've waited with folded hands. I had to be patient such a long time because I didn't want anything fraudulent. Maybe truth will be kind to me this once. Who's that, Auntie, who's that?

Aunt: Where, Jatin? No one is here.

Jatin: Go and look into that room. It seemed to me——

Aunt: No, child, I don't see anyone.

Jatin: But I thought I saw clearly——
Aunt: Ah, no, Jatin.

The Doctor enters.

Jatin: Who's that? Where did he come from? Is there any news?
Aunt: It's the doctor.
Doctor: Don't you sit there with him. He talks to you too much.
Jatin: No, Auntie, you can't. I can't let you go.
Aunt: All right, child, I'll sit right here in the corner.
Jatin: No, no. Sit beside me and hold my hand. God will take me from your hands into His.
Doctor: All right. It's all right. But don't talk. Now it's time to take that medicine.
Jatin: It's time! Do you come to deceive me again? Time is already past. I don't need sham consolation. Let's say good-bye, let's have all the farewells. Auntie, I've got you now. I want no sham of any sort. Sister Himi, sit beside me.
Doctor: So much excitement isn't good for him.
Jatin: Then don't excite me anymore.

The Doctor leaves.

The doctor's gone. Now come and sit on my bed. I'll lay my head on your lap.
Aunt: Sleep a little, my dear.
Jatin: Don't ask me to sleep. I still need to stay awake a little longer. Don't you hear? She'll come very soon. Somehow, everything is hazy. It's the twilight hour[3] of fortune, the twilight hour of my marriage. The door of the marriage room will open. Himi, sing that song now, "At the crossing of life and death."

Himi's Song

Beyond the crossing of life and death
You stand, my friend.

---

[3] Literally "the cowdust hour," the hour at which cattle are brought home in the villages so that a film of dust hangs between the beholder and the sunset.

In this untenanted sky of my heart
Your throne is flooded with light.
With profound hope, with joy
    I look to you with arms outstretched.
The silent night has touched your feet,
The darkness has spread the weight of its hair.
    What is this song that flowed from your *vina*
    To fill the world?
    This world is one with that tune—
      I am lost in the sorrow of that song.

Mani and her father enter.

Aunt: My son, Jatin, look, look up. She has come.

Jatin: Who? A dream?

Aunt: No dream. Mani, my son. It's your father-in-law.

Jatin (looks toward Mani): Who is that?

Aunt: Can't you recognize her? That's your Mani.

Jatin: Did the door open all the way?

Aunt: All the way.

Jatin: But don't put that shawl on my feet, not that shawl, not that one. Move it, move it.

Aunt: There's no shawl, Jatin. Your wife is lying at your feet. Lay your hand on her head and give her your blessing.

1925

THROUGH THE HAZE

(Ashpashta)

The pageant of life at the house across the way can be seen through these windows. That picture is drawn in lines and spaces, some visible, some invisible.

One day while he sat reading, Banamali's book lay still as his eyes wandered in that direction.

He saw that two unfamiliar persons had appeared upon the familiar canvas of that household. One was an elderly widow, the other a girl who might be sixteen or seventeen.

The old woman sat by the windowsill and braided the girl's hair, and tears ran down the girl's face.

Another day that person who had braided the girl's hair was gone. At the end of the day the girl leaned over an old photograph frame and, by the last light of the sun, polished it with the end of her sari.

Then the flow of her daily work could be seen through the window openings: lentils were sorted in a basket on her lap; betel nuts were opened, nut slicer in hand; her wet hair was shaken dry with her left hand after a bath; quilts were spread out in the sunshine on the veranda railings.

In the afternoons the men were at the office. Some young women took siestas, others played cards. In the dovecotes on the rooftops the cooing of the doves became muted.

At that hour the girl, feet outstretched, sat reading in the attic room on the roof. Sometimes she wrote a letter, with the paper resting on the book; her unbraided hair seemed to stop suddenly at her forehead, and her moving fingers seemed to whisper to the letter.

One day something went wrong. That day she wrote a portion of the letter, toyed with a part of the pen, while on the cornice a crow sat nibbling at the seed of a half-eaten mango.

Then it was as if a huge cloud tiptoed up and took its stand behind an absentminded new moon. The woman who entered was middle-aged. There was a thick bracelet on her plump wrist. Her hair was parted at the center of her forehead and a heavy vermilion mark was drawn at the parting.

She snatched that unfinished letter from the girl's lap. A hawk suddenly swooped upon the back of a dove.

The girl appeared no more on the roof. Sometimes late at night, sometimes in the morning, or in the evening, that house showed signs of an earthquake beating its head against the foundations.

Through the gaps between the windows across the way one could see the sorting of lentils and the preparation of betel nuts; from time to time the girl carried a milk pan to the water tap in the courtyard.

Thus some time went by. There came an evening in the month of Kartik when the earthen lamp glowed on the roof and the smoke from the stable writhed like a python and strangled the sky.

Banamali came in from outside, and as soon as he opened the window of his room, he saw that same girl standing quite still on the roof, her hands folded. In the Mullik family temple at the end of the lane lights were being waved before the image of the god and a gong was struck. After some time she lay prostrate; touching her head to the floor again and again, she bowed reverently. Then she was gone.

That day Banamali went downstairs to write a letter. When it was finished he went himself to put it in the mailbox.

That night as he lay in bed he began to wish that the letter would not be delivered. When he arose in the morning, he felt that he could not bear to look toward that house.

That same day Banamali left for Madhupur; he told no one where he was going.

He returned the day college classes began. It was evening. The house across the street was completely closed from top to bottom, completely dark. Where had everyone gone?

Banamali said to himself, "Let it go; it's just as well." He went into his room and saw a bundle of letters on the desk. At the very bottom of the pile was a letter addressed by a woman's hand, an unfamiliar handwriting, and stamped at the neighborhood post office.

He sat there with the letter in his hand. The envelope was still unopened. He merely held it up to the light. The writing inside was as hazy as the picture of the household across the street seen through the window.

Once, he brought himself to the point of opening the letter. Then he put it in a box, locked it, and vowed, "I shall never open that letter."

1919

THE OLD HOUSE
(Purono Bari)

1

That house belongs to people who for a long time were wealthy and now are poor.

Day after day it has been bruised by adversity.

Plaster has fallen from the wall; the sparrows scratch their claws on the broken floor and flap their wings in the dust; in the shrine of Durga the pigeons are gathered like a ragged rain cloud.

No one paid attention when on the north side of the house one panel of the door fell apart. The other panel, like a widow overwhelmed by grief, is thrashed by the passing wind, and no one notices.

It is a three-story house. Only five rooms are inhabited; all the rest are closed. It is like an old man of eighty-five; the padlocked memory of past days encompasses his whole life, the traffic of the present moves through only one room.

The house with its fallen plaster and bared brickwork stands beside the street like a mindless madman wearing a crazy quilt, paying heed neither to itself nor to others.

2

One day at dawn the weeping of women's voices arose across the street. We heard that the youngest son of the house, who earned his living playing Radhika in a theatrical troupe, had died that day at the age of eighteen.

The women cried for several days; then there was no more news of them.

After that all the doors were padlocked.

But on the north side that one widowed and battered door neither fell apart nor was closed; it slips awry like a broken heart and pounds in the wind.

3

One evening the excited voices of children were heard in that house.

We saw a red-bordered sari hanging from the veranda.

After all that time one part of the house has been rented. The tenant's income is meager, the children many. The tired mother becomes irritated, slaps them, and they roll on the floor crying.

A middle-aged maid works there all day long and quarrels with the housewife, says, "I'm leaving," but doesn't go.

4

In this part of the house repairs are made daily, a little at a time. Paper is pasted over the window; sticks are fastened into the gaps in the veranda railings; in the bedroom the broken window is propped up with a brick; the walls were whitewashed, but the evidence of black marks could not be covered.

In a planter on the roof terrace a sickly croton shrub suddenly appeared and was ashamed at being exposed to the sky. Next to it, a pipal tree growing through the foundation stands erect; its leaves seem to snicker at the shrub.

Here is the great poverty of great wealth. It lost its modesty in the attempt to hide its poverty with limited means.

No one has looked at the empty rooms on the north side. Still that unhinged door just thrashes in the wind, the breast-beating of a pariah.

1919

THE FAVORED QUEEN'S WISH
(Shuyoranir Shadh)

The Favored Queen thought that the hour of her death had come.

She felt suffocated, nothing pleased her. The doctor came with pills. He ground them in honey and said, "Take it." The Favored Queen threw it away.

The news reached the King. He quickly left his council and came. Sitting at her side, he asked, "What is the matter? What would you like?"

Haughtily she replied, "Everyone go away; call my friend."

The friend came. Taking her hand, the Queen said, "Sit down, friend. I have something to tell you."

The friend said, "Tell me just what you want to say."

The Favored Queen said, "The Rejected Queen had the use of three parts of my seven-part house. Then she had two, then one. Then she was put out of the palace.

"After that I forgot all about her.

"Then one day there was a color festival. We went to the temple in a peacock boat, the people in front, the lascars behind. On the right hand played the flute, on the left the drum.

"Just then I saw on the riverbank beside our route a hut near the landing, shaded by champak trees. Clitoria vines bloomed on its fence; before the door was a picture of Vishnu drawn in powdered rice. I said to my umbrella-bearer, Aha, whose house is that?"

" 'It belongs to the Rejected Queen,' she said.

"After I came home I sat down in the dark. I had not lit the lamp; I spoke to no one.

"The King came and said, 'What is the matter? What would you like?'

"I said, 'I won't live in this house.'

"The King said, 'I'll have a brick house with ivory walls

built for you. The floors will be made of powdered conch shells as white as foaming milk. I'll have the pearls from the beaches twined into a lotus garland.'

" 'My one wish,' I replied, 'is to live in a hut built on a riverbank, outside your garden.'

" 'Well, of course!' said the King. 'Who would have guessed that?'

"The hut was built. That house was like an uprooted wild flower. No sooner was it built than it began to droop. I went to live there. I felt only shame.

"Then one day there was a bathing ceremony.

"I went to the river to bathe. One hundred and seven ladies-in-waiting accompanied me. A palanquin was submerged in the water, and I bathed.

"On the way home I opened the door of the palanquin a little, and I saw a housewife passing by! She was like a flower offering! There were white shell bangles on her wrists; she wore a red-bordered sari. She had had her bath and carried a full water jar, and the morning light shimmered on her moist hair and on the wet water jar.

"I said to my umbrella-bearer, 'Who is that girl? Does she go to some temple to pray?'

"Laughing, the umbrella-bearer replied, 'Can't you recognize her? That is the Rejected Queen herself.'

"After I returned home I sat alone and spoke to no one. The King came and said, 'What is the matter? What would you like?'

" 'My one wish,' I said, 'is to go every morning to the river, draw water in an earthen jar, and carry it through the bakul-shaded streets.'

" 'Well, of course!' said the King. 'Who would have guessed that?'

"Guards were stationed in all the streets; the people were sent away.

"I wore white shell bangles and a red-bordered sari. I bathed in the river, filled the water jar, and brought it back. When I came to the door I felt so downcast that I broke the jar to pieces. I could not do what I had intended to do. I felt only shame.

"Then came the festival of Krishna.

"A camp was made in the pleasure grove by moonlight. The dancing and singing went on all night long.

"The next morning the howdah was mounted upon the elephant. Screened by its curtains, I was returning home when

I saw someone walking along the forest path, someone very young. Upon his head was a wreath of wild flowers. He carried a basket filled with water lilies, wild flowers, and garden greens.

"I said to the umbrella-bearer, 'Who is the heaven-blessed mother of the boy who has brightened the road?'

"The umbrella-bearer said, 'Don't you know? That is the son of the Rejected Queen. He is going to his mother with water lilies, wild flowers, and garden greens.'

"After I returned home, I sat alone, speaking to no one.

"The King came and said, 'What is the matter? What would you like?'

"I said, 'My one wish is to have water lilies, wild flowers, and garden greens every day; my son shall pick them and bring them himself.'

"The King said, 'Well, of course! Who would have guessed that?'

"I was seated in a golden palanquin; the boy came with a basket. He was covered with perspiration; he glowered angrily. The basket lay where it fell. I was ashamed.

"Then I did not know what happened to me.

"I sit alone, speaking to no one. The King comes every day and says to me, 'What is the matter? What would you like?'

"Even though I know what I lack, I am ashamed to tell it to anyone. That is why I have called you, my friend. To you I speak my last words: I want the sorrow of the Rejected Queen."

The friend, her hand at her cheek, asked, "Why do you say that?"

"Her bamboo flute played a tune," said the Favored Queen, "but I merely carried my golden flute. I wandered about and could not play it."

1920

THE PRINCE

(Rajputtur)

1

The Prince is about to leave his own kingdom, the land beyond the realm of the seven kings, for that land where no king rules.

That is the story of a time that has no beginning and no end.

In the city and village everyone else goes to market, keeps house, and wrangles; he who is our eternal prince leaves behind one kingdom after another.

Why does he go?

The well water stays in the well. The waters of the canal and the marsh are placid in canal and marsh. But the mountaintop water is not restrained at the peak, the water from the clouds is not curbed by the clouds. Who could keep the Prince within his own small kingdom? Having seen the endless plain he does not turn back; he goes beyond the seven seas and the thirteen rivers.

Men are born again and again as children, and again and again they hear this ancient tale for the first time.

The light of the evening lamp burns steadily; sitting silently, cheek in hand, the children think, We are that very prince.

Even if the endless plain comes to an end, there is still the ocean before him. In the middle of the ocean is the island where the Princess is held captive in the castle of the giant.

Everyone else in the world seeks money, seeks fame and pleasure, and he who is our prince has set out to rescue the Princess from the giant's castle. A storm arises, no boat is at hand, yet he seeks the way.

This is man's first and last fairy tale. Those who are newly born into this world must get from their grandmothers these eternal tidings: that the Princess is still captive, the ocean impassable, the giant invincible, and that one small man stands alone and vows, "I shall rescue the captive."

In the darkness of the forest outside, the rain falls, the cricket calls; the child sits, cheek in hand, thinking, I must get across to the castle of the giant.

2

Before the Prince lay the boundless ocean, like the blue slumber of a wave-tossed dream. There he alighted from his horse.

But as soon as his foot touched the ground, what happened! What magician had cast such a spell!

It was a city! Streetcars ran! The streets were blocked by office-bound cars. At the edge of the lane the flute-vendor tempted the naked children by blowing on a bamboo flute.

And see how the Prince was dressed! What manners! He wore an unbuttoned shirt, his dhoti was not very clean, his shoes were worn out. He was a country boy, going to school in the city, meeting his expenses by tutoring.

Where was the Princess?

She lived in the very next house. Her complexion was not like the champak flower; there was no shower of jewels when she smiled. She could not be compared to the stars of the sky; she resembled the nameless flowers that grew obscured by the grass after the first rains.

The motherless girl was her father's darling. He was poor and did not want his daughter married to an undeserving groom. The years closed in upon the girl; everyone criticized her.

The father died, and now the girl had come to her uncle's house.

A groom was found. He had considerable money, was considerably advanced in years, and his grandsons and granddaughters were numerous. There were no bounds to his bad temper.

The uncle said, "The girl is lucky."

At the time for the ceremonial marking with yellow ocher, the girl was nowhere to be found, nor was the boy next door.

The news came that they were secretly married. Their

castes did not correspond; only their hearts agreed. Every-one was critical.

The rich man promised his god a golden throne and said, "Let's see who can save this boy!"

When he was brought to court all the shrewd lawyers and all the experienced witnesses turned day into night with the help of the gods. How marvelous!

That day a pair of goats were beheaded before the god, the drums were played, and everyone was happy. Everyone said, "It is indeed the age of destruction, but honesty still survives."

3

There was much more to the story. The boy returned from jail. But the long road seemed to have no end. That road is longer than the endless plain, and it is friendless. How often he heard in the dark, "Fee, fi, fo, fum, I can catch the smell of a man." He was surrounded by the greed that devours mankind!

There was no end to the road, but there came an end to the walking. One day he reached that stopping place.

On that day there was no one to look after him. At his bedside only a merciful god kept watch. It was Yama.

At the touch of Yama's golden wand, what a change there was! The city vanished; the dream was shattered.

Instantly, the Prince appeared again. On his forehead was the timeless mark of royalty. He would break open the door of the giant's castle and free the Princess from her chains.

Age after age, the children sit on their mothers' laps and hear about the person who left home and crossed the endless plain. The waves of the seven seas roar in front of him.

In history his forms are varied; beyond history he has one form only—he is the Prince.

1921

MINU

1

Minu was brought up in West country.[1] As a child she had gone stealthily to pick the fruit from the mulberry tree beside the stone well, and she loved to be with the old gardener who weeded the lentil plot.

When she grew up and blossomed into youth, she was married. She had a son who died at birth, and the doctor said, "Who knows whether or not we can save her?"

It was then that Minu was brought to Calcutta.

She was very young. Like an unripe fruit, her immature heart firmly grasped the stem of the world. She felt a strong attraction toward anything fresh, anything green, anything alive.

Her courtyard in the country was eight or ten feet wide. That scrap of land had been her garden.

This garden had been like her own child. When she left it, the passionflower upon its fence already showed in its blossoming tendrils what it would some day become.

All the dogs of the neighborhood, tame and stray, had been fed and petted at her house. The one she loved most was a snub-nosed dog named Bhonta.

Minu had sat stringing colored beads for him to wear around his neck. That was left unfinished. The owner of the dog said, "Sister, you may take him along."

Minu's husband said, "Too much trouble. Leave him here."

2

Minu lay in a second-floor room in a rented house in Calcutta. The Hindustani nurse who stayed with her talked

---

[1] West country means west of Bengal.

incessantly; sometimes Minu listened, sometimes she did not.

Once Minu lay awake all night long. When the darkness faded a little at dawn, she could see that the champak tree beneath her window had blossomed and was covered with flowers. Its delicate fragrance came close to Minu's window as if asking, "How are you?"

How had that sun-starved tree, this mute child of the natural world, come to stand as if bewildered in the very small space between their house and the next?

The invalid Minu usually got up late. As soon as she was up, she would look toward that tree; one day there were no flowers to be seen. She said to the nurse, "Aha, nurse, for heaven's sake, dig around the base of this tree and water it a little every day."

Presently it became plain why there were no more flowers on the tree.

The morning light was breaking like a half-blown lotus; just then a Brahman worshiper, flower tray in hand, began to shake the tree, as a bandit landlord's bailiff collects rents.

Minu said to the nurse, "Quickly! Call that priest inside."

When the Brahman came, Minu touched his feet respectfully and said, "Reverend sir, for whom are you taking the flowers?"

"They are for God," replied the Brahman.

Minu said, "God himself has sent those flowers to me."

"To you!"

"Yes, to me. Whatever He has given, wasn't given to be taken back."

Vexed, the Brahman went away.

The next day when he began to shake the tree again at dawn, Minu said, "Oh, nurse, I can't bear the sight. Move my bed close to the window in the next room."

3

Across from the window in the next room stood the Raychaudhuris' four-story house. Minu sent for her husband and said, "Look there, look what a lovely boy they have! Won't you bring him just once and put him in my lap?"

Her husband said, "Why would they send the boy to a house as poor as ours?"

"Listen to that!" replied Minu. "When it comes to little boys, what difference is there between rich and poor? All laps are kings' thrones to them."

Her husband returned with this news: "The doorman said the gentleman of the house won't see me."

The next morning Minu called the nurse and said, "Look there, he's sitting in the garden playing all alone. Run and give him these sweets."

In the evening her husband came and said, "They are angry."

"Why, what has happened?"

"They said that if the nurse goes into their garden again, they'll surely have the police arrest her."

Instantly tears welled up in Minu's eyes. She said, "I saw it, I saw it. They took my sweets out of his hand. Then they slapped him. I can't live here. Take me away."

1921

THE JESTER
(Bidushak)

1

The King of Kanchi went to conquer Karnat. He was the victor. His elephants were laden with sandalwood and ivory, gold and jewels.

On the way back to his kingdom he flooded the temple with sacrificial blood.

As he returned from the ceremony, he wore a crimson robe; around his neck was a garland of hibiscus; on his forehead was the mark of bloodred sandal paste; he was accompanied only by his counselor and the jester.

At one place he saw some boys at play in a mango grove beside the road.

The King said to his two companions, "I am going to see what they are playing."

2

The boys had arranged dolls in two lines and were playing war.

"Who is fighting whom?" asked the King.

They replied, "Karnat is at war with Kanchi."

"Who is the victor?" asked the King. "And who is the vanquished?"

"Karnat is the winner," the boys said proudly. "Kanchi is the loser."

The counselor's face became grave; the King's eyes became bloodshot; the jester broke into laughter.

3

When the King returned with his soldiers, the boys were still playing.

The King commanded, "Tie the boys to a tree one at a time and cane them."

Their parents came running from the village. "They are stupid," they said, "they were playing games. Forgive them."

The King called to the general: "Teach this village a lesson so that it will never forget the King of Kanchi."

Having spoken, he went off to his tent.

4

In the evening the general came and stood before the King, bowed before him, and said, "Emperor, except for dogs and jackals, there is not a sound to be heard in this village."

"The Emperor's prestige has been maintained," said the counselor.

"Almighty God is the Emperor's ally," said the priest.

The jester said, "Emperor, give me leave to go."

"Why?" exclaimed the King.

"I am able neither to kill," said the jester, "nor to destroy. By the grace of God, all I can do is laugh. If I stay at the Emperor's court, I shall forget how to laugh."

1922

TWO BIGHA OF LAND

(Dui Bigha Jami)

Only two bigha of the land were mine. All the rest had been mortgaged.

"Do you understand, Upen?" said the zamindar. "I'll buy this land."

"You are a landlord," I replied. "Your holdings are endless. All I have is a place in which to die."

When the zamindar heard this he said, "Old fellow, you surely know that I have had a garden laid out; its length would equal its breadth if I had those two bigha of yours. You must give them to me."

With hands clasped at my breast and tears in my eyes I replied, "Please spare my poor homestead. That land is worth more than gold; seven generations of my family have lived here. Am I such a wretch as to sell this because of my poverty?"

The zamindar's eyes flushed red with anger. For a moment he was silent; at last he said with a cruel laugh, "Well, we shall see what happens."

A month and a half later I had lost my ancestral land and was turned out onto the road. A decree was handed down, everything was sold, and the bill of sale was fraudulent. In this world, alas, he who has most wants more! The king steals from all the poor. I thought to myself, God did not intend me to stay in this pit of avarice. Therefore, He deeded me the universe in exchange for two bigha of land.

I dressed as an ascetic and wandered from country to

country, the disciple of a holy man. I saw so many beautiful houses, so many pleasing vistas. Wherever I went, from mountain to ocean, from desert to city, I still could not forget, by night or by day, those two bigha of land. In the market, in the fields, on the road—I spent sixteen years this way. At last one day I felt a deep desire to return to my land.

Salutations, salutations to my lovely land, Mother Bengal —Ganga's banks and refreshing winds have soothed our lives. The fields stretch out unhindered, the dust of your feet is touched to the forehead of the sky, deep shadows are nests of peace for tiny villages. The leaf-screened mango grove is the playhouse of the shepherd. In the depth of night the pond's dark water is silent, unfathomable, and cool. Our love is deep and soothing as the night. The wives of Bengal, their hearts filled with sweetness, carry water home. At the word "Mother" our souls are restless and our eyes fill with tears.

Two days later at two o'clock, I entered my own village. I passed the potter's house on the south, I turned to the left. I saw the marketplace, Nandi's granary. I left the temple behind. Thirsting with anticipation, I came at last to my own house.

My heart was torn two ways as I returned; I looked all about. That same mango tree still stood beside the wall— there! I sat down beneath it and my pain was eased by tears. One by one, childhood memories arose. I recalled the summer storms, when no one slept at night; rising at early dawn and racing to pick up mangoes; those deeply savored, silent afternoons, a truant from school—

Alas, I thought, where else could I find that life again!

A sudden breeze sighed, the branches swayed, two ripe mangoes fell to the ground beside me. I thought, My mother knew me after all this time. I picked up those gifts of love and touched them to my forehead.

Then, alas, the gardener appeared, a messenger of doom with his hair bound up; at the top of his voice he heaped abuse on me.

"I have quietly given up all that I had," I said. "I have taken only two of his mangoes, and so much fuss over that!"

The gardener did not recognize me and held me down with his staff on my shoulder. He took me to the zamindar. The gentleman was fishing, surrounded by his courtiers. When he heard the story, he said angrily, "I'll beat you to death!" Everything the zamindar said was multiplied a hundredfold by the crowd of courtiers.

"Only two mangoes," I said. "Sir, I beg of you."

The zamindar replied with a smile, "You're a rascal dressed like a saint, a very canny thief." I laughed at this with tears in my eyes—this was my destiny! You, milord, had become the saint; now I was the real thief!

1895

THE SALE

(Mastakbikrai)

The King of Koshal had no peer; his renown encircled the earth. He was a constant refuge for the weak; he was father and mother to the poor.

When he heard of this, the King of Kashi flamed with injured pride. "My subjects consider him greater than myself! His ranks is less than mine, but he is more generous! All this religion and benevolence is a fraud. This is only his way of competing with me.

"General, prepare your arms and call out all the troops. The King of Koshal has the audacity to be more virtuous than I am!"

The King of Kashi went out in battle array; the King of Koshal was defeated. Grieved and disgraced, he left his kingdom and fled deep into the forest. The King of Kashi laughed and said to his assembled counselors, "Only those who have the power to keep their wealth can set themselves up as philanthropists."

The people wept and said, "The dreadful Rahu attacks even the moon! Lakshmi examines only the arm of the strong and pays no attention to virtue! We are fatherless!"

People everywhere sorrowed and said, "Shame on those who oppose the true friends of this world."

The King of Kashi was angry when he heard this. "Why is there such sorrow in the city?" he asked. "I am still here. For whom else would so many people mourn! He lost to me yet wants to be the victor! The scriptures say in several places: always put an end to the enemy. Counselor, let it be known in the city, proclaim it at all our boundaries: I shall give a hundred gold coins to him who brings in the King of Koshal."

Traveling day and night, the King's envoys carried the news to every house. Whoever heard them shut his eyes, bit his tongue, and shuddering, held his hands over his ears.

The King without a kingdom, dressed in the dirty rags of a poor man, wandered about the dense forest. One day a lone traveler came and tearfully inquired, "Oh, forest dweller, where does this forest end? I'm going to Koshal."

"It's an unfortunate land," replied the King. "You will regret going there."

"I am a merchant," said the traveler. "My ship has been sunk. How shall I live the rest of my life now, going from door to door with outstretched hand! I have heard everywhere that the King of Koshal is like an ocean of mercy; he is the protector of the helpless, the refuge of the poor. Now that I am poor, I shall call at his door."

The King smiled a little and checked his tears. After a moment's thought, he sighed and said, "Traveler, I'll show you the road to your heart's desire. You have come a long way with much sorrow; you shall have your wish."

The King of Kashi sat surrounded by his court. The long-haired ascetic came and stood before him. The King laughed and said, "What brings you here?"

The forest dweller answered softly, "I am the King of Koshal, and my palace is the forest. Whatever you have promised to the person who captures me, give to my companion."

The courtiers were astonished and the hall became very still. Tears came to the eyes of the armor-clad guards.

For a few minutes the King of Kashi remained silent. Then he laughed and said, "Oh, prisoner, you have continued to triumph over me by giving up your life. I'll crush that hope of yours. This time I shall win the battle; I shall return your kingdom to you, O Emperor, and I shall give you my allegiance as well."

The King of Kashi set the forest dweller, clad in his rags,

upon the royal throne. The crown was placed upon his disheveled head.

"Thou art blessed," the people said.

1897

THE REPRESENTATIVE

(Pratinidhi)

(Mr. Ackworth has published an English translation of several Marathi stories. This incident is taken from the introduction to that collection. Shivaji's saffron flag is known as *bhagoya jhenda*.)

One day at dawn Shivaji sat on the battlements of Setara Castle and saw Ramdas, his guru, begging from door to door as if he were a pauper.

What's this! thought Shivaji. Guruji with a begging bowl, he who has not a hint of poverty at home! Everything is at his disposal; the king falls at his feet. There's no end to his desires! This is a useless attempt to quench thirst by pouring water night and day into a vessel with a hole in it.

"I must learn," said Shivaji, "how much it takes to fill that begging bowl to the brim."

At once he took up a pen, wrote something, called his son Balaji, and said, "When my guru comes to the castle to beg, lay this note at his feet."

The guru went on his way singing. Horses, chariots, and pedestrians hurried ahead of him.

"Oh, Bhabesh, oh, Shankar," he sang. "You have given everyone a home. To me you have given only the open road. Annapurna, my mother, has provided for this world. The whole world lives happily. To me you are the Supreme Beggar, you have snatched me away from my mother and have made me your companion."

When he had finished his song and had had his midafternoon bath, he came to the castle door. Balaji paid his respects, laid the note at his feet, and stood aside. Curious, the guru picked up the note and read it. With deepest reverence, Shivaji had entrusted to him the kingdom and the capital city.

On the following day Ramdas went to the king and said, "My son, tell me what good it will do to give your kingdom to me? Have I your good qualities?"

"I would joyfully spend my life in your service," replied Shivaji as he paid his respects to the guru.

"Then put this sack on your shoulder," said the guru, "and go begging with me today."

Shivaji and the guru, begging bowls in hand, went from house to house. The children were frightened when they saw the king, ran home, and called out their parents. The man of incalculable wealth who embraces a beggar's austerity is like a stone floating on water. Shamefaced, the people gave alms with shaking hands. They thought it was a king's whim.

In the castle it struck two o'clock. The citizens left their work and rested. Shedding tears of joy, Ramdas played on the *ektara* and sang, "Oh, Lord of the Three Worlds, I do not comprehend your thoughts. You have no needs, yet you go begging from heart to heart, my Lord, asking everything from everyone."

At last, at the end of the day they had their evening baths on a riverbank at the city's edge. Contentedly they cooked the food that they had begged; the guru ate some of it and the disciple ate what remained.

Then the king smiled and said, "You have made a street beggar of me, to destroy my kingly pride. Your servant is prepared, do whatever else you wish. I shall accept any burden the guru gives."

"Then listen," replied the guru. "You have made a harsh vow, you must be prepared to carry it out. This is my assignment: in my name, on my behalf, take back the kingdom. Fate has made you the beggar's representative, a sovereign who is poor and indifferent to worldly desires. When you carry out kingly duties, remember that those duties are mine. You shall keep the kingdom but have no kingdom of your own. Then take my guru's robe, my son, and my blessing along with it. Make the ascetic's saffron mantle your flag."

Thus spoke Guru Ramdas.

The kingly disciple, head bowed, deep in thought, remained sitting on the riverbank. The cowherd's flute fell silent, the cattle returned to their shed. On the other side of the river the sun set.

Beginning the *raga* Puravi, absorbed in his improvisations, Ramdas sang, "Who are you that dresses me like a king, establishes me in this world, yet remains invisible? Oh, King, I have brought you your slippers, and I sit at the foot of your throne. Evening comes, how much longer must I wait? Come, oh, come to your kingdom."

1897

THE WRATH OF THE GODS
(Debatar Grash)

The news gradually spread from village to village: Maitra will go to the Ganges estuary for a ceremonial bath. A crowd of traveling companions gathered, children and old people, men and women; two boats stood ready at the landing.

Eager to acquire religious merit, Mokshada came and said, "O respected sir, I want to go with you." The young widow's request was difficult to deny; her sad eyes did not listen to reason.

"Where is there any more space?" Maitra said to her.

"I touch your feet,"[1] the widow said, weeping. "I'll make a little space somehow for myself to one side." The Brahman Maitra was touched, but still uncertain, he asked her, "What will you do with your child?"

The woman replied, "Rakhal? He will stay with my sister, Annada. After his birth I suffered for a long time from childbirth fever. I had no hope of life. At that time Annada

---

[1] A gesture of respect.

nursed him along with her own child and brought him up with great care. Since then the boy would rather have his aunt's affection than his mother's lap. He is unruly and listens to no one; if you discipline him his aunt comes with her eyes full of tears and takes him onto her lap. He would be more contented with his aunt than with his mother."

The Brahman consented. Mokshada promptly got ready and packed her belongings. She touched the feet of her elders; her girl friends floated on floods of farewell tears. When she came to the landing she found that Rakhal, having run ahead, was already aboard, sitting quiet and serene. "What are you doing here?" the mother asked.

He answered, "I'm going to the ocean."

"Going to the ocean! Oh, you naughty child, come down!"

With unwavering gaze, he said again, "I'm going to the ocean."

The more she tugged at his hand, the more he held onto the boat. At last the Brahman said affectionately, with a smile, "Let him stay, let him stay, let him come along."

The mother said angrily, "All right, I'll give you to the ocean." As soon as she heard her own words, her mother's heart, pierced by the arrow of remorse, cried out in protest. Closing her eyes, she cried out, "My God, my God!" Taking the boy on her lap, she caressed him lovingly, with blessing and penitence in her touch.

Maitra called her aside and spoke quietly. "For shame, never say such things."

So it was decided that Rakhal should go along. When the news reached Annada, she came running, saying, "Child, where are you going?"

Rakhal said, smiling, "Going to the ocean. I'll be back again, Auntie!"

Close to frenzy, Annada shouted, "Oh, sir, my Rakhal is such an unruly child, who will look after him? Since he was born he has never stayed long anywhere without his auntie. Where will you take him? Give him back!"

Rakhal said, "Auntie, I'm going to the ocean. I'll come back again."

The Brahman said fondly, "As long as I am alive, there is nothing to fear regarding your Rakhal. It is winter now and the rivers are calm. Many pilgrims are going together, there is no danger along the way. The trip will take two months. I'll bring your Rakhal back to you."

At the auspicious moment the name of Durga was invoked and the boat got under way. The womenfolk, tears in their eyes, were left standing on the bank. Amid the morning dews of autumn the village on the bank of the river Churni seemed to fill with tears.

The travelers reached their destination, performed their devotions, and returned together from the pilgrims' festival. Throughout the afternoon the boat had been tied to the riverbank, awaiting the incoming tide. Rakhal's curiosity was satisfied and his homesick heart turned longingly toward his aunt. Water—nothing but water—looking about him, he became unnerved. Smooth, sleek, treacherous, devoid of pity, greedy, fangs exposed, and cruel as a snake, the deceitful water seemed full of tricks. Thousand-hooded, panting and rumbling, it hungered ceaselessly for the children of the earth. O Earth, full of love but mute and motionless, eternal, ancient, enduring all tyranny, the abode of joy, soft and green, you stretch out your invisible arms, drawing man irresistibly, wherever he might be, toward your peaceful breast, which spreads as far as the horizon.

The restless child came repeatedly to the Brahman and asked in an eager voice, "Sir, when will the tide come today?"

Suddenly there was a swelling in the placid water. Both banks were alert and expectant. The prow of the boat swung about; groaning softly, it strained at the hawser. To the accompaniment of the water's gurgling song, the ocean's victorious chariot entered the river: the tide came. Invoking the name of God, the boatman cast off for the north. Rakhal came to the Brahman and asked, "How many days will it take to get home?"

They had gone four miles when, before sunset, the force of the north wind gradually increased. At the mouth of the Rupnarain River there was a sandbar. In the narrow river channel the current of the tide and the north wind battled in a towering rage. "Get the boat to shore!" the travelers shouted again and again at the tops of their voices.

Where was the shore? On all sides the maddened water, applauding with thousands of hands its own dance of destruction, foamed with spite and cursed the heavens. On one side the blue outline of the forest could be seen along the far-distant edge of the shore. On the other side the covetous, tormented, and ferocious ocean billowed in arrogant revolt toward the tranquil sunset. The rudder could not hold; confused and stupefied, the boat reeled like a drunkard. The bitterly cold wind mingled with the chill of fear set the men and women to shivering. Some were speechless, some wailed aloud, calling upon their loved ones. Maitra, ashen-faced, said his prayers. Rakhal trembled silently, his face hidden in his mother's bosom.

Then the beleaguered boatman called out to everyone, "One of you has cheated God and has not given what he promised. That's why there are such waves—this untimely storm. Listen to me right now: keep your promise. Don't play with the angry gods."

All that they had—money, clothes, everything—they threw unhesitatingly into the water. Yet, at that very moment, the water rose and gushed violently into the boat. The boatman repeated, "Listen now! Who is holding back what belongs to the gods?"

Suddenly the Brahman got to his feet. Pointing at Mokshada, he said, "Here is that woman who made over her own son to God, and now steals that gift from Him."

"Throw him overboard," the voices roared as one, all the travelers pitiless in their terror.

"Oh, revered sir," the woman pleaded, "save me, save me." Arms clenched, with all her might she held Rawhal to her bosom.

The Brahman bellowed in reprimand, "Am I your savior. You, a mother, were senseless with anger and gave your own son to God—after all that, am I to save him? Pay your debt to God. By breaking your word you would actually drown all these human beings in the ocean!"

Mokshada said, "I am a foolish woman. What I have said in anger—O God who knows my mind—that became the fact! When You heard it, didn't You understand how untrue it was? O God, did You only hear what I said? Didn't You hear the words of a mother's heart?"

While she spoke, the boatman and the oarsmen together took Rakhal by force, tearing him from his mother's breast. Maitra shut his eyes, and with teeth clenched and hands over his ears, he turned his face away. Who suddenly struck his heart with a lash of lightning, stung him like the sting of a scorpion? "Auntie! Auntie! Auntie!" The hopeless, helpless last cry pierced his covered ears like a flaming dart. The Brahman shrieked, "Stop, stop, stop!" At that instant he turned and saw Mokshada lying unconscious at his feet. For a moment the boy appeared among the boiling waves, his terror-stricken eyes open. Crying "Auntie!" he disappeared into the fathomless dark; only his weak fist appeared once in a last desperate effort, sought refuge in the heavens, and sank in despair.

"I will bring you back," the Brahman said, catching his breath. Instantly he jumped into the water and rose no more.

The sun set.

1897

THE LAST LESSON
(Shesh Shikkha)

One day the Sikh prophet Govinda sat alone, thinking about his life's story—that resolution that had manifested itself unfragmented and entire on the golden canvas of his youth, that prospect that encompassed all India, the prospect that today was shattered into a hundred pieces, diminished, filled with doubts, overwhelmed by difficulties.

Was it all a mistake? Is life, then, a failure? Racked by doubts, weary in mind and body, Govinda was deep in thought in the darkening evening; just then a Pathan came and said to him, "I'm leaving the country. Pay me for the horse that you bought."

Guru Govinda answered, "Sheikh, salaam. You will get the money tomorrow. Please go away now, brother."

"I want the money today," the Pathan replied in a rage. He seized Govinda's arm and abused him, calling him "Thief!" At that, Govinda suddenly drew a sword with lightning speed and in an instant had beheaded the Pathan. The ground ran with blood.

As he looked at the severed head, his handiwork, the guru said with a nod, "Now I understand that my time is up. The sinful sword made its own resolution today in this meaningless bloodshed. I have lost faith in my own strength forever. I must be absolved again and again for this sin, this shame—this will be the whole aim of my life."

Govinda took under his protection the young son of the Pathan. He watched over this boy and raised him as if he were his son. He taught him all that he knew of the scriptures and of scriptural scholarship. Early and late, the brave old guru played with the boy as if he himself were a boy. His disciples observed this and came to the guru saying, "What's this, master, what's this? This upsets us. Does any amount of care change the nature of the tiger cub? When he grows up, remember, Gurudeva, his claws will be sharp."

"That's what I want," the guru replied. "If I don't make a tiger out of the cub, what will he have learned?"

The little boy became a young man and was always at Govinda's side. Under his care the child had become a man. He followed Govinda like a shadow and served him like a son. He loved the guru with all his heart and stayed as alert as his right hand. All of Sikh Guru Govinda's own sons had died in war; now in his middle age the Pathan boy took possession of the Guruji's empty heart. When the wind drops a seed into the hollow of the blasted banyan tree, a sapling grows and thrusts its way upward; the old tree is covered by the branches of the new as its foliage spreads and flourishes.

Once, the young Pathan had touched the guru's feet in reverence and had said, "All that I have learned has been by your grace; now with your permission I will join the royal army and earn my living by my own efforts."

His hand on the young man's back, Guru Govinda said, "You still have one lesson of manhood to learn."

When the next day had waned, Govinda sat outdoors alone; he called the Pathan and said, "Take up your sword and come with me." The disciples shouted, "We'll all come, we'll all come."

"All of you go back," said the guru.

The two spoke no more; walking slowly, they went through the forest and along the riverbank. The red clay of the stone-strewn shore had been raked by the thousand fingers of the monsoon torrent. Gigantic sal trees stood in rows; in their shadow a crowd of infant trees jostled together reaching for pieces of the sky. The river was knee-deep, crystal clear, traveling in a single channel between banks of saffron-colored sand.

At the river's edge the guru made a sign; the Pathan stood

still. The purple light of the burnt-out day had reached to the western horizon like the wings of a bat flying quietly in the hushed sky.

The guru said to the Pathan, "Mahmud, come here, dig in this spot."

He dug in the sand and brought out a piece of rock with a mark the color of blood. Govinda said, "This red mark on the rock is your own father's blood. Here I struck off his head. I did not repay his debt, I gave him no quarter. Now the day has come. Oh, Pathan, if you would be a good son to your father, unsheath your sword. Kill the murderer of your father. Present a blood-offering to his thirsting spirit."

With the roar of a tiger, his eyes bloodshot, the brave young man leaped at the guru. The guru remained as still as a wooden image. Then the Pathan hastily threw aside his sword and fell at the guru's feet.

"Oh, Gurudeva," he cried, "even in fun, do not play this sort of game. By my faith I have forgotten my father's murder; all this time you have been father, guru, and friend in one. Let me keep that affection, let my vengeance remain suppressed and die out. Master, give me your blessing!"

After this outburst he ran panting from the forest. He showed no sign of returning; he did not pause. Two teardrops wet Govinda's eyes.

From then on the Pathan remained aloof. He did not come to awaken his guru at dawn in his solitary bedroom. He did not stand watch at the door all night, sword in hand. He was not seen hunting with the guru on the opposite riverbank. He did not come when the guru called.

One day Govinda and the Pathan began a game of chess. Neither knew that the day had ended. Mahmud was defeated again and again and became increasingly intent. Evening came, night spread about them. Their companions went indoors. Full night descended.

The Pathan played with his head bowed in concentration. Suddenly he was checkmated, and the guru struck Mahmud on the head. The guru said with a loud laugh, "He who is so cowardly as to play games with his father's murderer— how can he win?"

At once, with lightning speed the Pathan unsheathed a sharp sword and pierced Govinda's breast. Smiling, the guru said, "After all this time you have learned to take re-

venge for injustice. This was the last lesson. Now I bless
you, my son."

1898

GLOSSARY

AMLOKI: A bitter, astringent fruit used for medicinal purposes.
ANNAPURNA: The goddess of plenty, the giver of food.
ASHAR: A rainy month of the monsoon.
AYURVEDIC: An indigenous system of medicine still practiced in India.
BABU: Master, frequently suffixed to a person's name (e.g. Makhanbabu) as a sign of affection and respect.
BHABESH: Lord of the universe, also used as a personal name.
BHAGIRATH: Grandson of King Sagar who brought the river Ganges down to earth.
BHAIRAVI: A melodic mold in the Indian musical system; also a female ascetic of the Saiva Hindu order.
BHANTI: A flowering tree; also its flower.
BHOLANATH: A name of the god Shiva.
BHRIGU: A god of truth and purity.
BOU-KATHA-KAO: A bird (the name echoes its typical call).
CHAND: The moon.
CHAPKAN: An outer garment worn by men in India.
CHOGA: A loose upper garment worn by men in India.
DIPALI: Festival of lights during the fall in India.
DURGA: The household goddess, wife of Shiva.
EKTARA: A one-stringed musical instrument.
ESRAJ: A many-stringed musical instrument.
GANGA: The Ganges River.
JABA: The hibiscus flower.
JUDHISHTHIR: The eldest brother of the Pandavas in the epic *Mahabharata*.
KALI: The fourth age (of evil and destruction) as described in medieval Hindu mythologies.
KALIKAL: The age of destruction.
KALMEGH: A medicinal plant.
KARTIK: A military protector of the gods: also a symbol of a handsome man.
KATHA: Indian measurement equaling 80.65 square yards.
KHOOKI: Little girl.
KRISHNA: The eighth avatara and the divine leader in the Gita.
KRISHNA-PRATIPADA: A dark night of the moon.
KSHATRIYA: The warrior caste.
KULIN BRAHMAN: A favored class of Brahmans.
KUMBHAK YOGA: A special kind of Yoga that is supposed to give supernatural powers to the practitioner.
KUVERA: Lord of wealth in Indian mythology.
LAKH: The number one hundred thousand.
LAKSHMI: The goddess of prosperity.
MADHAVI: A flowering creeper with fragrant blossoms.
MAHADEVA: Another name for Shiva.

MARWARI: Inhabitants of Marwar, mostly traders and money-lenders.

NAIMISH FOREST: Mythological forest where visions appear to saints and others, and miracles happen.

NANDI: A disciple of Shiva.

NARADA: A mythological saint, famed for his wisdom, described as having a long white beard.

NATARAJA: Shiva as the divine dancer.

NEEM: A medicinal tree.

-PARA: Neighborhood (suffixed to the name of the area).

PARVATI: Another name for Durga, Shiva's wife.

PHALNA: Discarded, cast off.

PICE: A bronze coin, the smallest monetary unit in India.

PURANAS: Medieval religious texts.

PURAVI: An evening melody.

RADHA: Krishna's beloved, the chief among his devotees.

RAGINI: A classical Hindu melody.

RAHU: The mythological god who swallowed the sun.

RAM (RAMA): The king of Ayodhya, the hero of the epic *Ramayana*.

SAGE AGASTHYA: A saint of ancient India.

SANAI: A wind instrument traditionally played at weddings.

SANDESH: A candy made from milk and sugar.

SANNYASI: Hermit.

SARASWATI: The Hindu goddess of wisdom and learning.

SAVITRI: The ideal wife in Hindu legends who observed penances and sacrifices for her husband.

SHANKAR: One of the names of Shiva; also a great metaphysician.

SHIULI: A flower that blossoms in the early autumn in India.

SHIVA: One of the gods, an aspect of the Hindu Trinity (god as destroyer).

SIDDHESWARI: The goddess of fulfillment.

SONA: Gold.

SRAVAN: A month of the monsoon.

SRIKSHETRA: The temple city of Puri on the east coast of India.

SUDARSAN CHAKRA: The circular weapon of Vishnu (used by Arjuna in the battle of Kurukshetra in the *Mahabharata*).

TANTRIK MARRIAGE: An irregular form of marriage outside the main Hindu law.

TRIPADI: A metrical pattern of three lines in Indian poetry.

TRISHANKU: A mythological king who remained suspended in midair between heaven and earth.

URVASI: A goddess hymned in the Vedas.

VAISAKH-DVADOSHI: Twelfth night of the moon.

VINA: A many-stringed Indian musical instrument.

VISHNU: A god, one of the Hindu trinity (god as protector).

VRAJA: A site near the city of Vrindavan, where the milkmaids worshiped Krishna, the divine cowherd in Indian mythology.

VRINDAVAN: A pilgrimage site associated with Krishna.

YAMA: The lord of death.

SELECTED BIBLIOGRAPHY

I. Works by Tagore (translated into English by the author unless otherwise indicated)

A. Poetry

The Child. London: George Allen & Unwin, 1931.

The Crescent Moon. New York: The Macmillan Company, 1913.

Fireflies. New York: The Macmillan Company, 1928.

Fruit-Gathering. New York: The Macmillan Company, 1916.

The Fugitive. New York: The Macmillan Company, 1921.

The Gardener. New York: The Macmillan Company, 1913.

Gitanjali. (Introduction by W. B. Yeats.) New York: The Macmillan Company, 1952.

Lover's Gift and Crossing. New York: The Macmillan Company, 1918.

Poems. (Trans. by various writers.) Calcutta: Visva-Bharati, 1942.

Stray Birds. New York: The Macmillan Company, 1916.

B. Plays

Chitra. New York: The Macmillan Company, 1914.

The King of the Dark Chamber. (Trans. by Kshitishchandra Sen.) New York: The Macmillan Company, 1916.

The Post Office. (Trans. by Devabrata Mukherjee.) New York: The Macmillan Company, 1914.

Red Oleanders. London: Macmillan & Co., Ltd., 1925.

Sacrifice and Other Plays. New York: The Macmillan Company, 1917.

C. Essays, Letters, and Lectures

Creative Unity. New York: The Macmillan Company, 1922.

Glimpses of Bengal. (Trans. by Surendranath Tagore.) New York: The Macmillan Company, 1921.

Letters from Russia. (Trans. by Sasadhar Sinha.) Calcutta: Visva-Bharati Granthalay, 1960.

Letters to a Friend. (Ed. by C. F. Andrews.) New York: The Macmillan Company, 1928.

My Boyhood Days. (Trans. by Marjorie Sykes.) Calcutta: Visva-Bharati Granthalay, 1940.

My Reminiscences. New York: The Macmillan Company, 1917.

Personality. New York: The Macmillan Company, 1917.

The Religion of Man. New York: The Macmillan Company, 1931; Boston: The Beacon Press (paperback).

Sādhanā. New York: The Macmillan Company, 1913.

D. Novels and Short Stories

Binodini. (Trans. by Krishna Kripalani.) Honolulu: East-West Center Press, in cooperation with Sahitya Akademi of New Delhi, 1964.

Broken Ties & Other Stories. (Translated by author and W. W. Pearson.) New York: The Macmillan Company, 1926.

Gora. (Trans. by W. W. Pearson.) New York: The Macmillan Company, 1925.

The Home and the World. (Trans. by Surendranath Tagore.) New York: The Macmillan Company, 1919.

The Hungry Stones and Other Stories. (Trans. by various writers.) New York: The Macmillan Company, 1916.

Mashi and Other Stories. (Trans. by various writers.) New York: The Macmillan Company, 1918.

The Runaway and Other Stories. (Trans. by various writers.) Calcutta: Visva-Bharati Granthalay, 1959.

The Wreck. (Trans. by Anderson) New York: The Macmillan Company, 1921.

E. Collected Works

The Collected Poems and Plays of Rabindranath Tagore. New York: The Macmillan Company, 1949.

A Tagore Reader. (Ed. by Amiya Chakravarty.) New York: The Macmillan Company, 1961.

Towards Universal Man: A Collection of Essays. (Ed. by Humayun Kabir.) Bombay: Asia Publishing House, 1961.

II. Works on Tagore

Kripalani, Krishna R. *Rabindranath Tagore, A Biography.* New York: Grove Press, 1962.

Lesny, Vincenc. *Rabindranath Tagore, His Personality and Work.* (Trans. by George McKeever Phillips; Introduction by C. F. Andrews.) London: George Allen & Unwin, 1939.

Mukherji, Sujit. *Passage to America (Rabindranath Tagore in the United States, 1912–1941).* Calcutta: Bookland Private Ltd., 1964.

Radhakrishnan, Sarvepalli. *The Philosophy of Rabindranath Tagore.* London: Macmillan & Co., Ltd., 1918. Rev. ed.; Baroda, India: Good Companions, 1961.

Rhys, Ernest. *Rabindranath Tagore, A Biographical Study.* New York: The Macmillan Company, 1915.

Tagore, Rathindranath. *On the Edges of Time.* Bombay: Orient Longmans, 1948.

Thompson, Edward J. *Rabindranath Tagore: Poet and Dramatist.* London: Oxford University Press, 1926; rev. ed., 1948.

SIGNET CLASSICS from Around the World

THE DANCE OF SHIVA and Other Tales from India

A rich sampling of the many strands that make up the age-old tradition of storytelling in India. New translation by Oroon Ghosh. Foreword by A. L. Basham.

(#CT281—75¢)

THE MARK OF THE BEAST and Other Stories
by Rudyard Kipling

Fifteen of the finest of Kipling's timeless, vividly realistic tales, set in India, England, America, and Europe. Foreword by Roger Burlingame. (#CD246—50¢)

THE TRAVELS OF MARCO POLO

The enduring record of Marco Polo's thirty-five years of fabulous Eastern travel. Edited with an Introduction by Milton Rugoff. (#CD97—50¢)

CANDIDE, ZADIG and Selected Stories **by Voltaire**

Voltaire satirizes with ruthless wit the social, religious, and human vanities of his day in sixteen biting stories. A new translation with an Introduction by Donald Frame.

(#CD35—50¢)

RESURRECTION **by Leo Tolstoy**

The Russian master's final work tells the story of a young man who seeks salvation by following into exile the girl for whose career in crime he was responsible. Translated by Vera Traill with a Foreword by Alan Hodge.

(#CT63—75¢)

BURMESE DAYS **by George Orwell**

Orwell's first novel presents a scathing indictment of British Imperial rule, against a brilliantly rendered exotic background. Afterword by Richard Rees.

(#CD194—60¢)

THE LADY OF THE LAKE and Other Poems
by Sir Walter Scott

The narrative poem which brought Scott to the peak of critical and popular acclaim, and eleven additional poems. Foreword by Bartless W. Boyden (#CT147—75¢)

THE DIARY OF A MADMAN and Other Stories
by Nikolai Gogol

New translation by Andrew MacAndrew of the title story and *The Nose, The Carriage, The Overcoat,* and the historical romance, *Taras Bulba.* Afterword by Leon Stilman.

(#CP285—60¢)

HEART OF DARKNESS and THE SECRET SHARER
by Joseph Conrad

Two tragic stories—one of a tragedy at sea, the other of a man's deterioration in an isolated trading post in the ivory country—by one of the world's greatest writers. Introduction by Albert J. Guerard. (#CD4—50¢)

GULLIVER'S TRAVELS by Jonathan Swift

The four classic voyages of Gulliver, which make both a fascinating fairy tale and a bitter satire. With 30 illustrations by Charles Brock and 5 maps. Foreword by Marcus Cunliffe. (#CD14—50¢)

BOULE DE SUIF and Selected Stories
by Guy de Maupassant

A new collection of twenty-three short stories by the 19th century French master of this form. New translation by Andrew R. MacAndrew. Foreword by Edward D. Sullivan. (#CD240—50¢)

TYPEE by Herman Melville

Based on Melville's stay in the Marquesan Islands, this novel offers a beautiful description of the natives' uncomplicated way of life, in contrast with the harsh aspects of civilization. Afterword by Harrison Hayford.
(#CP238—60¢)

THE GOLDEN SERPENT by Ciro Alegria

The lyric story of the Indian farmers of the Peruvian Andes, whose livelihood depends on the turbulent Maranon River. Translated with Afterword by Harriet de Onis.
(#CP114—60¢)

AN OUTCAST OF THE ISLANDS by Joseph Conrad

Set in the tropical jungle of a South Sea Island, the story of a white man whose career of treachery among the natives leads to final self-betrayal. Afterword by Thomas C. Moser. (#CD239—50¢)

THE POEMS OF FRANCOIS VILLON

The strength and lyric beauty of Villon's poetry is recaptured in this brilliant new translation by poet Galway Kinnell. (#CT288—75¢)